Choosing Elites

CHOOSING ELITES

ROBERT KLITGAARD

Basic Books, Inc., Publishers   New York

Library of Congress Cataloging in Publication Data

Klitgaard, Robert E.
  Choosing elites.

  References: p.228
  Includes bibliographies and index.
    1. Universities and colleges—United States—Admission.
2. Universities and colleges—United States—Entrance
requirements.   3. Prediction of scholastic success.
4. Prediction of occupational success.   I. Title.
LB2351.2.K57 1985   378'.1057   84–45304
ISBN 0–465–01106–3

Which of a number of varying individuals is to be judged superior to the rest depends upon the criterion which is applied, and the criterion is a matter of ethical judgment. That judgment will, if it is prudent, be tentative and provisional, since men's estimates of the relative desirability of initiative, decision, common sense, imagination, humility and sympathy appear, unfortunately, to differ, and the failures and fools—the Socrates and St. Francis—of one age are the sages and saints of another.

R. H. TAWNEY
Equality

Contents

Preface

HOW YOUNG PEOPLE are chosen for the fast track says a lot about a university or a corporation or, for that matter, a nation. It is a sign of how the institution thinks about efficiency, about mobility and justice, about incentives, and indeed about the need for a fast track at all.

It is one thing to describe or criticize the selection of various such "elites"— elites in the sense of "the choice or best of anything considered collectively, especially of a group or class of persons" *(The Random House Dictionary)*. It is another, and I think more difficult, task to say what we would do if we were in charge. The prescriptive question is the one I hope to clarify here: How should we choose a few from among many capable young candidates for a university or a job?

The answer leads in several directions. We need to think hard about the objectives of selection, and how those objectives fit in with the mission of our institution. We need to know what sort of information helps to make better predictions about which candidates are most likely to fulfill our objectives, and we need to use that information effectively. We may want to give weight to the representation of various social groups, such as those from certain races or regions; we then need to trade off the benefits and the costs of such representation to arrive at the optimal extent of preferential treatment.

This book provides *frameworks* for decision making about objectives, prediction, and representation. The frameworks are not answers; indeed, their major qualitative purpose is to show how our choices depend on our values and on various features of an institution's specific situation.

Many of the issues treated here are relevant to a range of selection problems characterized by rationing of scarce positions, vague objectives, imperfect information, and issues of incentives and equity as well as efficiency. I emphasize the interesting and important problems attending "prediction at the right tail," that is, prediction among an already self-selected sample with outstanding credentials. I talk about admissions at Harvard and other selective universities, but much of what I say applies to personnel selection in business and government, screening systems in medicine and elsewhere, the design of contests, and even to professional sports teams making draft choices. In a narrower vein, aspiring students and their parents will find information here about how selective universities admit students. I also try to unpack some of the mysteries of standardized test scores—just what they predict and are good for.

I am indebted to many people for their help. Terri Bergman, Susan Davis, and James Hammitt provided research assistance. Many admissions officers and faculty members at Harvard helped me to identify key issues and learn how admissions is done; descriptions in chapter 2 are based on admissions policies in the late 1970s and early 1980s. On parts of one or another draft I have benefited from the advice of Derek Bok, Robert Coulam, Mia de Kuijper, Laurence Dougherty, Christopher Edley, Nathan Glazer, Richard Herrnstein, Fred Jewett, Emmett Keeler, Martin Kessler, William Kruskal, Herman Leonard, Richard Light, Glenn Loury, Calvin Mosley, Frederick Mosteller, David Riesman, Thomas Schelling, Russell Simpson, Michael Stoto, Gregory Treverton, Dean Whitla, and Richard Zeckhauser. Along the way I received valuable information from Irv Broudy, Henry Braun, Donald Powers, James Maxey, Winton Manning, Leonard Ramist, John Rolph, Robert Solomon, Warren Willingham, and Kenneth Wilson. Erin Clermont's recommendations clarified the exposition in many ways. And Constance Tuton patiently provided the very best of secretarial assistance.

The help of these friends and colleagues has led to many improvements, but perhaps not as many as they hoped. I have not been able to incorporate all of their useful suggestions, and acknowledging these generous people by no means implies that they agree with my analyses or conclusions. The views expressed here are personal and do not necessarily reflect the official policies of Harvard University.

Choosing Elites

1

How Should Elites Be Chosen?

AT A CONFERENCE RECENTLY, I spoke about the difficulties of admissions at Harvard. I was not describing getting into Harvard, but the flip side of that problem: how difficult it is for the university to decide which among many superbly qualified applicants should be accepted. How should this elite be chosen? One of the conference's organizers captured the audience's reaction in his summary remarks. "As for Harvard's problems," he said, "I wish we all had them."

Most universities probably envy Harvard's dilemma. Its College and various graduate schools and departments select students from very capable candidate pools—perhaps among the ablest groups of applicants in the world. Harvard's problem is not everyone's. And yet, selection at Harvard is an archetypal instance of a quite general social issue. If a few highly valued positions or opportunities are to be allocated among a large number of aspirants, how should this be done? What objectives should be sought? If, as is usual, one has only imperfect information on the candidates, how should this information be used? What if certain subgroups are disproportionately excluded by selection according to individualistic criteria? As a society evolves—or the institutional objectives shift or the applicant pool changes—how should selection policies also evolve? How, in short, should one choose an elite?

Why Selection at the Right Tail Is Difficult

The questions of selection involve much more than simply screening out prospective failures. True, even that is not a trivial undertaking, because people are unpredictable. But both conceptually and practically, it is more difficult to select at the "right tail" of the distribution of talent.

By the phrase right tail, I am referring to the right-hand portion of the bell-shaped curve that is often used to symbolize a distribution of desired attributes or abilities (see figure 1.1). The problem of selection at the right tail occurs when most applicants for a job or grant or other position are well qualified, falling at the right tail of the distribution of qualifications. When professional football teams select draft choices from a pool of players, all of whom are big and fast and excelled as collegians, it is selection at the right tail. So is the choice of who among many deserving patients will receive liver transplants. Examples abound in hiring, the awarding of contracts from bids, the design of contests, and—the instance that is the subject of this book—the selection of students by top universities.

Selection at the right tail, or "choosing elites," is difficult for a number of reasons. First, the objectives of the admissions process often become much harder to define, just as many times the objectives of the very best universities are often more difficult to derive.

Several years ago, I interviewed a number of deans from graduate schools of education. I asked each dean about the mission of his school—

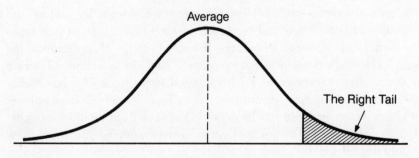

FIGURE 1.1
Bell Curve Distribution of Desired Characteristics

how he thought about his school's niche in the educational world. One pointed out that at his eminent school, the mission was unclear. Other schools, in particular state universities, could simply look at the job market, assess its needs for personnel and training programs, and adjust both curriculum and student body accordingly. But students at his school almost always would get jobs. His task, as he saw it, was to lead the profession, to anticipate needs, to create flexible educators who could respond to changing conditions. True, one could say, "We are training future leaders of the educational profession." In this sense the school did have a "clear mission." But he pointed out that it was a long step from there to the choice of programs and curricula, and to the specification of the characteristics of desired students.

But wouldn't this dean simply want the best students, in the academic sense? He didn't, and neither do most admissions committees at Harvard. Intellectual distinction is usually only one of many criteria considered. "Less than half of those admitted to Harvard Law School each year," writes one of its assistant deans, "are obvious admissions in the sense that their qualifications are demonstrably and clearly 'better' than those presented by all other candidates."[1] And this is the very school about which a distinguished Harvard law professor could write, "Indeed, the Harvard Law School in particular has prided itself over the years—and has been praised—for its almost single-minded commitment to a meritocratic admissions policy."[2] Simply put, "merit" at Harvard and other highly selective universities is not confined to academic merit as measured by past performance (grades and honors) and future potential (aptitude test scores). One official description cites these additional criteria used at the Law School: leadership, evidence of outstanding performance in nonacademic fields such as journalism, professional plans and motivation, and creating a class with "diversity" along the dimensions of geography, college, work experience, and "race and ethnic background." "Apart from identifying those candidates whose qualifications are truly exceptional," some members of the admissions committee would say that "*the* major responsibility of the Committee is to insure reasonable diversity among the remaining choices for educational and professional reasons."[3]

In this sense, to talk as I will about selection at the right tail, as if talent or ability had only one dimension, is to use only a rough metaphor, because many attributes matter. Across schools and departments at Harvard, desired student characteristics vary widely. The Medical School aims to select and train the future leaders of the medical profession, not just medical researchers, but also practitioners of various stripes. The Business School tries to identify future general managers, who are characterized not only by academic talent but by energy, interpersonal skills, and leadership ability. The College worries about a balanced class. All students must have academic talent, and some students are admitted almost exclusively on that basis, but the College values a diverse set of attributes and factors, such as athletic ability, artistic talent, leadership, demographics, and whether one's parents attended or teach at Harvard.

To cite these policies is not to prejudge their correctness. The point is that other universities may not have as much scope to go beyond academic competence. Other institutions may be so constrained by their applicant pools and their curricula that they have little leeway for considering the characteristics of the ideal student, or the ideally diverse group of students, or the ideal future professional.

But as a university moves beyond academic criteria that may be clearly and intuitively linked to the major work of an academic institution, the selection problem grows complex. Philosophical, scientific, and practical questions multiply. How should valuations of applicants be constructed and constrained? Should the admissions process define the characteristics of ideal professionals? Should admissions be considered a prize to reward achievements to date? Admissions criteria create incentives for potential applicants and sometimes for secondary schools. Should these effects be factored in, and if so, how? If including nonacademic criteria leads to a more costly admissions process and allows personal biases to enter, how far is it wise to go?

Such questions are clearly bound up with an institution's educational philosophy. The answers depend on its idea of what sorts of people make a social and academic contribution, on what it teaches, on what its competitors do, and on its conception of fair play and due process. To define what an institution should be trying to do in its admissions process is full of complexity. Think of the problem as "choosing an elite," and watch the classic issues of social justice and efficiency kick into play.

Selection at the right tail is difficult for a second set of reasons. The descriptors of past achievement and the predictors of future success are often instruments designed to measure rather large differences across the distribution of talent. For example, grades may do fairly well at separating "average" performance from "good," and "good" from "excellent." But when applicants are at the right tail and have mostly "excellents," then their grades will obviously not give much help to an admissions committee trying to decide among them.

Universities often ask for letters of recommendation. If most applicants are outstanding, or if most of their weak-kneed recommenders cannot, in this age of open files, bring themselves to say less than that, the value of the information may be minimal to an admissions committee.

Even aptitude test scores have this problem of efficiency at the right tail.

6

True, many standardized admissions tests discriminate across at least six standard deviations of whatever they measure and allow hundreds of possible scores. But as we shall see, these tests are designed to provide greater effectiveness in distinguishing among various shades of "average," and in separating "average" from "good" and "excellent," than in discriminating among those at the right tail.

Selection at the right tail is difficult for a third reason: the stakes are high. The most selective positions are often the most valued; admission brings joy and prestige, rejection a sense of failure and exclusion. For a variety of good and bad reasons, most of us distrust exclusiveness, which is associated with elitism and all its pejorative connotations. Consequently, we apply stricter standards of fairness and "relevance" to selection procedures at the right tail. True, the cost to an applicant of not being admitted to Harvard is not as high as not being admitted to a top university in many other countries, simply because the American educational system has so many alternatives, so many paths. But because Harvard is one of the best, others watch. They may watch as applicants, to know what to study and what activities to pursue. They may watch and apply pressure, as interest groups or alumni or faculty sometimes do. They may watch as fellow educators, in order to emulate, to justify or excuse, or to rethink. Or public leaders may watch, for the purpose of setting public policy, as Justice Powell did in citing Harvard College's admissions policy as exemplary in his opinion on the Bakke case.

A Changing Environment

Selection at the right tail is further complicated by changes in the external environment over the past decade or so. These changes have affected the applicant pool, the objectives of admissions policies, and the usefulness of various predictors and measures of achievement.

SUPPLY, DEMAND, AND THE APPLICANT POOL

Demographic trends and changes in labor markets influence how many potential students there will be and what they will wish to study. Population forecasters say that the number of college-aged youth in America will decline by about a fifth from the mid-1970s to the mid-1990s. Enrollments may not decline this much, because a higher proportion of college-aged youth will enroll in college, older students may return to the university, and more foreign students will probably apply. Some projections of college enrollments even call for modest increases nationwide over the next decade, although most forecast a decline. Most experts see a leveling off or a mild decline in enrollments in the professional schools, and enrollments in graduate schools of arts and sciences may drop sharply.

If the number of young eligibles is down, so is the number of young and able eligibles. Increasing participation rates will augment the total number of applicants, but this will not help much at the top end of the ability spectrum, since most of the very able are already college-bound. In some ways, then, selective institutions like Harvard could be hit hard. True, most parts of Harvard will probably continue to have more qualified applicants than slots. But if the absolute number of young people who are "very able"—define that as you will—goes down by a fifth, the quality of Harvard's applicant pool will also decline. The recent golden age of selectivity, when the postwar baby boom pumped unprecedented numbers of extremely talented applicants into the university system, is temporarily over.

Changing conditions in labor markets have sent applications to the major professional schools soaring. But the "minor professions"—as sociologist Nathan Glazer terms education, public health, divinity, and others —will probably not fare so well.[4] Already at these schools at Harvard, it is often the case that over half the applicants are admitted. Academically talented undergraduates will probably be less likely to pursue a Ph.D. degree program and enter academic careers than in the past.

These changes in demography and labor markets will affect applicant pools, even at highly selective institutions. Consequently, they will affect what universities can feasibly attain via their choices about admissions policies.

CHANGING EDUCATIONAL OBJECTIVES

Environmental changes have also affected the objectives of admissions policies. The most important development has undoubtedly been the rise of *affirmative action* policies, which motivate Harvard and other universities, sometimes under threat of government penalties, to admit some members of certain minority groups, and some women, who are ostensibly less qualified in academic terms than other applicants. The result has been a dramatic increase in minority representation at selective universities, and important new issues face admissions committees.

Because of this changing environment, Harvard's policies have shown dramatic shifts. The College suddenly admitted many more blacks for the class of 1972, partly as the result of a greater recruitment effort among heretofore underemphasized sources of black talent and partly as the result of giving racial "diversity" more weight as an objective than in the past.

The College long before had pioneered the idea that a diverse class enhances the learning experience. But exactly how racial diversity contributes to the educational process, and how one might know whether 2 percent, or 7 percent, or 12 percent black enrollment was the right amount, has remained the subject of much emotion but little analysis. The number of women has also moved markedly upward, resulting in lower academic qualifications for some entering Radcliffe students than in the past. The proportion of women admitted to Radcliffe/Harvard was increased from about one in five in 1971 to about two in seven in 1975, as the result of a presidential policy directive. The admissions offices were merged in 1975–76.[5]

The Business School provides an interesting example of changing admissions policies. In 1969, the faculty voted to "admit candidates from disadvantaged minorities to the first year of the program in the greatest number consistent with the effective functioning of the program."[6] Operationally, this was defined as taking all minority students who had a 75 percent or higher chance of passing the first-year curriculum. The enrollment of black students sharply increased to about seventy per class. But when fewer than 75 percent of the blacks actually passed and the ensuing consequences for black and white students were deemed unfavorable, the school shifted its strategy. It began recruiting harder for blacks and other minorities but enrolling fewer. The number of blacks in the entering class dropped sharply from 1972 to 1973. Only now are the number of black admits back to the level of 1972, despite over twice as many minority applicants. But fewer blacks now fail.

At other selective universities, too, admissions committees struggle over the definition and implementation of affirmative action. At most schools and departments, affirmative action entails admitting minorities or women with lower grades and test scores. Some justify that practice by citing the educational benefits of racial diversity in the student body. Others cite a perceived need for more minorities or women in a certain profession or discipline. It is fair to say that every faculty finds this a vexing issue, where pressures from interest groups are severe and clear-cut policy statements are difficult, even dangerous.

A second change in the environment, *critiques of academic credentialing,* has affected the objectives of admissions. Over the past ten or fifteen years, several studies of higher education have argued that what is learned at universities is unrelated to later success in life. Instead, the mere credential is what makes a difference. Variations in academic attainment, it is contended, matter little. Universities instead function as diploma mills, filters, screens, and socializers. If this argument, which we shall examine later, is true, then admissions decisions become even more important and controversial. For if universities affect social welfare more as gatekeepers than as transmitters of knowledge, then decisions to admit and reject become paramount in determining a person's life chances. Indeed, the academic mission itself is brought into question—are scholastic credentials and aptitudes mainly pretenses, however unwitting, to preserve and legitimate existing social and racial strata? If so, should the objectives of university admissions policies—particularly at high-profile gatekeepers like Harvard —be recast?

A third change in the environment is *declining academic standards.* According to objective indicators such as achievement test scores and subjective reports from high schools and colleges across the country, academic standards in America are slipping. The causes are unclear. Part of the decline stems from the increased enrollment and testing of academically weaker students. But this is only part of the answer, as even the test scores of valedictorians and salutatorians declined considerably from 1960 to 1977.[7] From 1976 to 1981 alone, the number of students in the United States scoring above 750 on the mathematics portion of the Scholastic Aptitude Test dropped from about 12,000 to about 6,500. The numbers scoring above 750 on achievement tests in biology, German, and French also dropped about half. In English composition, 5,235 students scored above 750 in 1976; the number fell to 1,484 in 1981.

In such circumstances, it might be argued that some universities should set high academic standards, and that by their doing so, the erosion in academic values could be halted. In the late 1940s and 1950s, a time of rising academic values and large numbers of applicants for scarce positions, selective universities like Harvard could afford to provide nonacademic leadership and to demonstrate the multiple roles of the university. But in a time of academic deterioration and overcapacity in the higher education system, Harvard might provide the greatest service by reaffirming the primacy of academic values. On this view, far from recasting academic standards in light of their alleged uselessness in current American society, such standards should be strengthened with the purpose of reinforcing academic standards throughout the educational system.

PREDICTORS

If objectives must be reexamined because of changes in the external environment, so must the predictors and measures now used by admissions committees. I am referring to standardized aptitude and achievement tests, previous grades, and letters of recommendation. All three have suffered in recent years.

Test scores are required by most universities, even though in many institutions the actual scores are seldom used to reject applicants.[8] All accredited law schools require the Law School Admissions Test (LSAT). Eighty percent of the business schools require the Graduate Management Admissions Test (GMAT), and almost 70 percent of graduate schools of arts and sciences mandate the Graduate Record Examination (GRE).

Attacks on standardized tests are not new,[9] but it is hard to match recent critiques for detail and depth of feeling.[10] Two basic criticisms are made. The tests are said to be poor predictors of later academic performance, and later academic performance is said to be a poor predictor of success in life; so, in the language of the testers, the tests lack predictive validity. Second, the use of current tests is alleged to discriminate against applicants from minority groups and lower-class backgrounds. In other words, tests are said to add little and take away a lot.

Assessing such arguments turns out to involve complicated methodological and empirical questions. The answers may well be different for very selective universities than for less selective institutions. The issues badly need clarification, and the use of test scores in admissions requires fundamental reexamination.

Apart from test scores, grades have also been criticized. A student's previous grades in school are also widely used by admissions committees to gauge both aptitude and academic preparation. But the late 1960s and 1970s witnessed an unprecedented inflation in college and high school grades. Moreover, grades are notoriously inexact and unreliable, even within the same course. Add the problems of comparing grades across courses, fields, and schools, and it is not surprising that grades are problematic both as predictors and as measures of academic success.

Letters of recommendation are another piece of information used by admissions officers. Serious questions can and have been raised about validity and bias of personal recommendations. In the 1970s, these perennial questions emerged again with the passage of the Buckley Amendment, which gave students the right to see information contained in their student files, unless that right was explicitly waived. According to many letterwriters and admissions members, the result has been vaguer and more inflated letters. Even when the right has been waived, the candor and therefore the value of recommendations is said to have declined.

Thus, the use of test scores, grades, and recommendations has come into question. Too often, though, little is said about what might replace these allegedly flawed predictors. Seldom is the general problem of imperfect prediction analyzed in all its messiness and uncertainty. Almost never does one encounter a balanced and constructive treatment of how to select at the right tail.

Selecting Elites Outside the University

Many of the problems we have been discussing are not confined to selective universities. Consider the selection of entry-level officials in government. What characteristics should be sought in civil servants? How should we decide among a highly qualified pool of candidates which few are best suited? How should we measure and weight such attributes as ability, experience, character, representation of geographical regions and races and constituencies, and so forth? And there is a practical question: What information is available, or could be made available—and at what cost—to help in making the selection?

The same kinds of problems emerge when AT&T or Texas Instruments selects entry-level managers; when the Presidential Management Intern Program chooses young people to enter a fast track in public administration; or when the Los Angeles Raiders make their selections in the National Football League's draft of college seniors. In broader terms, these situations share several characteristics:

- *The absence of a perfectly effective market.* Large-scale hiring followed by large-scale firing is costly or even impossible, just as admitting all applicants and then flunking out those who are not up to standard is thought to be costly and undesirable. A certain number of slots need to be filled, and for various reasons *ex ante* predictions need to be made of who will be most likely to fill them best.
- *Fuzzy, imprecise objectives.* It is difficult to quantify exactly what is sought in an ideal candidate, in part because many attributes matter.
- *Questionable predictors of later performance.* For wide receivers in football, one's time in the 40-yard dash is an important criterion. Those running slower than 4.8 seconds—only a few young men are able to run faster—need not apply. But the top fifty, say, wide receiver prospects eligible for the draft each year run the "40" faster than 4.8. How should their relative speed be weighted? Should the fastest be the first chosen? Or at some point, does being even faster no longer matter so much, compared to other attributes like size, "hands," intelligence, dedication, and character?
- *Certain subgroups performing better on selection criteria than others.* Does this mean the criteria are biased in favor of those groups and against others? To what extent should subgroup membership be weighted separately in selection, and why?

Obviously the selection problems differ in important ways as one moves from higher education to government to business to sports. As I will emphasize later, no one system of selection will be right for every context. But one may nonetheless observe and study their common features.

Selection at the right tail takes one into philosophy and economics, statistics and politics, tradition and ritual, and a tangle of sensitive institutional nerves. By examining these complexities in the context of a selective university, I hope to provide a framework of use to others interested in how to choose an elite.

An Overview of the Book

In chapter 2, I describe how admissions policies work. What objectives do various schools and departments have as they do the choosing? What do admissions people think they are accomplishing? How do their objectives translate into operational criteria? What procedures are used?

Several findings will emerge. First, various admissions committees differ greatly in the procedures and criteria they use. This might not seem surprising; after all, there is no reason that the desired qualities of a prospective doctor should be the same as those of a lawyer or a chemist or a minister. What is surprising is that the differences in procedures and criteria are not explainable by differences in goals. Policies are not derived in even a moderately explicit way from a careful specification of each institution's differing objectives in the selection process. A second finding is that the objectives of selection are remarkably vague. Admissions officers readily admit—and faculty review committees frequently lament—that admissions policies are not spelled out, that they can vary remarkably from year to year, that members of the admissions committee may disagree diametrically on the aims to be pursued. Many admissions officers, who are often also professors, confess puzzlement not only about what various criteria being used really "mean," but also about what the admissions process itself should be seeking.

Moreover, as one member of a committee that reviewed admissions at the Harvard Medical School wrote, "There is a striking lack of outcome audits, of feedback, and of studies that verify the validity of the assumptions and decisions of the admissions committee."[11] This observation applies to the other admissions committees, too. It is remarkable how little systematic information is used by admissions people in making their judgments.

I say all this as a former admissions chairman. It is a provocative exaggeration to say that we make these important decisions without clear objectives, without relevant feedback, and without accountability to students, faculty, and alumni. But it is almost that way. Indeed, that it is that way may be well and good; I do not wish to prejudge appropriateness. But it does mean that in considering more generally how elites should be chosen, one will not be able to turn to Harvard, or to other universities I know, for a careful elaboration of objectives, criteria, and procedures.

These findings lead to the question posed in chapter 3: What should the objectives of selection be? Obviously, the objectives depend on a number of specific features of the situation: what society rewards and what the selector thinks it should reward; what the institution itself deems valuable; what is taught and how; and who applies or would apply under alternative selection schemes. I examine several archetypal approaches to the selection problem. First, there is the market mechanism: Why not treat the education as just another commodity subject to market forces? Why not an auction? Second, why not allocate the scarce slots randomly?

Third, I analyze a more complicated alternative, where the institution attempts to calculate the social value added of its education for the different applicants, choosing those applicants for whom the social value added is highest. "Social value added"—the value to society, reflected in later-life performance, that an education provides—is a fiction. I presume for the sake of clarifying philosophical issues that one has perfect information about this obviously problematic concept—an assumption relaxed in later chapters. Discussing this alternative leads down a number of fascinating trails; it raises fundamental questions of the just society, of the deserving individual, and of the importance of academic values.

These issues are not resolved in chapter 3. Indeed, I conclude that such questions are not "soluble," in the sense that no answer is demonstrably superior. But I try to provide a framework for the inevitably value-laden discussion of objectives—a framework that might elevate many currently unproductive discussions, and that might also be helpful in reorienting policies in the face of social and educational change.

Chapters 4 to 7 deal with more practical, but no less fascinating or complex, questions. Suppose we wish to select an elite according to certain objectives, but, contrary to the assumption in chapter 3, we do not have perfect information about which candidates fill the bill. We must predict which among a pool of young men and women are most likely to be the best students or the best lawyers or the best doctors—or which are most likely to lend a hand in changing society or the professions in ways we deem desirable. What is known about how to do that predicting? What attributes of young people predict what sorts of later "success," and how well?

A good deal of the debate over admissions policies focuses on narrow versions of these questions, as noted above. Critics of standardized tests argue, with statistical studies in hand, that the tests don't predict, or don't predict well enough, either academic or later-life success. How should we evaluate such issues? What does the actual evidence show? But the issues raised are much broader than the statistical relationships between test scores and later grades or later income. These chapters apply also to a larger domain. Suppose we have an objective that we wish to pursue in choosing an elite; suppose, lamentably, that we have to predict which applicants will best pursue that aim. How should we assess how well we can predict, and how we might make better predictions?

Chapter 4 leads off on these questions. It is mainly methodological. What is attempted is a primer of how to think about and carry out predictions in the context of selection at the right tail.

Chapters 5 through 7 build on this primer. They review the state of the art of predicting various forms of academic (chapter 5) and later-life success (chapters 6 and 7). How well do various widely used criteria for selection actually predict various kinds of later success of interest? Do other criteria, now seldom used, have promise?

Several surprising, and I confess to me disheartening, results emerge. I find that even at the right tail standardized test scores usually do quite well —and usually better than any other criteria—at predicting academic success at selective universities. I provide different ways to think about what "quite well" means, and I realize that others may not apply that value-laden descriptor to the same evidence.

I also find that popular criteria such as interviews, letters of recommendation, extracurricular activities, and other indicators of "leadership," "character," and "personality" do poorly in predicting various kinds of later-life success. Moreover, the review in chapter 7 of other possible criteria such as direct measures of interests and personality, concludes that, for the most part, they would not be useful in choosing an elite. Evidence about the current state of the art does not support the idea that using such measures would enhance the prediction of any of various forms of later-life success. They may have predictive powers, but at present there is not good evidence to that effect.

I do discern a significant relationship between various academic variables and various sorts of later-life success. I am not willing to use the value term "important" to describe this relationship. But I am willing to bet, based on current evidence, that for young men and women test scores and grades forecast later success in business, law, medicine, and academia better than existing measures of personality, character, leadership, or diligence.

I find these results unsettling. I have always viscerally distrusted test scores and grades. And I feel intuitively that given two able young people I could forecast, on the basis of an interview and letters of recommendation and essays and extracurricular achievements, who would be more successful in later life (along a range of definitions of "success"). Perhaps you feel the same way about your ability to predict, but the evidence about you and me is not in. Let me put my finding this way: No system of using such nonacademic criteria can be shown, for large numbers of young people, to choose consistently and significantly those who will be most "successful," judged along several criteria of success.

Before trying to transform these findings into recommendations for policy and research, I turn in chapter 8 to another major aspect of choosing elites, the problem of group representation. As the archetypal case, I consider the differential performance of black and white students in America on measures of academic achievement. What are the existing differences in performance, especially at the right tail? To what extent are those differences due to biases in the measures? What are the educational benefits of a "diverse" student body? What are the educational costs? What are the implications for choosing the elite? The results once again surprised and distressed me.

In the final chapter, I return to the larger questions. Armed with descriptions of existing practices at elite universities, with a framework for considering the objectives of selection, with the evidence about how well we can predict many sorts of later-life contributions, and with an appreciation of the problem of group representation, how should we think about choosing an elite? By the nature of the problem, there is no one right answer; it depends on many features of a particular situation, which I try to spell out. Moreover, reasonable people disagree on the objectives of selection, which depend so much on value judgments, and even one's own value judgments may change as society and the educational system do. My own tentative conclusions carry no final authority. The further development of measures of success and predictive criteria for selection may well render obsolete many of my empirical findings. I hope so. But in the meantime, I hope that the evidence and analytical frameworks I provide will be helpful in a wide array of policies for choosing elites.

2

How Admissions Works

HOW do selective universities choose students? What objectives do they have? How are these objectives translated into specific criteria and procedures? In answering these questions, I will focus primarily on the admissions processes of the university I am most familiar with, Harvard.

There is no one Harvard admissions policy. Like most universities, Harvard is a collection of institutions. It includes a college, nine professional schools, and over forty departments and divisions in the Graduate School of Arts and Sciences (GSAS). These institutions vary dramatically in their admissions policies. Consider these differences in criteria and procedures, all within the same university:

Test scores. The Harvard Divinity School and certain programs in other faculties do not require admissions tests. At other schools and at Harvard College, certain test-score thresholds seem to exist, below which almost no student is admitted. The weight given to test scores above the threshold varies considerably across schools and departments. Why?

Alumni preference. The Law School gives virtually no weight to the off-spring of Harvard alumni, while the College and Medical School admit academically qualified alumni children more frequently than other applicants. Why?

Diversity. The College stresses the diversity of its entering class among many nonacademic dimensions. Personal qualities such as leadership, initiative, social skills, and special talents affect an applicant's likelihood of being admitted to a substantial degree. But at the GSAS and the Law School, personal qualities play a much less important role. Why?

Interviews. The Medical School gives two interviews each to about 1,000 of its over 4,000 applicants. The College urges all applicants to be interviewed, usually by alumni. But the Law School, Business School, and other professional schools do not use interviews. Why?

Essays. The Business School and the College place a great deal of emphasis on a series of essays written by the applicants. The other professional schools and graduate departments also require essays, but fewer of them, and they give the essays much less weight. Why?

Publicity of criteria. The Law School publishes a table for prospective applicants (as well as alumni and faculty members) that shows the probability of being admitted, given various grades and test scores. Some admissions committees keep this information secret, even from faculty members. Why?

Admissions committees. The College and the Business School rely heavily on professional admissions officers to decide who gets in. The Medical School, Kennedy School, and GSAS rely almost entirely on faculty members. Students sit in on some committees but are excluded from others. Why?

The whys turn out to be not easy to answer. When those of us who do admissions are pushed about why we aim for this and not that, why we employ one measure and not another, or why we use the particular procedure we do instead of some other—well, most of us confess that we wish we knew more.

Around Harvard and at other universities I know, the whys and wherefores remain remarkably vague. As one study of the Harvard Medical School's admissions system lamented:

> The Admissions Review Committee is aware of the absence of hard data bearing on the relative success or failure of our present process of selecting applicants for admissions to Harvard Medical School. Each procedure used in the selection of students has its strong advocates and detractors but the arguments advanced for or against a given procedure are based more on custom, emotion, and "instinctive feelings" than on scientifically accepted facts.[1]

Someone interested in how to choose an elite will not find an explicitly worked out and empirically justified policy for doing so anywhere at Harvard. Instead, one discovers divergent views, strongly held but seldom validated in ways that academicians would validate propositions in their chosen fields of study, and procedures that persist out of habit and custom.

This may not be a defect in practice. I do not wish to prejudge the correctness of existing policies and procedures, nor of course should one contend that policies should be the same across institutions. But it does mean, I think, that the lessons we can learn from Harvard about how one should choose an elite are limited—perhaps primarily a reminder of how difficult, political, and controversial such decisions inevitably are.

I will proceed impressionistically rather than exhaustively, in part to spare the reader and in part because some information about what goes on is confidential. We will look at the policies followed by several Harvard faculties in the early 1980s, outlining their objectives, criteria, and procedures for admissions. We will also see how Harvard's policies compare with those of other institutions. I hope this will be of use to aspiring students, as well as to those interested in the general issue of choosing an elite. I hope to illustrate with examples how much the research of the sort described in the next chapters is needed for selection at the right tail.

The Kennedy School of Government

OBJECTIVES

Let's expose my glass house first. I will focus on the two-year Masters Program in Public Policy, a program whose first class was graduated in 1971. The Kennedy School of Government expanded rapidly in the 1970s, and the Public Policy Program was its leading edge. The school had a grandiose aim: to create a new profession of public policy and management. Admissions policies would be crucial. As sociologists Christopher Jencks and David Riesman observed:

> It is easier to change a profession by recruiting apprentices than by changing the rules of their apprenticeship. Professional schools have their students for only a few years, and they can do only so much with whatever raw material they get. But to the extent they are overapplied and can select their raw material according to some preconceived plan, they can influence the profession they serve decisively.[2]

Two big questions arose at the start of the Public Policy Program. Suppose you wanted to train future leaders in the public sector. What should you teach them? And whom should you select? Notice that these questions are not independent, though at times they have been treated that way.

The curriculum came first. Its guiding idea was to combine the analytical techniques of the hard social sciences with a rigorous concern for management, politics, and ethics. The Kennedy School was quantitatively rigorous, and in order to pass, students had to have aptitude for quantitative work.

Those selected in the first years of the program were indeed academically impressive. But a sense of unease emerged. Was the Public Policy Program really producing future leaders and change agents? Or was it instead graduating analysts and staff people, who might not play as central a role in government and politics as the school's mission entailed?

When I became admissions chairman in 1978–79, Dean Graham Allison expressed his concern bluntly: "Find us more winners. Certainly academic ability is important, but so are leadership and character. We have to raise our admissions standards." The job, he said, was to select future leaders in government. But who were they?

DESIRED CHARACTERISTICS

Classic arguments ensued when we set out to raise admissions standards. Some members of the admissions committee believed that academic criteria should predominate. The smarter the candidate, the more he or she would learn. Top-flight analysts were being sought in government—at one point, President Carter had seven Ph.D.s in economics in cabinet-level positions. Lowering intellectual standards would be shortsighted, since then the very best students would no longer want to come. Lower academic standards, some said, would make us less distinct from other public policy programs, and it would disenchant the faculty. Finally, there were doubts about identifying "winners." Who could tell? Why not admit the smartest candidates—many of whom were in fact excellent on other dimensions—then at least we would know what we were measuring.

Others countered that we were too academic, both in our curriculum and in our admissions decisions. Too few students seemed like the sorts of people who would someday run a large agency. Test scores and grades said little if anything about future promise in public affairs. By stressing quantitative aptitude, the school had turned down disproportionate numbers of women and minority applicants—an unfortunate outcome for a leading school of government.

Values were at issue, but so were facts. As with most admissions committees, there were plenty of hunches but little systematic information. We decided to undertake a number of studies. First, we examined the criteria that our predecessors had implicitly used in admissions decisions. Table 2.1 gives some of the results. For a typical candidate, a 116-point increase in the Graduate Record Examination quantitative score raised the chance of admissions about 45 percentage points (from 16 percent to 61 percent). In contrast, excellent letters of recommendation made no statistically significant difference (this result is not shown in the table). Was this what the committee wanted?

Second, the committee studied the predictors of academic success at the school. In the three core courses taught by the case method, neither college grades, test scores, letters of recommendation, or any other variables significantly predicted first-year grades. But in core courses in economics, statistics, and analytical methods, the quantitative test score was powerfully related to success—to a lesser extent, so were college grades. Applicants with GREQ scores below 650 had a dangerously high chance of failing these quantitative core courses.

Third, the committee tried to assess the qualities of successful public managers and politicians. A survey of faculty members identified fifteen public policy graduates with successful public careers, who were then contrasted with fifteen graduates who were on no one's list of successes. The successes turned out to have had much higher test scores, more leadership positions in college, better recommendations, more athletic letters, higher grades, and so forth—in short, they were better on almost every dimension. The committee also examined the literature on the personal qualities of top managers, including their "cognitive styles" and "motivation." Furthermore, personality tests were given on a voluntary basis to our students and faculty. (One professor turned in his test saying, "Now you know more about me than I do.")

Fourth, the committee tried to think rigorously about the issue of "diversity" in the student body. What combination of students—or types of students—would lead to the greatest educational benefits? How much affirmative action was the right amount? Senior faculty members and some students were interviewed. A memorandum on the subject was prepared,

TABLE 2.1

How Changes in Admissions Criteria Affected Admission Chances

A typical applicant to the Public Policy Program at the Kennedy School of Government had Graduate Record Examination scores of 649 verbal (GREV) and 639 quantitative (GREQ), had a college grade average of 3.4, and was a major in science or economics. This applicant had a 16 percent chance of being admitted. What would be his or her chance if:

GREV were 102 points higher?	18 percent (2 points higher)
GREQ were 116 points higher?	61 percent (45 points higher)
Grades were 0.38 higher?	35 percent (19 points higher)
Political science major?	9 percent (7 points lower)
Humanities major?	9 percent (7 points lower)

NOTE: Changes in GREV, GREQ, and grades represent one standard deviation within the public policy program's applicant pool.

circulated, and discussed. Although there was no agreement on the appropriate dimensions or the optimal degrees of diversity, the committee did give the matter considerable attention.

The committee did other things, too. It targeted certain underrepresented groups for intensified recruitment: minorities and women, scientists, graduates of small colleges, and foreign students. It had meetings, in advance of the admissions cycle, to discuss objectives and the results of its studies.

The outcome of all this was a moderate shift in policy. The committee paid more attention to personal characteristics than in the past. For example, more weight was given to evidence of leadership and social commitment—although committee members didn't know much about how to measure or weigh such evidence. Some very smart students were rejected because their essays or recommendations made them sound poorly motivated, egocentric, or immature. Indeed, the committee rejected over half of those who scored between 700 and 800 on the GRE quantitative test, and a third of those who scored above 800. One short-term result, I think, was a notably more likeable class.

But who knows? Did we give up too much academically? We could have chosen so that every student admitted scored over 700 on the GRE quantitative, instead of three-quarters of those admitted. We could have raised our average GREQ by about 40 points and the tenth percentile of the class by about 40 points. Would that have been important? Should we have given even more emphasis to affirmative action? What had we gained by using our highly subjective impressions of "leadership potential" and "character"? Were we on to something important, or were we kidding ourselves?

PROCEDURES

Our procedures can be quickly summarized. In 1979–80, the Public Policy Admissions Committee included seven faculty members and administrators. Each application was read by at least two committee members. The applications included scores on the Graduate Record Examination, transcripts, three letters of recommendation, and three long essays. Each reader wrote a descriptive paragraph, which became part of the cumulative sheet on the applicant; gave the applicant three ratings (on "intellectual distinction," "leadership potential," and "personal character"); and gave the applicant an overall rating from 1 to 5 (1 = clear admit, 2 = strong candidate, 3 = marginal, 4 = reject, and 5 = clear reject). Applicants not rejected by the first two raters received from one to four additional reads. Then the overall ratings were averaged. The top 150 of the 500 applicants were discussed by a subcommittee, which made tentative decisions on about 75 and brought them and the remaining, toughest 75 candidates to the full committee for discussion and vote. The full committee met for a whole day and evening to make the final decision. Afterward, we went dancing.

Harvard College

The Public Policy Program at the Kennedy School of Government is relatively new, and my admissions committee had virtually no studies or accumulated experience to guide us in choosing our elite. It was perhaps not surprising that we remained unsure of what we were doing in admissions. But what about Harvard College, the oldest component of the university and one renowned for its admissions system? What were its objectives, criteria, and procedures?

OBJECTIVES

In official prose, the College describes its goals as "to prepare a diverse student body with a wide variety of excellences to maximize their talents and ultimate contribution to society."[3] This preparation is primarily academic. According to Harvard President Derek Bok, the most important mission of the College is to transmit knowledge.[4] Many studies show that knowledge is most readily transferred to the most academically capable students, as measured by previous grades and standardized tests.

But knowledge transmittal is only one of the College's objectives. Harvard also wants to produce future leaders in the public sector, business, and the professions. The Ford Report of 1959, which reviewed the College's admissions policies, said that the ultimate objective was to select and perpetuate a fellowship of intelligent, educated people of high character who would loyally serve their college and their country. Leadership depends not only on intelligence, but also on "character" and "personality." And talent, as it matters to society, has many dimensions. Thus, purely academic objectives are not the only ones.

DESIRED CHARACTERISTICS

But how should one translate the vague and noble aims of Harvard College into specific criteria for admission? What nonacademic attributes should count and how much? The answer is, no one knows—although there's a lot of rhetoric around. A former dean of admissions and a member of the admissions committee tried to explain matters this way:

> The reason for emphasizing our concern for other qualities and factors is that exceptional style of any kind is rare. It is because we have the good fortune to be able to choose from an academically powerful applicant group that we can acknowledge exceptional strength of any kind that seems relevant to Harvard's broad educational mission. And it is the rareness of all types of first-rateness that makes us anxious to maintain, if we can, something like the current spread of measured ability at the College.[5]

But what are the "other qualities and factors," "exceptional style," and "types of first-rateness"? Things can quickly get subjective:

> The contrasts in viewpoint about the personal rating (what qualities make a man outstanding?) and the fact that there are many composites which merit outstanding ratings, make the assessment process difficult. "A touch of greatness," was what one counselor ascribed to an applicant, "the simple charm of ingenuousness," "the organized effective energy and the irascibility of a Henry Ford."[6]

Indeed, the ascertainment of the desired qualities sometimes sounds almost mystical, as in the words of another former dean of admissions:

> We're looking for collective power; but we have obliged ourselves to look for it in many different areas and many different ways, so when that power comes in, it spontaneously has blend and diversity—which is in itself attractive, but not something we have to pursue consciously.[7]

One implication does seem clear to most admissions officers at Harvard College: We must go well beyond objective academic criteria. One could offer several justifications for doing so. The so-called objective measures might conceal "a pretty dull and bloodless or peculiar fellow," and contrary to what some would presume, selecting along such measures would not lead to the academically most talented class. Former Dean of Admissions Wilbur Bender put the argument this way:

> The student who ranks first in his class may be genuinely brilliant. Or he may be a compulsive worker or the instrument of domineering parents' ambitions or a conformist or self-centered careerist who has shrewdly calculated his teachers' prejudices and expectations and discovered how to regurgitate efficiently what they want. Or he may have focused narrowly on grade-getting as compensation for his inadequacies in other areas because he lacks other interests or talents or lacks passion and warmth or normal healthy instincts or is afraid of life. The top high school student is often, frankly, a pretty dull and bloodless or peculiar fellow.

What I am trying to say is that a deliberate policy of one-factor selection might produce in our student body not more students of first-rate intellectual power, but fewer.[8]

Another justification was even more subtle. The most academically able students might not want to join a college that selected on purely academic criteria. As David Riesman contended:

Many young men of 17 or 18 who will end up as scholars and researchers do not know this of themselves in high school, and are put off by a college that seems monolithically scholarly, since they cannot then make such a commitment. . . . In fact, I have known quite a few highly intelligent students who have chosen to come to Harvard because the Cambridge-Boston ambience offered a greater variety of alternatives if academic intensity proved unsatisfying in competition with the enclave of the University of Chicago.[9]

Or one could justify departures from academic criteria on political grounds. What Deans of Admissions Bender and Chase Peterson called "constituencies important to the College" would be unhappy if only the most academically talented were chosen.[10] One needed to appease the alumni, the private schools, the Cambridge/Boston community, and, more recently, the minority groups.

But the most celebrated of Harvard College's justifications concerns "diversity" in the student body. Admitting some students with less academic talent actually enhances, rather than dilutes, the overall educational experience. The less qualified students, through their "diversity" in nonacademic dimensions, actually improve the learning environment for the more qualified, and possibly vice versa. Contrary to appearances, then, there is no academic trade-off in admitting some football players, minorities, graduates of prep schools, and others who are less qualified academically than some who are rejected. Departures from academic merit can be defended not only politically or socially, but on academic grounds.

Dean Bender stated the case eloquently:

In other words, my prejudice is for a Harvard College with a certain range and mixture and diversity in its student body—a college with some snobs and some Scandinavian farm boys who skate beautifully and some bright Bronx pre-meds, with some students who care passionately if unwisely (but who knows) about editing the Crimson or beating Yale, or who have an ambition to run a business and make a million, or to get elected to public office, a college in which not all the students have looked on school just as preparation for college, college as preparation for graduate school and graduate school as preparation for they know not what. Won't even our top one-percent be better men and better scholars for being part of such a college?[11]

Fred Glimp, who succeeded Bender, pushed the theory a step further with his "search for the happy bottom quarter."[12] Inevitably, he observed, 25 percent of the entering students would end up in the bottom quarter of the class. If they were former academic stars, they would be unhappy —perhaps they would even be broken by the experience. So, intentionally admitting less academically able students as "the bottom quarter," who were strong in sports or social life or the arts and would therefore not care so much about their academic standing, would make everyone's educational experience happier.

These justifications, though vague and not spelled out quantitatively, have become part of the mores of Harvard College admissions. Perhaps because many potentially vocal interests have been appeased in one way or another, and because the selection process is shrouded in secrecy, few have questioned the justifications for departures from straight academic criteria. Some observers have complained that "leadership" and "diversity" are too subjective. In a controversial doctoral dissertation, Penny Feldman observed:

> Beyond the use of ascriptive standards, the admissions process is subject to criticism for its use of broad discretionary power. As readers of this thesis are informed of the subjective evaluations made by individual committee members and of the degree of individual discretion involved in the advocacy system, some have already and others are likely to question the equity of the admissions process.[13]

Some asked whether the use of vague "personal characteristics" would allow whims and biases to influence admissions. Some of Bender's stereotypes do chafe:

> Would Harvard become such an intellectual hot-house that the unfortunate aspects of a self-conscious "intellectualism" would become dominant and the precious, the brittle and the neurotic take over? . . . The question is, what happens to the atmosphere and the values of an institution and how do its students react on each other when an entire undergraduate student body consists of "gifted" individuals? There is some profane amateur opinion that the percentage of bearded types tends to go up with the increase of the average IQ. And anyone who has survived the feline atmosphere of a Phi Beta Kappa chapter meeting when the Junior Eight or the Senior Sixteen were being chosen must have some concerns.[14]

And what seems admirable "diversity" to an admissions committee at one point in time may not sit well later. At the time Dean Bender was writing about diversity at the College, he noted that almost 90 percent of alumni sons were admitted and deplored the limited progress in incorporating low income families. (Dean Peterson later stated that in 1960 only 3 percent of the student body came from "the lower half of the nation's social strata.")[15] Dean Bender never mentioned race as an aspect of diversity, but by 1968, the underrepresentation of blacks and other minorities was perceived as a major lack of diversity. The number of freshman blacks at Harvard suddenly jumped from about 2 to about 7 percent. By 1968, less than half of alumni sons were being admitted—a figure that has continued to decline.

Obviously, value judgments are at issue here. But factual questions are also important in deciding how much diversity of what kinds we should prefer. First, what are the facts about current procedures? How much do various nonacademic criteria matter to a candidate's chance of being admitted? Second, how much is lost in academic terms, and how much gained in other ways, by emphasizing diversity?

Current data are kept confidential, but earlier studies are helpful. Dean K. Whitla examined the relationship between various measures, committee ratings, and admission:

Measures ⟶	Committee Ratings ⟶	Admit/Reject
Test scores	Personal	
Grades	Academic	
Recommendations	Extracurricular	
Interviews	Athletic	
Essays	Overall	

Whitla used statistical analysis to combine measures into variables for "academic" and "personal" attributes. He found that personal attributes were more important than academic ones in determining admission.[16]

To underscore this point, consider the use of the committee's academic ratings in admissions. Extensive data are only available publicly for the Harvard College class of 1975,[17] which included only men (Harvard and Radcliffe admissions offices were not merged until 1975). In that year, 51 applicants were academically rated 1, the highest rating; 50 were admitted. In addition, 608 applicants were rated on the lowest categories of 5, 6, or 7, and 604 were rejected. Of the 1,747 applicants rated 4, only 173 were admitted.

The great uncertainty resided in applicants academically rated 2 or 3. Within this group, nonacademic factors were crucial. Table 2.2 shows the probability of being admitted for various subgroups, given an academic rating of 2 or 3. The table gives some rough idea of the "weights" accorded to various kinds of diversity for the College class of 1975.

TABLE 2.2

Probabilities of Admission for Subgroups of Candidates With Academic Rating of 2 or 3
(Harvard College Class of 1975)[18]

Applicants with Academic 2 or 3	N	Probability of Admission (%)	Probability Increase Over Other Applicants with Academic 2 or 3 (%)
Total	4,244	30	—
Alumni son	1,223	60	33
Black	96	73	45
Athlete*	396	64	38
Private school	1,233	37	10
"Scientist"**	658	33	4

NOTE:
*Athlete = athletic rating of 1 or 2 (possible college varsity player).
**Scientist refers to a perspective major in engineering or physics. According to the rating code for the class of 1975, an academic rating of 2 was defined as: "Strong scholastic ability. Will do solid honors or magna work." A 3 rating was: "Good solid student; probably will do honors work."

Figure 2.1 shows the actual class chosen compared with a class if chosen on the basis of verbal scores on the Scholastic Aptitude Test (SAT). Notice that the entire class would have been above 690 on the SAT verbal, compared to fewer than 35 percent in the actual class. The average SAT verbal score would have been about 60 points, or 1.2 standard deviations, higher; the tenth percentile would have increased by about 100 points, or more than 2 standard deviations.

This is one crude way of estimating some academic costs of the College's deviations from strictly academic criteria in admissions. It remains a question how much these costs matter. There is also the question of what the ostensible gains in "character" and "diversity" were worth. We shall look at both issues in later chapters.

PROCEDURES

In the late 1970s, applicants submitted transcripts, letters from principals and teachers, SAT aptitude and achievement tests, and several essays. This information, together with the required interview reports, was read by at least two members of the admissions committee. Applicants were divided by "dockets," which separated areas of the country and cities, particular private schools, and foreign candidates for purposes of the first analysis. These divisions facilitated comparisons among similar candidates and permitted members of the committee to specialize on schools in particular areas. Dockets also encouraged diversity. Targets for numbers of students from each docket were established in advance.

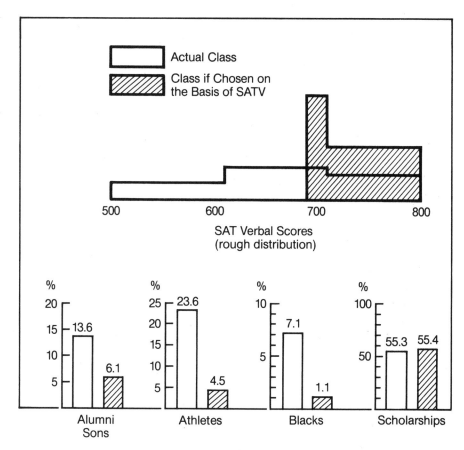

FIGURE 2.1

Admission If Based on SAT Verbal Scores [Harvard College, Class of 1975]

Applicants were categorized by letter code according to what a 1977 faculty review of admissions called "personality type":

S = First-rate *scholar* in Harvard departmental terms (will usually be a "1" academic)
D = Candidate's primary strength is his academic talent, but it doesn't look strong enough to qualify as an S (D comes from "diller dollar second-rate scholar")
A = *All-American*—healthy uncomplicated athletic strengths (though not necessarily a varsity prospect here) and style; perhaps some extracurricular participation, but not combined with top academic credentials
W = *Wheel*—Mr. School: significant extracurricular and perhaps (but not necessarily) athletic participation plus excellent academic record
K = *Krunch*—main strength is athletic; prospective varsity athlete

29

P = PBH Style—real social concern and action (PBH stands for Phillips Brooks House, a service organization at Harvard)
B = Boondocker—unsophisticated rural background
C = Creative—in music, art, writing, and so forth
T = Taconic—from culturally depressed background, usually includes low income
L = Lineage—Candidate probably could not be admitted without the extra plus of being a Harvard son, a faculty son, or a local boy with ties to the university community

Readers gave the candidates an overall rating from 1 to 5, where 1 was a clear admit and 5 a clear reject. In addition, readers contributed four other ratings—academic, extracurricular, athletic, and personal—and a summary descriptive paragraph.

Subcommittees of five to ten people then considered the candidates. Clear admits and rejects were set aside. For each candidate, an "advocate" on the committee presented the case for acceptance. From around February 15 until March 20, subcommittees met six or seven days a week, and many nights. Thereafter, the full committee met daily through early April to deal with the most difficult cases. Those who have participated in or studied this process are impressed by—and proud of—the enormous effort expended and the integrity of the process.[19] The 1977 faculty review concluded:

> All these analytic breakdowns by origin as well as personality type have facilitated the Committee's task of representing the major interest groups who are important in the mix to be represented at Harvard such as alumni, private schools, scientists, blacks, athletes or the like. These and other constituencies with supporters among the Harvard administration, the faculty, the alumni, or in the public scene cannot be ignored. The result is a process wherein the Admissions Committee of staff and faculty members try to achieve multiple goals using multiple criteria, flexibly applied. This procedure is made as sophisticated and responsible as possible. It weighs an applicant's individual strengths carefully while also considering his membership in some broader constituency.[20]

The Harvard College admissions committee is composed primarily of professional admissions officers led by a dean and a director, with modest participation by a few faculty members. Penny Feldman described these officers in 1975:

> For the most part, committee members who were Harvard undergraduates are the product of the norms of personalization and categorization first instituted in the 1920s. Neither the "brilliant students" nor the "truly original and independent and imaginative minds" who are sometimes admitted to Harvard, they

were, rather, among the students who were admitted for other reasons: for their "goodness or loyalty or energy or perceptivity or a passionate concern of some sort."

They share in common a belief that they can identify the nuances in individual character and ability which make for a successful career at Harvard College, for they were all successful themselves. They are strongly and personally inclined to continue the practices which brought them to Harvard and to define success in terms of personal adjustment, some contribution to extracurricular life, and academic competence rather than academic superiority.[21]

The admissions process is costly. In 1982–83, the College's staff for admissions and financial aid cost about $600,000 a year, of which about $450,000 was for admissions work alone. Dean of Admissions Fred Jewett estimated that if folders were given only one reading and committee discussions were eliminated—as at some schools—about half of the $450,000 could be saved. An additional $10,000 would be saved from the $40,000 computer time budget by such a move.

The Graduate School of Arts and Sciences (GSAS)

Over forty separate departments, divisions, and committees in the Faculty of Arts and Sciences offer graduate degrees, mostly Ph.D.s. Each establishes its own admissions standards and procedures. Although a central office in GSAS handles some of the administrative details, there is no homogeneous admissions policy. Nonetheless, broad objectives are shared, and many departments face similar, vexing problems.

OBJECTIVES

"The most basic mission of the Graduate School," said a recent memorandum on admissions policies, "is to provide guided intellectual development in a specialized area of scholarship, leading to independent research and original contributions to a field of study."[22] Departments are searching for creative and original minds who will eventually advance knowledge in their fields. To a degree unmatched elsewhere at Harvard, the objective is to reproduce the faculty. Doctoral training resembles a research apprenticeship. Even an applied field like psychology, where clinical and other professional jobs exist, states its objective unequivocally: ". . . to train research psychologists to carry out original research on a wide variety of psychological phenomena. . . ."

DESIRED CHARACTERISTICS

Various attributes receive different weights in different departments. Indeed, even within a single department, members of the admissions committee judge candidates differently. "We attempt to use everything in the folder—grades, GREs, personal statements, and letters," noted one professor. "Different individuals weight them differently. No instructions are offered as to how to make these judgments."

My impression after examining the admissions policies in several departments is one indicating subjective appraisal by faculty members with little help from empirical studies or from clear departmental guidelines. The essence of a "policy," insofar as one exists, is not the delineation of desired attributes and appropriate weights for imperfect measures, but a process designed to involve a variety of faculty members in choosing their future students.

The most important criteria are usually prior grades and test scores. Most departments try to factor in the difficulty and type of courses taken as well as the college that the applicant attended. "Evidence of analytical skills and writing ability is important," said Professor Sidney Verba of the Department of Government. "We often look for some demonstrated skill in difficult analytical tasks—high test scores in mathematics, a high grade in a course in the hard sciences, et cetera."[23]

Test scores are required by most, but not all, departments. In many cases, the verbal and mathematical aptitude scores are given weight but achievement scores in the particular fields are only marginally important. Only a few departments seem to use "cut scores," or particular thresholds below which candidates are only cursorily screened. One that does this is the Psychology and Social Relations Department. Internal studies over the years have shown that students with combined verbal and quantitative GRE scores below 1,300 have often had academic problems. The current procedure gives such applicants only one read, and generally they are rejected.

Test scores may matter too much. Professor Duncan Luce of the Psychology and Social Relations Department colorfully described the situation:

> Despite the fact that all of us know that with GREs above 1300 there is little or no correlation between them and graduate performance, it is irresistible to pay attention to the numbers. They have a magic simplicity.[24]

Letters of recommendation are required, but there is widespread skepticism about their value. "They are hard to judge and hard to read," said one chairman. "I write lots of recommendations myself and have frequently lied through my teeth. Some people write good recommendations and are honest, but more are like myself, they are jellyfish. I never say anything bad about a student." Another agreed:

> The letters may be useless or worse. There is such an inflation of superlatives that most contain no information of use. Moreover, there is a tendency to search for signs or hints of something negative, and I fear that we are penalizing some applicants because some of the letter writers are less in command of the language than others are. In a few cases where we know the letter writer, there probably is useful information. I have serious doubts about the worth of asking for them, at least in the way we now do it.

Students are asked to write essays about their career plans, academic interests, and so forth. When the essays are sublime or ridiculous, they can make a difference. Still, many professors doubt the usefulness of essays.

A few departments interview the most promising applicants. Professor Gwynne Evans described the situation in the English department:

> Dissatisfied with the extent to which it was possible to judge a candidate solely on the basis of an application folder, the English Department three years ago added the extra final step of a personal interview. Although the process is costly, . . . the department feels that a number of gains outweigh the cost, gains for the candidate as well as for the department. In the first place it allows us to evaluate a student's promise as a teacher and scholar much more immediately than course grades, GRE scores, or letters of recommendation allow (especially since score grades tend to be inflated and letters of recommendation, because of the Buckley amendment, more wisely cautious or laudatory than ever). Second, apart from permitting us to assess a student's actual knowledge, critical sophistication, and preparation (what kind of impact, in other words, four years of undergraduate learning, and in many cases graduate study, has in fact had on his or her mind), the interview gives us an opportunity to observe how a student handles himself (or herself) in a situation in many ways analogous to that which he or she will be facing both as a graduate student and as a teacher—a kind of exchange of minds.[25]

Few departments worry about "diversity" or "balance" in an entering class, with two exceptions: academic subfield and race. The subfield matters in some departments but not others. In 1980, for example, the Department of Psychology and Social Relations divided applicants according to their prospective specialties, such as cognitive development, psychobiology, sensation and perception, personality, and so forth. The faculty from each subfield then rated the candidates. Then the department's admissions committee gave an overall ranking. This procedure has since been abandoned. The English department steadfastly avoided any balancing acts. "We don't just want medievalists looking at medievalists," Professor

Evans noted, explaining why the 220 applicants were distributed among the entire admissions committee. "We want the best from a professional point of view. If the best is a medievalist but we need a modernist, that's too bad. We take the medievalist."[26]

Regarding minorities, GSAS built in incentives to admit them. Each department was given a quota of financial aid by GSAS. But minority students did not count against the quota. GSAS in effect picked up the tab for minority students without charging the departmental allocation. Nonetheless, little weight was apparently given to minority status (and perhaps a very little to women). Only one percent of the 817 admits for fall 1980 to GSAS were blacks. Four percent were "East Asian," and none was a member of another minority group.[27]

Other dimensions of diversity—such as geography, athletics, artistic talent, and so forth—are spurned. Sometimes "personality" matters. But here it is not a question of screening in people with desirable traits, but of screening out those with psychological troubles or attitudinal shortcomings, as judged by the committee members.

PROCEDURES

In 1980, most departments employed a three-stage process. A first reading or two eliminated about half the applicants. Then the admissions committee met to decide who among those remaining were admissible. Finally, the admissible ones were ranked by the committee and passed along to the GSAS admissions office. The key features of this process were: (1) faculty members made up the admissions committee, not professional admissions officers or students; (2) when they made their decisions, the committees did not know about the financial situation of applicants; and (3) the financial aid system turned out to mean that a low-ranking but admissible candidate who could pay his or her own way would be able to come to Harvard in lieu of a candidate who was much higher ranked but without funds.

The procedures are described in a GSAS memorandum:

> After a department completes its initial review of all applicants, the files of applicants found clearly inadmissible are returned to the [GSAS] Admissions Office, and deny letters are mailed under the signature of the Director of Admissions. The department then ranks #1, 2, 3, etc., the remaining applicants according to desirability. Not all ranked candidates will be offered admission. Offers of admissions are made according to a predetermined number of openings in the department and the availability of financial grant-in-aid funds for the department. Normally, candidates will be admitted in order of their placement on the rank list. However, if a department runs out of grant funds before running out of spaces, further offers of admissions are made only to those applicants who

can demonstrate self-support for the first two years of graduate study. In these cases some lower-ranked applicants may be admitted because applicants ranked higher could not demonstrate sufficient assured resources.[28]

The Law School

OBJECTIVES

A recent issue of the Law School's Register elaborates on the oft-cited goal of "teaching students to think like a lawyer."

> The Law School seeks to impart the enduring principles of law, legal philosophy and the historical development of legal institutions, rather than emphasize the mastery of legal detail and memorization of terminology. The goal is to develop the student's ability to analyze the web of facts at the core of a problem, and then to solve that problem using legal methods. The faculty believes that a firm understanding of judicial principles and reasoning better equips students to deal with new legal problems as the law changes and evolves.[29]

DESIRED CHARACTERISTICS

In comparison with other professional schools, law schools tend to rely more on academic criteria and less on "personal characteristics." Over the years, the Harvard Law School has carried out careful studies of the correlates of first-year grades, and these results have been utilized in the admissions process. Predictions are based on Law School Admissions Test (LSAT) scores and on college grades that have been statistically adjusted by the law school to reflect the fact that, say, a 3.6 grade average from one college does not predict the same law school grades as a 3.6 from a college with higher standards. In the early 1980s, the tests and adjusted grades were combined into an "admissions index" (AI). Briefly, the AI used an average of LSAT scores on the old 200–800 scale and the adjusted college grade-point average (where $4 = A$, $3 = B$, $2 = C$, and so on) multiplied by 200, so that grades became roughly comparable to the LSAT. Then:

$$AI = \frac{(200 \times \text{adjusted grades}) + \text{LSAT (old scale)}}{2}$$

For example, a student with an adjusted college grade average of 3.6 and an LSAT of 680 would have an AI of 700, the same AI as a student with a 3.0 adjusted grade average and a perfect 800 LSAT score. The AI is used

35

to separate candidates at the outset and is closely related to the admissions committee's final decision.

The Law School has in the past informed prospective applicants, faculty, and alumni about selected aspects of its admissions process. For example, a 1978 article in the Law School's alumni magazine not only described the process, but gave a table showing the probability of being admitted given various values of the AI.[30] The data from that table are the basis for figure 2.2.

Notice how important small changes in the AI were in the 700 or 740 area. For example, in 1978 a student with a 3.6 average from Harvard College and a 720 LSAT score had an AI of 720 and about a 40 percent chance of being admitted. If the same student had a 3.7 grade average, the chance of being admitted jumped to over 60 percent. A student with a 3.7 average and a 740 LSAT score had about an 80 percent chance of getting in.

The AI is not the only criterion. The committee considers personal

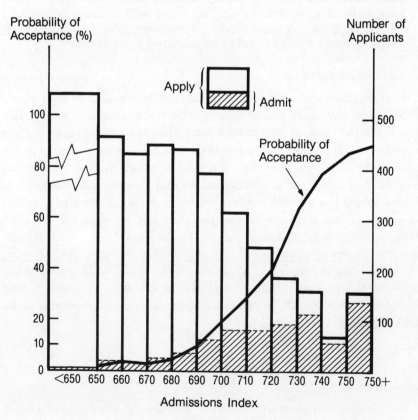

FIGURE 2.2

Applications and Acceptances by Admissions Index [AI] Harvard Law School, 1978

characteristics thought to be important for a successful legal career. Motivation is sometimes a factor—as one member of the committee put it, "I'm partial to people who persuade me that they really want to become lawyers." The faculty is ambivalent about trying to assess "leadership" and "personality." On the one hand, applicants are told "We also try to assess a number of intangible qualities—energy, ambition, sound judgment, and high ideals."[31] On the other, some professors and deans worry that these other dimensions are unclearly related to later legal success, are difficult to define and measure, and may screen out "the unorthodox thinker, the maverick, the curmudgeon." A leading faculty member described the dilemma this way:

> First-year grades are our set baseline of success. We would love to have other measures of success, say as a lawyer. But we tend to believe that first-year grades measure analytical ability. We know that other things matter in being a successful lawyer, but a good measure of pessimism is in order about our ability to measure those other things. . . . For success in the real world, you have to worry about many other qualities, such as getting along with people or the ability to collaborate or the ability to organize one's own activities and the activities of others. . . . But entering into such traits might lead to misunderstanding, since we are admitting people to a training program and not to a job.

Diversity matters: among the considerations that affect decisions are race, geography (Cambridge and far-flung areas like Wyoming get preference at the margin), economic disadvantage, unusual work experience, and sex. No "diversity points" are given for athletics, artistic talent, prep schools, appearance, and so forth. Relatives of alumni are given far less preference than at the College or even the Medical School.

> Since the vast majority of faculty and alumni had no forbears closely connected to the School, perhaps some would have been excluded had significant preferences been given for those "connections." The fear is also expressed that many of the extraordinary candidates whom the School would most like to have as students would view such a preference as unfair and would not seek admission in competition with other less qualified candidates who had the proper "connections."[32]

There are no prescribed policies or explicitly agreed-upon criteria for the committee to follow:

> Factors that are considered strongly by one member of an Admissions Committee have been considered irrelevant or negative by other members. Committee decisions involve compromise and persuasion which complicate attempts to analyze the results of those decisions. Furthermore, membership on the Committee changes significantly on a two- to four-year cycle. Factors that one

Committee emphasized regularly may be weighed sparingly by another Committee.[33]

This also holds for "diversity," which is not obtained according to a fixed formula but as the natural by-product of individual decisions.[34]

The Law School also requires a personal statement, letters of recommendation, and a "college questionnaire." There are no interviews. The essay gives the candidate a chance to "present themselves and their qualifications as they wish." But as an assistant dean observed, "Most candidates do not use these opportunities to very good advantage."[35] Letters of recommendation discuss both academic and personal qualifications. They are usually inflated:

> Although writers of these recommendations are cautioned to be specific and to state the facts on which their academic judgments are based, the vast majority of academic recommendations are very general and not helpful to the Admissions Committee. Most authors of academic recommendations feel great pressure to be advocates. By trying to make each candidate appear to be a budding Holmes or Cardozo, they make most candidates sound very good but very much alike.[36]

But despite these shortcomings:

> About half the members of each entering class would not have been admitted but for one or more letters of recommendation that provided essential information or strongly supported or supplemented information found elsewhere in the application materials.[37]

PROCEDURES

In the early 1980s, the committee was chaired by a professor and included three assistant deans and two other professors. Specially trained readers assisted with applicants with AIs below 650, the bottom half of the 7,000 person applicant pool. A preliminary grouping of applicants was done on the basis of the AI, as table 2.3 describes.

The committee met weekly from December to April and made admit, hold, and reject decisions at each session. Approximately 400 applicants were discussed by the entire committee. About 150 of the 750 slots were withheld till the end for the final round of applicants and those on hold from earlier sessions. The process was grueling. Each faculty member on the committee read about 1,000 applications; the assistant deans read even more.

TABLE 2.3

Screening at Harvard Law School (1978)[38]

Approximate AI	Applicants	%	Procedure	Admitted (%)
725+	500–600	8	Read by an assistant dean and a professor. If both vote admit, the applicant is accepted. Otherwise, the applicant is given further reads and discussed by the committee.	75+
700–725	600–800	10	First read by an assistant dean. If accept, then two faculty members read and if they agree, the applicant is accepted. If deny, then other assistant dean reads; if both deny, then rejected. Otherwise, the candidate is discussed by the committee.	30
650–700	1,700–2,000	25	First read by an assistant dean. If reject, then rejected. If accept, then goes to two faculty members for reading.	5
650	3,500–3,800	50–60	First read by a specially hired reader, not a member of the committee. Unless the candidate is a minority or has outstanding personal attributes, he/she is rejected after being "reviewed" by a member of the committee. Those 10–15 percent passed along are read by committee members and discussed.	under 2

NOTE: Total applicants about 7,000; total admits about 750

The Medical School

OBJECTIVES

Compared to the College and to Harvard's other major professional schools, the Medical School has a small entering class—only about 165 positions. Despite its relatively small numbers, the school has not specialized like some other medical schools. Instead, it looks for future leaders in all areas of medicine:

> Harvard does not seek to train primarily scientists for research or primarily clinicians for the practice of medicine or primarily teachers. Rather, a goal of the educational program is the development of highly qualified physicians capable of providing leadership in their chosen fields, no matter how diverse.[39]

It has proved difficult to agree upon the specific desired characteristics of Harvard Medical School students, with two exceptions: the objective of 20 percent minority representation and a quota of 25 students per class for the Harvard-MIT joint program in Health Sciences and Technology. A review of the school's admissions process was blunt: "In other areas policy is poorly defined or inconsistent, or non-existent".[40]

Academic criteria are paramount. A candidate "must present evidence that his or her academic achievement and other credentials are of such quality as to predict a high degree of success in the graduate study of medicine."[41] Applicants have to satisfy various prerequisites: a year of biology, two years of chemistry, a year of calculus, a year of physics, and a year of English composition and literature. (A new subcommittee is looking into the possibility of relaxing these prerequisites in various ways.)

The Medical School also values "character" and "motivation." "Within a large and diversified pool of applicants," explained a 1979 review of the admissions system, "the objective is to attempt to single out those individuals whose academic performance is accompanied by a constellation of moral qualities which include integrity, maturity, commitment to society, capacity to relate to people, and broad human interests."[42] Once again, the word "leadership" is current, as in these guidelines for interviewers:

> Ideally, we seek evidence of native intelligence, judgment, maturity, imagination and leadership. Is the student rigid or flexible and adaptable? How well will the applicant relate to people? Is the applicant a broad and well-informed young citizen, or is he or she narrow in academic and extracurricular interests? What is the ultimate potential as a physician? . . . It is our aim to select for Harvard truly outstanding young men and women destined to be leaders in medicine.[43]

Some sorts of "diversity" count and some do not. Racial diversity is especially important. "The minimum goal should be a representation of minority groups in the student body at least equal to the proportion of these minority groups in the population of the U.S.A. at large."[44] Women are actively recruited. Between two equally talented candidates, an edge is given to faculty or alumni offspring. Candidates from geographically diverse colleges and hometowns are given a marginal boost.

Other sources of diversity are ignored. Future career choice is unimportant:

> It is neither wise nor feasible for the Admissions Committee to try to select students according to predicted future needs of society. . . . In the consideration of a given applicant it is unlikely that his or her essay, lifestyle, academic or extracurricular records, or even the reactions of discerning interviewers will give

evidence adequate to permit the prediction of his or her future professional career.[45]

An applicant's undergraduate major is considered when assessing quality of mind, but the class is not balanced by a varied group of majors. Unlike the College, athletic and artistic success are not counted among the valued dimensions of "first-rateness." Foreigners are "discouraged" in spite of the diversity they might add on the grounds that the United States does not have enough facilities to train its own citizens.[46]

PROCEDURES

In 1980, the *Harvard Medical Alumni Bulletin* published a lengthy account of the prevailing admissions process. Several features are worth highlighting: (1) the system of subcommittees (including one designated for minorities, which has since been discontinued); (2) the participation of students (about one fifth of the admissions committee) and faculty (the remainder); (3) the elaborate system of two interviews each for almost 1,000 finalists; and (4) the lack of uniform criteria for screening, interviews, and final voting.

Judgments are based on all available information, including the academic record, MCAT scores, the essay, extracurricular activities, and letters of recommendation. . . . If an application had only one rating of ten it was examined by a third screener. Thereafter, all subcommittee chairmen had the opportunity to review the applications. The chairman of the minority subcommittee reviewed all pertinent candidates with a rating close to ten. The applications were then assigned to subcommittee IV [for minority students], and the remainder were distributed to subcommittees I, II, and III on the basis of the college of origin. Through years of experience, the subcommittees have learned how to interpret the grading systems and letters of recommendation of different colleges. As a result of the screening process, the applicant pool was narrowed to 926, a four-fold reduction that is believed to be about the maximum possible on the basis of the material received.

All 926 students had two interviews. Interviewers included all members of the admission committee and the subcommittees, and for regional interviews outside of Boston, alumni/ae together with subcommittee representatives. Every attempt was made to assure that at least one interviewer was a member of the subcommittee to which the particular applicant was assigned. The second interviewer was chosen at random. . . . The interviewers seek evidence of integrity, ability to relate to others, leadership qualities, broad human interests, and emotional maturity. The applicants were given scores of from 10, if outstanding, to 6 or less, if unsatisfactory.

Whenever possible, each application was presented to the appropriate subcommittee by the member who had functioned as an interviewer. Details of each application brought to light family background, academic record, MCAT scores, the essay, extracurricular activities, letters of recommendation, and the reports of the interviews. General discussion followed with special attention being paid to contradictory information. The subcommittees' deliberations were facilitated greatly by prior experience with the characteristics of the school of origin and its premedical committee. Thereupon, the applications were either rejected, put on hold, or passed on to the full committee. Applications on "hold" were decided upon in subsequent meetings.

It is important to note that the total number of applicants forwarded by the subcommittees to the parent committee was about twice those finally accepted and that the subcommittees provided no ranking of their respective applicants. This procedure guaranteed true merged competition of applicants from all the subcommittees. The highly rated applications forwarded from each subcommittee were then randomly assigned to members of the main admission committee. Each member addressed the strengths and weaknesses of the candidates assigned to him or her, again with detailed consideration of socioeconomic backgrounds, school records, MCAT scores, essays, recommendations, collateral activities and impressions from interviews. . . . After a general discussion, a vote was taken, with options of "accept," "hold," and "reject." The number of votes in each category for each applicant was recorded, followed by more discussion and a final vote.[47]

The Graduate School of Business Administration

OBJECTIVES AND CRITERIA

"The basic objectives of our admissions function have changed very little over time," noted a faculty report in late 1976.[48] A 1974 faculty review cited a 1970 committee, and that committee in turn had referred to a 1957 report. "The 1957 legislation is still today the guiding policy of the Admissions Board," the 1976 report states, "except that the policy is now applied to men and women alike."[49] Notice the emphasis on outstanding personal characteristics:

The admissions policy of the Business School is to select from applicants for admission those men whose character, intellectual capacity, seriousness of purpose, maturity, leadership potentialities, willingness to assume responsibility, and other favorable personal qualities best fit them to be trained for administrative positions in business. The Admissions Board will seek to minimize the number of failures throughout the program by selecting for admission only men reasonably likely to complete the MBA Program satisfactorily and to be effective administrators after graduation.[50]

The faculty committees that reviewed admissions in 1970 and 1974 were more explicit:

42

The recruitment of well-qualified applicants to the MBA Program is the first stage of a long-term educational process. Our goals for admissions are obviously related to the product that we want to emerge from the education process and to the education process itself. . . .

In terms of output, we want to have alumni who will:

- be leaders in our society and economy,
- view organizations as effective means of achieving social purposes,
- provide managerial talent for both American and foreign businesses and for other organizations,
- provide a broader socio-economic-cultural base from which leaders, managers, and administrators are drawn.

In terms of the educational program itself, we want to have students who will:

- improve themselves by increasing their skills and thus expand their potential roles in our economy,
- contribute to the learning process of their peers by bringing their background, knowledge, and experience to bear on case discussions both in and outside the classroom,
- share with the Faculty an interest in the subject matter, concepts, and skills which constitute a curriculum in business administration, and energetically participate in the learning process,
- have the ability to perform well academically.

The evaluation of applicants is based on three main areas: (1) academic ability, (2) past and potential administrative achievement, (3) those personal qualities necessary for outstanding achievement in management.

Given that the School must select an entering class from a large number of applicants, most of whom possess the basic qualifications to benefit from the MBA Program, we agree with previous statements on the evaluation of applicants to identify those individuals who are outstanding in several of the following characteristics: intellectual aptitude, entrepreneurship, peer leadership, demonstrated concern for social issues, non-academic achievement (either administrative or non-administrative), and other distinctions.[51]

There are no longer "pools of applicants for which lower standards are accepted." In the past, the Business School had such pools for military officers, women, students from developing countries, and disadvantaged minorities. In 1969, the faculty voted to "admit candidates from disadvantaged minorities to the first year of the program in the greatest number consistent with the effective functioning of the program."[52] All minorities with no more than a one in four chance of flunking out were admitted. In 1970, minority groups were not mentioned in the recommendations, being replaced by "educationally disadvantaged groups."[53] But later reports—in 1974 and 1976—stressed the goal of 10–12 percent minority representation. The faculty also called in 1970 for explicit preference for applicants from "foreign countries other than those in Western Europe or those in which English is the principal language."

The rigors of the first-year curriculum require good mathematical aptitude, which is measured in part by scores on the Graduate Management Admissions Test. Particular academic preparation is not required. Most entering students have business experience; often young applicants are rejected with encouragement to reapply after gaining business experience.

In addition to grades, test scores, and recommendations, applicants submit seven essays. The essays are considered an invaluable tool of assessment. In their length and importance as an admissions criterion, essays probably play a more significant role at the Business School than anywhere else at Harvard. Personal interviews are not used.

PROCEDURES

The admissions board is made up of professional admissions officers. Most are recent graduates of the Harvard Business School, who work on the board for a few years before entering a career in the private sector. In 1979–80, each voluminous application received a "preliminary application review," where the candidate was given three "PAR ratings" to summarize his or her promise as a general manager. Then the application was read by two members of the board and reviewed before a final decision was made by the director.

New board members are often "broken in." Some may be asked to read old folders and relevant literature and report to the director their impressions of the appropriate criteria for admission. There is no substitute for reading essay after essay: "You have to read about six hundred applications before you get a handle on how to judge the candidates," a past director said. As elsewhere at Harvard, there is no formal training for admissions committees.

From 1969 to 1975, a "second-stage" process allowed minority students, who were rejected in the strictly competitive regular admissions process, to be given a second review reading by a special subcommittee of the admissions board based on a different standard of admissibility, namely whether they had a sufficient chance of completing the MBA Program.[54] This process was abolished in 1976, but affirmative action is still stressed. Minority readers may be sought to help place the applicant's achievements in context. "Under an open admissions policy, recruitment and financial aid become the only instruments through which we can improve minority enrollment."[55] According to the faculty, the old system had several undesirable outcomes:

44

- Too many second-stage admits ended up at the bottom of the class. Yet they might have done well at many other business schools.[56]
- Other minorities felt stigmatized by the second-stage process, as if future employers were being told that Harvard had two sorts of students.[57]
- Fair grading may have been hindered by the faculty's desire not to fail disproportionate numbers of minorities.[58]
- The pressure to find higher quality minority students "might be unjustifiably diminished" by admitting less qualified minorities through the second-stage process.

The Afro-American Student Union also recommended that "all special review processes for minority applicants should be eliminated."

In the 1970s, the faculty approved a 4 percent minimum quota of students from non-English speaking countries. This was later abolished as superfluous; that percentage was easily met without special considerations.

Admissions at Other Universities

Harvard has other professional schools, and they exhibit their own idiosyncratic policies and procedures. But without reviewing other Harvard examples, I trust an important message about selection at the right tail is already clear: the range of policies and practices is extraordinary. Objectives, desired characteristics, and admissions processes vary remarkably, even among the faculties of a single university.

This lesson applies to other highly selective universities as well. Across institutions, one discovers greatly differing policies. Within categories, however, such as medical schools or law schools, there are some common practices. For example:

Selective colleges. In a survey of 1,463 colleges, only 13 percent called themselves "competitive," admitting fewer than half of "those applicants who meet some specified level of academic achievement." Academic criteria are important. But like Harvard College, these schools value personal characteristics, alumni relations, and ethnic diversity. To assess these attributes, admissions committees use interviews, student essays, letters of recommendation, and extracurricular activities. Seldom do students participate in admissions, and most colleges rely on professional admissions officers more than faculty members.[59]

As an example of which nonacademic characteristics matter and how much, consider table 2.4. At these three selective colleges, the most important determinants of admission besides academic criteria were membership in a minority group, having an alumni parent, living in the local community, and having an "outstanding" interview. Extracurricular activities almost never had statistically significant effects.

Graduate schools of arts and sciences. Like Harvard, most schools select primarily on the basis of intellectual attributes. Personal characteristics matter little, with the exception of race—in one survey, "minority group admissions was deemed the foremost issue facing graduate schools."[61] Faculty members make the admissions decisions in most cases. Only a small fraction of graduate departments conduct studies of the performance of those admitted. As at Harvard, departmental practices vary widely, and the admissions process seems chaotic compared to colleges and professional schools.

Law schools. Like Harvard, most law schools group applicants with an admissions index based on predictors of first-year law school grades. Also, like Harvard, many law schools talk of the need for diversity, character, personality, and other variables, but these characteristics do not affect

TABLE 2.4
How Nonacademic Characteristics Influence Admissions[60]

	Percentage Point Increase in the Probability of Being Admitted at:		
	Williams	Colgate	Bucknell
Background Characteristic			
Female	0	0	−1
Minority Group	53	46	51
Disadvantaged	18	6	−1
Geographical diversity (state)	—	10	10
Local resident	26	9	26
Parent:			
Prominent	3	−3	−2
Highly educated	2	0	0
Alumni	36	31	47
Personal Achievement			
Community activities	3	4	−7
Athletic	5	1	4
Leadership	3	10	7
Creative talent	5	4	2
Essays:			
Writing quality	17	7	9
Content	11	12	2
School recommendation	3	12	5
Teacher reference	3	10	2
Outstanding interview	23	17	30

NOTE: The numbers indicate the extent of advantage or disadvantage that groups with various characteristics have in admissions, assuming comparable high-school academic ranks in class and Scholastic Aptitude Test scores.

admissions decisions much compared to professional schools elsewhere. Admissions are primarily determined by two major considerations: predicted first-year grades and race. Surveys show that admissions directors are reluctant to make selections based on the supposed attributes of successful lawyers.

> If admissions directors wished to select those persons likely to become successful lawyers, they would first have to decide how much to measure such success and how to predict it. Such double guesswork generates arbitrary admissions criteria dependent largely on the biases of the persons devising them, and it is hardly surprising that the responses of admissions directors to questions eliciting their views on nonobjective criteria were vague and highly generalized.[62]

Interviews are rarely used. Essays and recommendations are solicited, but they usually receive little weight.

Medical schools. Most are highly competitive in academic terms. Studies show that the most powerful predictors of being admitted are grades in science courses and scores on the science portion of the Medical College Admissions Test. Almost all medical schools require college courses in biology, organic and inorganic chemistry, and physics; the vast majority of applicants accepted are science majors. Most medical schools favor graduates of the undergraduate school of the parent university.

But like Harvard, despite heavy emphasis on academic excellence in science, most medical schools talk a lot about the importance of "personal qualities" and have aggressively pursued affirmative action. Interviews are the preferred means for assessing personal characteristics—this despite numerous challenges in medical schools of the reliability and validity of personal interviews.[63] Letters of recommendation and essays are also solicited. As at Harvard, most medical school admissions committees are dominated by faculty members, but students often participate.

Business schools. "Probably more than in any other discipline, actual work experience is highly valued" by business school admissions committees.[64] As at Harvard, experienced students are thought to contribute more to the learning of their classmates, particularly in courses taught by the case method. But success in an early job is also thought to correlate with success in a managerial career. More than in other major professions, business schools try to select on the basis of attributes associated with top professionals. Predicted first-year grades are not the main criterion, although academic talent is important, particularly analytical aptitude. Admissions committees give great weight to their subjective appraisals of social and interpersonal skills, initiative, tenacity, and the ability to get things done. Only about a quarter of business schools interview at least half of their applicants; instead, essays and recommendations are heavily weighted. Most graduate schools of business utilize professional admissions officers.

Unresolved Questions

WHAT SHOULD BE SOUGHT IN CHOOSING AN ELITE?

A remarkable feature of selection policies is how vague they are. Many admissions officers and faculty review committees readily admit that policies are not spelled out and may vary from year to year depending on the committee, and that often individuals on the same committee weigh attributes completely differently.

This is not necessarily a shortcoming. Those who work in admissions may have an abiding confidence in our "clinical judgment" of merit. But upon reflection, the idea that selection shall be left to specialists' judgments seems simply to beg important questions. Surely, most academicians would be uncomfortable in accepting such an argument applied to other areas of public policy or educational policy: "Let us specialists decide, and let us do so subjectively and secretly, with a minimum of accountability." It seems an awkward stance in admissions policymaking and elsewhere. Even if politics and ritual and judgment inevitably play a role in the shaping of decisions, so too should careful thought about the objectives being sought.

Questions of objectives in choosing an elite have received too little attention. Chapter 3 attempts to sort out the issues involved and to create a framework for more effective discussions of the objectives of selection.

WHICH CRITERIA AND MEASURES SHOULD BE USED AND HOW?

Once we decide what we want, we face the problem of measuring it and predicting it. Various sources of information are used in various ways in admissions processes. How valid, reliable, and biased are test scores, grades, interviews, recommendations, and the rest in measuring and predicting various outcomes of interest? Might other sources of information be worthwhile? What kinds of "diversity" in the student body enhance the learning process, and how much? If we care about later success in life, how well can we predict it, and how much can we enhance it?

As we have seen, reviews of admissions processes at Harvard often lament the lack of data pertinent to these questions. It is remarkable how little systematic information is used by admissions committees in making their judgments and predictions. As Dr. Gertrude Murray, an alumna of the Harvard Medical School who participated in the 1978–79 review, noted: "There is a striking lack of outcome audits, of feedback, and of studies that verify the validity of the assumptions and decisions of the admission committee."[65]

The situation may be even worse in Great Britain:

> Here again British universities have lacked the initiative and boldness needed to carry out even the preliminary research which would tell them something about the applicability of these methods in relation to their needs; their whole approach has been a mixture of smugness and self-satisfaction hardly justified by the results.[66]

"Smugness" is probably not the best explanation. As we shall discover in chapter 4, empirical research is particularly complicated and methodologically perilous in the context of selection at the right tail. Simply put, we are raising hard questions that are hard to study. After reviewing the methodological difficulties and, I hope, resolving a few of them, we shall examine in chapters 5, 6, and 7 how well various criteria predict "success" of various kinds at the university and in later life.

HOW SHOULD "DIVERSITY" AND REPRESENTATIVENESS BE CONSIDERED?

As we have seen, admissions committees find this question particularly troubling. Important ethical questions are raised. To what extent should members of particular ethnic groups be advantaged in the selection process? Table 2.4 indicates that at Williams, Colgate, and Bucknell, minority status adds 40 or 50 percentage points to the probability of being admitted. Is this the extent of preference we want? More? Or less?

There are also many issues of fact. Are standard academic criteria biased against certain groups? How much does it "cost" in academic terms to admit more members of underrepresented groups? How should one analyze these trade-offs, particularly at the right tail? These questions are addressed in chapter 8.

WHAT ADMISSIONS PROCESS SHOULD BE FOLLOWED?

Admissions criteria are so vague and subjective that basic questions are raised about how decisions should be made and by whom. How should an admissions committee be held accountable? Should policies be clear and publicly known? How much influence should constituencies be allowed to have in the process? Can the process be made fairer to individuals and subgroups of interest? Can it be made less costly/more efficient?

We might even ponder a couple of radical questions. Given the problems of predicting success and the expense of the admissions system, why not admit more students and flunk them out more readily? Or why not select randomly among applicants who are above a certain threshold of admissibility? These last questions provide a convenient entry point into the next chapter.

3

The Objectives of Selection

THE FIRST QUESTION to ask about selective admissions is why it should be selective at all. Most people feel ambivalent about selectivity. On one side, we laud excellence, recognize its scarcity and utility, and endorse admissions on the basis of merit rather than ascriptive characteristics. On the other, we worry that a merit system and educational stratification may breed a privileged caste. Selectivity has unpleasant connotations of elitism, unfairness, snobbishness, and uniformity.

This ambivalence may make us wish we did not have to choose, but we do—don't we? After all, universities like Harvard have many more candidates than places in the entering class. So do employers for which there are more applicants than jobs. Only some can be accepted, and someone has to decide who they will be.

There may be a way out. Think of the problem as follows: Places at Harvard are a product, or a service. That product experiences excess demand. Our job, in effect, is to ration that excess demand. But why ration at all? Why not raise the tuition or expand the enrollment until supply and demand are equal?

This supply and demand approach is, I believe, a useful one for considering just what sort of "product" the university wishes to produce and, consequently, how it might begin to define the objectives of an admissions policy. (Similar questions could be devised for the analogous problem of an employer choosing employees.) To work through this approach, we could use some formal economic models, but that might be a bit dry. Consider instead an economist's fable on the evolution of the Harvard College admissions process from 1985 to 2010.

In 1988, the functioning of the selection mechanism underwent a revolutionary change at Harvard College, when the first auctioning system went into place. The new policy was lauded as "a major leap forward" by the university president.

"It will enable candidates themselves to judge the value of a Harvard education," the president said in his annual report. "It promises to bring the College a more secure financial base, with no loss to our academic values."

The policy was proposed in 1986 by a faculty review committee led by several members of the economics department and the vice-president for financial affairs. Its detailed report, which included many simulation models of classes chosen under different rules, contained several key points:

First, most applicants to Harvard were academically qualified. Moreover, the admissions office had stated on numerous occasions that "all Harvard graduates are successful" and that "grade-point averages are poor indicators of performance at Harvard or in later life." It was also argued that, except for premedical students, it was virtually impossible to predict of any eighteen-year-old his or her future career choice or likely social contribution. From these facts and opinions, the committee concluded that candidates who were qualified to do Harvard academic work—an estimated 90 percent of those who applied at that time—should be valued equally in terms of the admissions process.

Second, the committee examined students' motivations for pursuing higher education. Applicants were posited to maximize their individual "utilities," which were modeled as a sum of each student's estimate of his or her net value added from a particular education (computed in terms of discounted earnings streams from the various choices) and of the "consumption value" of the education. Students and their parents could be presumed to know these utility functions better than Harvard admissions officers. Therefore, because to Harvard all academically qualified candidates were identical, scarce spaces ought to be allocated to applicants who would receive the highest utility from them.

Third, however, the committee recognized that one could not simply ask applicants how much they wanted to come to Harvard. "Experience with statements of desire in student essays has shown them to be unreliable measures." Theoretical arguments were also used to show that candidates would have an incentive to inflate statements of their utilities, if they thought Harvard were admitting students on that basis. Thus, the committee asked that "market forces be harnessed here as elsewhere in our society."

The first auction for admissions was thereby conceived. It had two parts. A determination was made of the candidate's ability to do Harvard-level academic work, based on high-school grades and test scores. For those who qualified, a sealed bid, backed by a bank guarantee, was obtained. The bid stated how much the candidate was willing to pay to attend Harvard for a four-year period.

When news of this plan first leaked to the college newspaper, it was greeted with widespread derision. Indeed, an assistant to the dean, who had worked on the report and was identified with it in the Crimson, *was blasted as a "crass materialist," and student activists pasted his office over with Monopoly money.*

In those days, "selling out" was an expression of scorn and disapproval. Although elementary economics was the most heavily subscribed course on campus, many students and, to be fair, some faculty members from the humanities and the abstract physical sciences, did not readily understand the idea of different utilities for different students and the Pareto optimality of an auction. For the most part, the faculty members were assuaged when the financial implications of the new policy were made clear. Humanists were promised more library facilities and assistant professors, scientists more laboratory equipment and assistant professors.

Additionally, 150 places in the entering class were reserved for those applicants with the very highest test scores and grades, with scholarships depending on their need and not on their bids. This number roughly corresponded to the number of remarkable "scholars" admitted on that basis alone in previous Harvard College classes.

Despite the controversy, the president and corporation endorsed the report in 1987, and it went into place for the class entering in 1988. Data on actual bids received were kept in strict confidence, so the detailed workings of the new system are even now unknown. Rumor has it that the highest bid in the first year of operation was $1.3 million for four years, with several other bids alleged to be over $1 million. Tuition revenues soared upwards, though not by as much as the most optimistic members of the Harvard economics department had forecast.

Despite the financial success, there were complaints, and these resulted in a substantial change in the process in 1990. The new auctioning system was criticized as unfair to poorer students, who could not afford to bid as high as students from rich families. Supporters of the untrammeled auctioning process responded by saying that the distribution of wealth and income was decided by society, not by Harvard, through its system of economic rewards, inheritance taxes, income taxes, and transfer payments. It would be presumptuous and improper, it was argued, for Harvard as an institution to take a stand on the proper income distribution in the nation as a whole. In any case, the argument went on, poorer students could get loans, based on their future earnings potential.

But critics eventually won out, thanks to an award-winning doctoral dissertation that examined the workings of the capital market. If it could be shown that loans were not readily available to students with little income but great promise, then the efficiency arguments in favor of the auction were weakened. The thesis precisely documented such imperfections. Fortunately, the federal government was also moving in the direction of guaranteed loans for college, which were made feasible by a new repayment enforcement procedure controlled by the IRS and the FBI. The new dean of admissions explained, "No one could any longer object to auctioning on the grounds of inefficiencies caused by imperfect capital markets."

A major challenge to the auctioning system occurred in 1996. Faculty members complained that academic values were in decline, and they blamed it on the new admissions process. "Those most willing to procure a Harvard education are not those best fit to take advantage of our intellectual resources," said an open letter signed by a substantial proportion of the professoriat. Even with the 150 "scholars" admitted annually without regard to bids, the average level of academic performance had dropped, and a noticeable shift in tone had occurred. Students did not value the life of the mind as much. The result, it was argued, affected research as well as teaching. Despite the increase in facilities and junior faculty occasioned by the increased tuition revenues, a few professors had sought jobs at universities with a more academic atmosphere.

In short, all students should not have been valued equally just because they "can do the work at Harvard."

The problem was given to a faculty committee representing a range of disciplines. Their proposal, delivered in 1998, revised the auctioning system. "The university should recognize that though tuition is a valued attribute, it is not the only one. Students contribute in nonmonetary ways to the welfare of the university. These different 'benefits' that students bring to Harvard can be traded off in a fair and rational way."

Using detailed faculty surveys to estimate the trade-offs, the committee envisioned a two-part process. As before, applicants would submit bids. But an admissions committee would independently rate candidates in terms of predicted academic performance. A "trade-off surface" was constructed that defined an exchange rate between increases in willingness to pay and decreases in academic performance. In effect, the difference between a prospective magna and a prospective cum laude graduate was given a dollar value. Candidates with the highest total "value" to Harvard were admitted.

This proposal, complete with a complicated mathematical structure understood fully by only a few members of the committee, was endorsed by the corporation later that year and put into effect for the class entering in 2001. The new admissions process had higher costs, and these were immediate debates about the appropriate predictors of academic performance. But the new system also had an unforeseen benefit. Prospective students could no longer be sure that a bid somewhat higher than last year's lowest accepted bid would ensure their admission because their predicted academic performance would also be taken into account. But, as in the years before the auction, the estimation of an applicant's "predicted rank list" was shrouded in secrecy. As a result, applicants were uncertain of where they stood and bid much more. Tuition revenues soared even as willingness-to-pay was demoted from the sole criterion to one of two.

However, from 2002 to 2004, the new system came under attack from a variety of quarters. It was argued that additional criteria be added to the assessment of a student's contribution to Harvard. Tuition and academic performance were undeniably good, but so were other attributes. The proposals included weightings for:

- *Athletic excellence, with the highest weights given for skilled positions in football and large basketball players with touch. Points were also given to other excellent players in these sports and hockey, down to no points for projected junior varsity squash players.*
- *Musicians, particularly violinists and pianists, with the possibility of negative weightings for enthusiasts of electric guitars and snare drums.*

- *Persons of great physical beauty, who would "enhance the lives of other students and help dispel unflattering stereotypes about Harvard."*
- *Relatives of Harvard faculty members, with somewhat fewer points for the offspring of administrators.*
- *Those interested in the classics and other undersubscribed majors.*
- *Applicants afflicted with various physical and social handicaps, who deserved special preference even in cases where a Harvard education could not be expected to overcome those handicaps.*

Professors and graduate students undertook a number of studies to quantify the many trade-offs implied by these multiple attributes. But faculty members, administrators, students, and alumni could not agree among themselves or with each other on the appropriate weights. Indeed, posing the questions openly made people increasingly uncomfortable. By 2004, the philosophical foundations of the College's admissions system were, in the words of the dean's annual report, "a shambles."

The current system was introduced in its earliest form in 2006. Recognizing that no universally acceptable weighting scheme could be devised, officials designed a political process for admissions.

The president summarized the basic idea. "In a free community, unanimity is seldom feasible, nor perhaps is it desirable. Fair and democratic mechanisms must be devised to reflect the widely varying values of the university's citizens."

It was administratively impossible for each "citizen" to vote on each prospective student, but there could be a vote on desired distributions of characteristics of students. Each senior faculty member, for example, was given 300 "points." He or she could allocate those points across valued student attributes. For example, a faculty member could use up 30 points on each of ten applicants with the attribute "potential summa in Greek literature." Or he or she could place 50 points on one applicant with the attribute "superior quarterback"; 20 points on each of ten students of "outstanding ability in the performing arts"; and 1 point on each of fifty students with the attribute "congeniality: 'glue' among the student body."

This new political method of selection has already undergone several modifications, and major issues remain in debate. How much "voting weight" should be allocated to the College's various constituencies? How can the true preferences of "voters" be elicited without strategic voting? Should voting blocs be allowed? Should voters be permitted to sell their points to other voters?

The next decade should be full of advances on these questions, and no doubt further changes will be in order. But one lesson of the recent history of Harvard admissions is clear. As the last dean of admissions said after failing to win reelection to the deanship, "Designing an admissions system is a many-headed beast of a problem."

Alternatives to Selective Admissions

The fable of future admissions policies contains the nucleus of a market-based approach to the selection problem, which is to say, not to select at all but to use pricing as the means of overcoming the problem of excess demand. The fable also indicates why many of us are uncomfortable with the microeconomic approach, at least in the case of selection systems for higher education.

It is true that there is a market for higher education. It is also true that an institution, especially a university that fancies it is selecting and training a future elite, has other values. It cares about the nonfinancial contributions that its students make to the institution's health and reputation, such as through their academic excellence. A university has academic values, apart from economic ones.

The fable reminds us that many people care about still other characteristics of students. Besides money and academic values, there are a host of social, demographic, and personal attributes of applicants. We may be looking for people who will undertake certain careers or achieve particular sorts of success after graduation. We may disagree on which attributes should be used in selection; as the fable points out, it is probably too much to expect unanimity on which characteristics should matter and how much. But we agree that the criteria should go beyond how much a student is willing to pay. The simple economic idea of an auction somehow violates our notion of a university.

The uneasiness we feel is, I think, the same one reflected in a Harvard *Crimson* reviewer's comments on a book by former Harvard President Nathan Pusey. *The Age of the Scholar,* said the reviewer, revealed a president committed "to preserving poetry, people and God in his university against the inexorable logic of the cost-efficiency ratio." Isn't it a mistake to treat a university education as a commodity, despite the markets for research, faculty members, and even students surrounding us? McGeorge Bundy criticizes the views that "graduate education is a form of investment in human capital, with the benefits primarily private, not public," and "research results are a commodity that the agencies can purchase as necessary from universities or any other competent supplier." He argues:

> It would be hard to misunderstand the matter more thoroughly. . . . Neither basic research nor the university that is its principal American home can flourish if subjected to the tests and values of the commercial marketplace.[1]

Doesn't history reveal the fragility, and the importance, of academic values in the face of economic forces? Former Yale President Kingman Brewster's criticism of an auction model somehow rings true:

> There are relatively few institutions whose education does conspicuously offer a special career advantage, and they must be convincingly open to free, competitive admission *based on merit.* Assessing the merits of individuals—particularly at the half-blooming age of seventeen or eighteen—will involve many subjective judgments about character and motivation which, of course, no test scores or grades should obscure or override. But I really believe that more fundamental to the survival of our way of life in this country than the race to the moon or the size of the missile arsenal will be our ability to sustain the widespread conviction that in a society based on private property and contract, a society governed by a federated republic, success is at best related to effort, at worst dependent on luck, and as little as possible rigged by either private status or public favor.
>
> If the Yale privilege, and the springboard to a headstart which it offers, were to be rationed by inheritance, if it were to be auctioned in return for financial support, if it were to be conditioned by racial or social or economic preference, we would by that measure be dealing a very serious blow to the "opportunity sense" that is the greatest heritage and the greatest promise of the country.[2]

Even if the tuition charged by private institutions does in part reflect what the market will bear; even if there are analogies between scholarships and the economist's concept of price discrimination; and even though money can be translated into academic inputs (such as books, laboratories, research grants, and professorships)—even so, almost no one in American higher education has advocated an auction-based admission policy. Such a policy does "solve" the problem of excess demand; raising the effective price of the education does clear the market. But somehow it doesn't seem right.

Before exploring further this uneasiness with the market model, let me briefly cite three other ways that we might escape from having to choose elites.

Another traditional economic remedy for excess demand is to increase the supply. It would not be an unprecedented move. Higher education has often grown in order to meet increased demand. As the demand for higher education rose nationally in the 1950s and 1960s, the supply side responded, even at Harvard. And in the early 1970s, when the demand for graduate training in arts and sciences showed signs of decline, Harvard responded by cutting the size of many departments. Quantity can be varied. When qualified applicants outstrip available positions, why not simply enlarge the university?

Several answers might be given, but are seldom made explicit, in my experience. We might talk about diseconomies of scale. The cost of an education may rise if the student body is expanded—especially in the short run because of limitations in physical capacity. The benefits may decline, because of internal travel costs, greater impersonality, and so forth. Nonetheless, many other successful universities are much larger than Harvard.

More important, I think, is that a larger Harvard would presumably include less capable students. The quality of Harvard students would decline, affecting both the level of intellectual activity and the value of the Harvard credential. The latter result might or might not be a social loss, but it would probably be opposed by those already owning Harvard credentials.[3] The former possibility was encountered in the fable, and again the point is reinforced that many constituents do not value equally all students who can do the work at Harvard and are able to graduate. But notice that a number of empirical questions arise here—economies of scale in education, the extent and effects of lower academic standards from expanded enrollments, and so forth. They deserve careful study before we accept or reject this idea.

Another alternative to selective admissions is a lottery. It could be among all applicants, or it could be constrained by the requirement that only applicants who are judged able to pass be included in the pool. If we were unable or unwilling to distinguish among those in the pool, random selection would seem the fairest way to ration the scarce commodity of admission. It would also be inexpensive. But David Riesman amusingly describes student resistance to various allocation mechanisms for freshman seminars and "elite concentrations":

> Yet in discussions with students I have not found support for any system of rationing of scarce Harvard resources. . . . Nor is there support for a lottery, which students regard as too impersonal and denying them the opportunity to plead their own particular case. There is a widespread belief today that there are no real scarcities, and if one is denied an opportunity it means only that one is discriminated against or that monopolists are holding out on one.[4]

More important, most people reject random admission on the grounds that students do differ. Most of us believe that we can distinguish, even among those who can do the work at Harvard. Students seem to differ in terms of what the university can offer to them and what they can offer to it. This again is an empirical question deserving careful study.

There is a final alternative to selective admissions. Why not push the decision process forward in time? Would it not be fairer and more efficient to give students a "tryout"? Why not admit many more students and, after a trial period, flunk out those deemed least worthy?

In essence, this is the strategy followed by many state universities and some graduate departments of the University of Chicago. It was the policy of the Harvard Law School until the mid-1930s. In his 1978 Annual Report, Arts and Sciences' Dean Henry Rosovsky surfaced it as an alternative for consideration in graduate admissions. How should we think about the pros and cons?

•   Some gains in average performance can be reaped. Presumably, performance in the first year (or other trial period) is more highly correlated with overall performance at Harvard than is high-school performance. Thus, selecting on the basis of the trial period will result in fewer "mistakes" and a higher level of performance. As we shall see in chapter 4, the magnitude of the gains in performance depends on the variance in overall performance, the relative strength of the correlations, and the selection ratio.

•   The costs of testing and admissions will decline, because less selectivity is necessary. On the other hand, flunking out entails costs for students (and for the university, if tuitions do not cover educational costs). Students may gain from the trial period, but usually educators assume that those who flunk out represent lost resources. One might argue that if students are willing to take the chance, we should not count their investments as a loss. Others disagree.

•   Some gains in the representation of students from disadvantaged backgrounds will probably ensue. For example, the correlation between test scores and social status is generally higher than the correlation between college performance and social status. A trial period will give students from lower-status backgrounds a greater opportunity to demonstrate their talents.

•   Under the tryout system, students may work harder. Just as economists posit that competition breeds better performance, so might educators argue that the fear of flunking out will engender higher levels of academic attainment in college (although perhaps less attainment in high school). On the other hand, the tryout system may lead to too much competitiveness, anxiety, and other negative effects. Also, universities may lack the will or the desire to tell a large number of students they must leave; in effect, it may be thought preferable to have admissions officers say "no" instead. (My inquiries at the University of Chicago and other institutions where high proportions of students flunk out failed to produce either studies or a consensus of informed opinion on these phenomena. The literature on institutional studies of particular colleges also turned up a blank on these questions.)

How should one study these questions? What are the important dimensions of the choice among admissions policies? Consider an ideal world in which we know everything about the applicants. Assume that we have perfect measures of their past academic achievements, personal characteristics of all kinds, aptitudes and interests, and any other information deemed pertinent. To sharpen the points even further, suppose that we also have perfect information about the applicants' future attainments. We already know how much they would learn and grow in the university, if admitted. We also have perfect forecasts of their later-life contributions and of a university's value added to those contributions. In this ideal world of perfect information, whom should we admit?

Let me suggest a framework as a baseline for discussing how we should choose an elite: We should select students to *maximize the value added* of the education an institution provides. "Value added" is a term familiar to business people and economists. It refers to the difference between the value of the raw materials and the value of the finished product; that is, the increment of value that the production process creates. Applying this metaphor to education, the value of the raw materials would be the later-life contributions of students who did not receive the education in question, and the value of the finished product would be the later-life contributions of identical students who did receive that education. But I wish to enlarge the value-added metaphor, for by "value added" I mean several things:

A. The value of the education to the student *in terms of a utility function,* given his or her characteristics and alternative educational opportunities. Here we would gauge how much difference choosing one set of students instead of another would make to the valuation of their later social contributions of various kinds.

B. The value of the student to the university itself, given his or her characteristics. Here we would presumably enter in the student's financial, academic, "diversity," and other contributions to the university, while that person is a student or perhaps as an alumnus or alumna (alumni contributions, and so forth).

C. The value of various incentives that the choice of admissions policies creates. The incentives affect those who may, and may not, apply to a given university, and they also affect secondary schools, faculty, admissions process, and the job market.

D. The *intrinsic value* of selecting certain kinds of students. We might wish to reward virtuous students, or to obtain different degrees of representation in the student body of various groups of interest—races, sexes, regions, nations, and so forth. We might have already captured these benefits in the calculation of A, but we might value these attributes in and of themselves.

This framework suggests that we treat the institution as a production process whose value added is to be maximized. The choice of students affects the value the university will add. Through the incentives an admissions policy creates, there may also be repercussions beyond the student body, which should also be taken into account. The basic economic intuition is, I hope, clear—although as we shall see, the multifaceted problem contains a number of interesting complications. And without giving away too much too soon, the economic objective of maximizing social value added is subject to a number of penetrating objections.

We will tackle parts A to D in turn. Then I will try to summarize the discussion with a framework that I hope will be valuable in considering the objectives of selection.

A. The Social Value Added of the Education for Students' Later Lives

Harvard College has combined two traditions: a concern for academic excellence and a desire to serve society. In the words of the Ford Report of 1960:

> The ultimate goal of any admissions policy for this College is . . . to put Harvard's strengths to the best possible service of the nation by selecting and training those candidates best fitted to take advantage of what Harvard has to offer.[5]

If we follow these traditions in choosing students, we want high academic standards. But we also want well-rounded, moral, practically adept people. We want to train experts in the most profound scholarship and the most advanced technologies, and for these tasks, only the intellectually ablest would seem to do. But we also want to cultivate our students, to create men and women of ample vision who will be able to play a leading role not only in academia, but in all walks of life.

There is a tension here, which Max Weber recognized in a more general context. "Behind all the present discussions of the foundations of the educational system," he wrote, "the struggle of the 'specialist type of man' against the older type of 'cultivated man' is hidden at some decisive point."

> The term "cultivated man" . . . is understood to mean solely that the goal of education consists in the quality of a man's bearing in life which was *considered* "cultivated," rather than in a specialized training for expertness. The "cultivated" personality formed the educational ideal, which was stamped by the

structure of domination and by the social condition for membership in the ruling stratum. Such education aimed at a chivalrous or an ascetic type; or, at a literary type, as in China; a gymnastic-humanist type, as in Hellas; or it aimed at a conventional type, as in the case of the Anglo-Saxon gentleman. The qualification of the ruling stratum as such rested upon the possession of "more" cultural quality (in the absolutely changeable, value-neutral sense in which we use the term here), rather than upon "more" expert knowledge. Special military, theological, and judicial ability was of course intensely practiced; but the point of gravity in Hellenic, in medieval, as well as in Chinese education, has rested upon educational elements that were entirely different from what was "useful" in one's specialty.[6]

The expert is competent along one, often theoretical, dimension; the gentleman is multidimensional, with personal qualities that enable him to rule. In our ideal, Harvard's scientists should be eminent, its scholars distinguished, its professional schools and college the training ground of future leaders in business, government, and the professions. But in Weber's terms, the "expert" should not drown out the "gentleman."

Knowledge and learning should be applied to the public good. President Charles Eliot, for example, warned in his inaugural address that without a university to select its leadership and to cultivate the special mental habits necessary in every special endeavor, America courted disaster.[7] Harvard historically has behaved as if its contribution to social welfare is greatest if it stresses high academic standards *and* educates those who will play prominent roles in the world.

These two goals are not identical. The most academically capable individual may not be the most capable in the real world. Nor will the student with the highest *academic* value added always be the one with the highest *social* value added due to the education. These are important distinctions to have in mind when considering the objectives of selection.

It helps me to think of a sports analogy. Suppose you have a basketball training institute and wish to maximize your contribution to the sport. You are not replacing the instruction received at each team's training camp, nor are you providing on-the-job training; you have a school. You choose your curriculum, academic standards, pedagogical techniques, tuition fee, and admissions policy simultaneously.

If you wish to train players who will make the most difference to basketball, neither your students nor your curriculum should be chosen solely on academic grounds. You do care about how teachable—how academically competent—your basketball students will be. But if contributing to the playing of basketball is your objective, then you should also select on the basis of the attributes important to playing basketball—such as height and quickness and coordination. Before applying this metaphor to university admissions, two additional points should be noted.

First, the value added of what your school offers depends on what your students would have achieved without you. Other basketball schools may exist; if so, you have to compare the value to basketball of what students learn from you with the value of what students would have learned elsewhere. This is the economic concept of *comparative advantage.* Compared to no schooling, your basketball school might add the most basketball utility to relatively ignorant basketball players of average talent. But suppose for the sake of the distinction I now want to make that other schools are already available to train average basketball players and none exists to handle truly excellent players. Because your value added calculation should include what other educational options are available to your candidates, you should take very able players. Even if your absolute advantage is with less talented players, your comparative advantage may be with the more talented ones. To maximize your contribution to the sport, you should follow the logic of comparative advantage.

Second, you must consider your exact mission within the world of basketball. In the example , I assigned your school the mission of training basketball players. But you might instead wish to train coaches or officials or sportswriters. If so, then height and quickness and coordination will probably not matter to you, as they probably have little effect on value added in these professions. Other personal qualities may now become important.

These are elementary distinctions. And yet, in my experience, these points are often forgotten or misunderstood in discussions of selection policies. How do they apply to selective universities? Like President Eliot, we may recognize that our primary contribution is intellectual value added for students of high academic ability and achievement. We believe that only very able applicants can survive the curriculum; that academically talented students stimulate each other's learning and the faculty's research output; and that in some fields only academic power and creativity matter for society's sake—say, in the training of theoretical physicists.

But at least in the cases of many undergraduate colleges and the major professional schools, the objective is to train most students for leadership roles in society. Leaders in medicine, law, and business tend to possess nonacademic skills of various kinds. Such skills may not be teachable (at the university) or acquired later—by analogy, think of the basketball player's speed, height, and coordination—though some may. Thus, we obtain a first conclusion: To maximize the social value added of a university education, students should in part be selected because of these other traits and skills, which will in part determine how successful they become in later life.

A second lesson, however, has a different slant. Based on the logic of comparative rather than absolute advantage, we might end up selecting the intellectually ablest students even in fields where nonacademic attributes are important for later-life success. It might be that "average" students would learn almost as much at an "average" university as at a university like Harvard, whereas academically gifted students might learn much more at the latter than the former. In this hypothetical case, the change in social value added from going to Harvard might be greater for the academically ablest students than for average ones.[8]

Third, our calculation of value added depends on what part of a profession we are serving. A former dean once noted that in past times Harvard's professional schools of education, divinity, and perhaps public health were not primarily training "main-line professionals" like teachers and ministers—by our analogy, basketball players. Instead, in those days at least, these schools at Harvard specialized in educating professors, critics, "gadflies," and others, who might be compared with our coaches, officials, and sportswriters. If this point had validity, it might be interpreted as follows: Even though teachers and ministers should be selected in part on nonacademic attributes important to success in these main-line professions, we need not value those attributes if we are training academics and scholars within those professions.

Difficulties with Social Value Added as an Objective

The idea of maximizing the value added of the education to students' later social contributions is attractive. But it faces a number of difficulties. We can calculate value added, if at all, only in society as it presently stands. We may not approve of the skills and attributes that society rewards, nor the amounts involved. Should we look at the kinds of people who succeed in the current, imperfect world—and end up educating the powerful because their influence guarantees the highest educational value added? Or should we instead select students as if the world were ideal—as if the wise would rule and the meek would inherit and accidents of appearance and personality did not matter?

Let us examine several hypothetical examples that pose serious problems for the theoretically attractive notion of "social value added":

Example 1. Suppose you are admissions director for a school of government that trains future public leaders. The school has judged that the skills it teaches are particularly useful to society when in the hands of the powerful and influential. A small increment in the economic skills of a future cabinet official is worth more to society than a great increment in the economic skills of a student who will become a routine bureaucrat. This is your definition of value added.

Two candidates compete for a single slot. One is the son of a cabinet minister from an oil country and a member of the royal family. He is ticketed for a powerful post simply by dint of his family connections. The other applicant is from a small, democratic country. He dominates the first candidate on all academic and personal criteria. But because his country is fairly ruled, and besides, he has no important family connections, he will not become a minister (or his chance of becoming a minister is 5 percent compared to the royal candidate's 95 percent). Whom do you admit?

The royal candidate in this case has a higher social value added given the education you provide; yet even granting this, many people would feel uncomfortable admitting him over the other applicant. Two reasons may be given. First, the society in which he will serve is, in our ideal, unjust, perhaps even corrupt. Second, the family connection that turns out to be crucial is not alterable, by either candidate.

Example 2. Suppose you were the chairperson of admissions for a chemistry department in 1940. You must choose one of two competent applicants. The first, who happens to be a Jew, is slightly better than the second, in terms of future scholarly performance, but only if he gets a job. You are aware that the job market is anti-Semitic, so that educating the second candidate turns out to have the highest expected value added to scholarship and society. Whom would you admit?

As in the first example, most people would be reluctant to follow the argument from social value added. By hypothesis the society is unjust, and the deciding trait is not alterable.

Anti-Semitism is not a fictitious aspect in making choices:

> The limitations in the job market for Jews were used by various graduate schools as reasons for curtailing admissions on the assumption that they would be unable to place their Jewish graduates. Albert Sprague Coolidge of the Harvard chemistry department told a Massachusetts legislative committee shortly after World War II that his department had followed such a policy.[9]

Example 3. If one's social class background affects one's later-life contributions, should the selection process take it into account? In the ninth century, the prominent Chinese statesman Li Ti-yu argued against the prevalent system of allocating government positions according to examinations. This method ignored social value added:

> The outstanding officials of the government ought to be the sons of the highest officials. Why? Because from childhood on they are accustomed to this kind of position; their eyes are familiar with court affairs; even if they have not been trained in the ceremonial of the palace, they automatically achieve perfection. Scholars of poor families, even if they have an extraordinary talent are certainly unable to accustom themselves to [the palace's routine].[10]

If this were true of contemporary America, would you tailor your admissions policies accordingly, admitting more upper-class students in order to maximize the social value added of the education you provide?

These three examples remind us that if a society is deeply biased or unfair, selection according to "social value added" may reinforce the injustices. But perhaps we should instead admit those for whom the education would have the highest value added in a just, meritocratic system. But how idealistic should we be? How much of our imperfect society's structure and preferences should be reflected?

Example 4. Consider the case of female scientists. Let us suppose, for discussion's sake, that the following statements are true:[11]

- Women in the top ability quartile go on to college about as often as men of similar economic and ethnic backgrounds.[12]
- Women are accepted by similar colleges at the same rates as men.[13]
- Women are as likely as men to be admitted to and receive fellowships from top-ranked Ph.D. departments.[14]
- Once women attain their Ph.D.s, they publish and are cited much less than men. In a sample of 565 male and female scientists who received their doctorates around 1957, the median number of publications over the next twelve years was 8 articles for men and 3 for women. The median number of citations was 50 for men and 17 for women.[15]
- Differences in publication rates are not explained by marital status, employment at a college or a university, IQ, or prestige of department affiliation. For example, unmarried women averaged 5 articles over the twelve-year period, compared to 9 for unmarried men.
- The academic labor market for women is "unbiased," in that hiring prospects, promotions, and quality of department are unaffected by sex, when publication rates and quality of doctoral department are taken into account.[16]
- Finally, publications and citations are considered workable proxies for the quality and quantity of academic work and not biased against women.[17]

Supposing these "facts" to be true, we can ask a hard philosophical question. If women were likely to be less productive scientists, other things being equal, and if the scientific reward system (jobs, publications, and so forth) were not sexually biased, should we favor male applicants over female applicants?

Many people would be uncomfortable showing preference for males, even supposing the value-added argument favors it and that the scientific reward system is fair. We may not wish to select on the basis of an unalterable characteristic when no clear causal mechanism connects the characteristics and the outcome. In other words, because there is no appealing theory or ideology to explain why women of equal intellectual ability and family obligations would perform less well, we would resist using sex as a predictor. Or we may have a theory to explain the result but not believe it to be a good normative basis for admissions decisions. Sociologist of science Jonathan Cole writes:

> It is possible that in order to account for the correlation between sex status and the rate of scientific output, it may be necessary to look outside the institutional structure of science, to examine carefully the prior experiences and socialization processes affecting women in the larger society—which may dampen motivation to succeed and influence their publication performance after they enter science.[18]

We may believe, for example, that discrimination or socialization at an early age accounts for women's underproduction in science. Just as in the first examples we might not wish to echo future prejudice or future injustice in our admissions decisions, so we might not wish to reinforce past discrimination or past injustice, refusing to allow it to affect our utilitarian framework. Simply maximizing "social value added" is not an appropriate objective.

Our problem, then, is how and where to draw the line in "accounting for" injustices or efficiencies. What sorts of existing individual and group inequalities will we permit to enter into our maximizing calculations for the future? How will we recompute the appropriate values of all sorts of future contributions to society? Do we need a complete definition of the ideal society and a theory of which attributes would be most valuable in it?

Example 5. So far, we have seen that even if family connections or religion or social class or sex affect the social value added of education, we are reluctant to allow these attributes to affect admissions. What about race? Say you are admissions director at a selective law school. You have evidence showing that the greatest social value added of your school's degree occurs in the case of members of disadvantaged ethnic groups. On average, you believe, such graduates do more to promote social justice than other graduates. Should you give preference to such groups?

For the sake of argument, suppose you say yes. You have no problem justifying greater efforts to recruit and give preference in admissions to students from such groups. But you ask how far you should go. Given your school's relatively small but important share of the market for lawyers, perhaps it would make sense to specialize in minority students. Why not devote all your school's resources to the disadvantaged? And if not all, how much? Would you decide the optimal extent of admissions preference on the basis of calculations of social value added?

Finally, suppose a colleague proves that, because of current affirmative action policies in hiring, minority group graduates have even better prospects than you have calculated. Should you admit even more minorities?

Example 6. Sometimes the use of certain sorts of predictors causes problems. Suppose, as several studies have shown, that physical appearance—independent of measures of academic ability and past achievement—helps predict whether a person will reach a position of leadership. Tall people, slender people, and attractive people would, other things being equal, have a higher social value added from your university's education than ugly, obese, or short people. Should the former, therefore, be given preference in the admissions process?

If tall, attractive applicants are not to be given preference, are some determinants of social value added "irrelevant" to you? Which ones? Why? Because you believe society is "biased unfairly" against the unattractive? If so, do you believe there is bias against the timid, the unconfident, and the person who does not enjoy social gatherings? Should you therefore not give any weight to self-confidence, social skills, and *savoir faire?* Giving weight to these attractive dimensions of personality and social skills may impinge against the admission of some brilliant scientists.[19]

Example 7. Again, you have perfect information. You have two applicants for whom the social value added of the education that you provide is equal. You can admit one of the two.

John has come very far because of his efforts. He is tenacious, works very hard, and exploits his abilities to the fullest. Bert only makes a middling effort, but he has outstanding native gifts and social advantages. Should you give preference to John? Does effort deserve more credit than advantages for which the candidate can, in some sense, claim no responsibility? Presumably not everyone would agree with Confucius's answer:

> Those who are born wise are the highest type of people; those who have become wise through learning come next; those who learn by sheer diligence and industry, but with difficulty, come after that. Those who are slow to learn, but still won't learn, are the lowest type of people.[20]

These questions raise the old philosophical problem of just deserts. According to philosopher John Rawls, rewarding effort may end up rewarding privilege:

> The precept which seems intuitively to come closest to rewarding moral desert is that of distribution according to effort, or perhaps better, conscientious effort. Once again, however, it seems clear that the effort a person is willing to make is influenced by his natural abilities and skills and the alternatives open to him. The better endowed are more likely, other things equal, to strive consciously, and there seems to be no way to discount for their greater good fortune. The idea of rewarding desert is impracticable.[21]

This example reminds us again that defining "social value added" involves issues of justice.

These seven, difficult examples raise fundamental objections to the economist's idea of maximizing the value added of the education provided. That idea takes society's existing reward structure as given. It also takes as given the "system" that prepared different candidates differently for the university. If the reward structure is unjust, shouldn't an admissions policy work to overcome it, rather than reinforcing it? And isn't an admissions policy fair and efficient only if it "corrects" for disadvantages not under the candidate's control?

These questions make it clear that an admissions policy ultimately cannot avoid philosophical questions of justice and moral desert. When an institution considers its objectives in choosing an elite, it must evaluate its educational mission and how that mission fits with the workings of society. Admissions policies are in the broadest sense political, depending as they do on our values and our understanding of the functioning of the social and educational system. Some might argue that an elite university should play an overt role in promoting social change, in part by defining a just social order and admitting those students most likely to contribute to it. This might mean admitting more of the poor and disadvantaged, or more of those with altruistic ideals. Or, with a different conception of the desirable social order, it might imply a preference for students from aristocratic backgrounds. Or another alternative: The university should declare itself for the primacy of academic values and intellectual excellence—even if these are insufficiently rewarded in the current social system—and should select its students on those grounds alone.

I have argued that it may be myopic to admit students solely on the basis of academic criteria—at least myopic if you are concerned about the social contributions your students will make in their later lives, and if you have perfect information. Now we see that it may also be unsatisfactory to admit students on the basis of a calculation of the value added your education provides to their later lives, because that value added is affected by past and future imperfections in society that you may not wish to reinforce. There is no easy escape. You can declare that you will admit those with the highest levels of academic achievement, or those through whom your education will have the highest social value added, but complicated arguments of value are necessary to justify either choice.

You might think that philosophers could help you sort out the arguments here, and you would be right, to a degree. The selection problem has received some attention in recent years from philosophers, especially on the question, "When is preferential treatment for minorities justified?" The best analysis I have found is Alan H. Goldman's book, *Justice and Reverse Discrimination,* which examines the analogous selection problem of a firm allocating scarce job openings among an abundance of applicants. He derives what he calls the "right" of the most qualified candidate to be accepted. Who is the "most qualified" for a position? The person with the highest "performance or predicted performance along some socially useful (nonarbitrary) scale."[22] In part, Goldman justifies his conclusion "on grounds of increased welfare for all members of society," an argument that economists would find congenial. But Goldman goes beyond the economist's utilitarian approach. He also bases his conclusion on "a right to equal opportunity to succeed through socially productive effort," which in turn he derives "from the most fundamental right to have one's interests considered equally with those of others."[23] He argues against a libertarian approach, where a school can admit whomever it pleases with no philosophical compunctions, and an egalitarian approach, which asks that an admissions policy redress social and innate inequalities in awarding scarce positions.[24]

But Goldman does not describe which among many possible "socially useful (nonarbitrary) scales" should be used to measure who is "most qualified." He does talk about the philosophical status of arguments for the redress of prior social injustices, and he does consider whether effort or innate capabilities should be rewarded. But he does not, and perhaps no one can, link up "socially useful" with a description of the just society. He does not provide an operational answer to the problem of choosing an elite.

My own conclusion is that philosophical argument is unlikely to provide an answer. Such value questions have proven notoriously difficult to resolve. This does not, however, mean that we should throw up our hands in intellectual despair. Analysis can advance normative discussions, even if it cannot resolve them. We can hope to provide a kind of roadmap to this terrain, so that blind alleys and notorious potholes may be avoided.

Before trying to put together such a roadmap, other dimensions of this policy problem besides "the value added of the education in students' later lives" have to be considered. It is to the second of the four dimensions described on page 60 that we now turn.

B. The Value of Students' Contributions to the University

We have been speaking of candidates until now in terms of their value added *from* a university education. We must now consider their value added *to* the university and its objectives. These contributions include tuition and later financial support, nonacademic contributions to university life, and academic contributions to the university. They also include students' educational contributions to each other.

About three-quarters of American private four-year colleges state that a candidate's "ability or inability to pay attendance costs" is not considered in the admissions process.[25] Nonetheless, just as scholarships are costly, tuition revenues are undeniably valuable. Another benefit of choosing one student over another involves different expectations of their future financial contributions as alumni. We may decide not to count financial benefits in the admissions process, but only at the cost of leaving out one of the differences among students that eventually add value to the university.

A second category of students' value added to the university is the variety of nonacademic contributions students make during their years there. Some nonacademic activities are considered valuable, but it is hard to know how to take account of them in admissions. In the case of college sports, we might say that these sports have a value of their own, and excellence here as elsewhere is to be sought. Then why not admit the truly great halfback who turns out to have little academic merit as we might admit a gifted mathematician who is uninterested or incapable in sports? Why do we feel indignation toward colleges that lower academic standards for top athletes? Is it because we believe that these other contributions to the life of a university, though valuable, should not count as criteria for admission? If we believe they should count "a little," how do we draw the line between a little and a lot?

Third, and to some more important, we must weigh in students' contributions to the generation of knowledge and the promotion of academic values. Besides the social value added of an education to the future careers of graduates, universities value the creation of new knowledge and the preservation of culture. Students are said to be an important part of that process, even those who do not go on to academic careers. They contribute to the generation of knowledge. The academic tone of a university may greatly be affected by the average (and spread) of academic preparation, motivation, and ability in the student body. Apart from incentive effects in attracting able faculty members—we shall discuss these shortly—an able student body may create a climate in which a given faculty is more productive in its research and dissemination of knowledge and culture. And the academic excellence of a student body, just as the excellence of a faculty, may create a beneficial standard for the society and other universities. I have found no empirical studies of these phenomena, although interviews with faculty members and others show that such issues are matters of passionate belief. Again, questions of values and fact intertwine.

"DIVERSITY" AND EDUCATING EACH OTHER

It is often noted that students educate each other, and sometimes it is argued that a more diverse student body has educational advantages. But homogeneity may also help, depending on the attribute. The desired diversity is usually described in terms of different academic interests, geographical and socioeconomic backgrounds, extracurricular skills, political and other opinions, sex, and race. But homogeneity may be preferable in terms of a relatively tight band of academic achievement, a common commitment to scholarly activities and education in general, high moral character and strength, and age. How should your admissions process take account of the various benefits of diversity and homogeneity?

To begin, notice that people disagree on the desirable degree of diversity, in part depending on their educational objectives but also depending on their assessments of matters of fact. Some universities choose to specialize in certain disciplines—Harvard would be unwise to admit a student whose heart was set on a degree in geography, as that department no longer exists. Some colleges primarily serve members of particular religions or races, such as Bob Jones University, College of the Sacred Heart, or Howard University. Some accept only women, or only men. Some universities believe their resources are put to best use by educating the most intellectually able students. Others concentrate their efforts on raising up those of relatively low achievement. Some colleges want a diverse student body, while others value homogeneity. In other countries at various times, universities have admitted only students of certain political persuasions or socioeconomic backgrounds, in order to serve social as well as educational objectives.

Scale also matters. Is the desired diversity to be sought at the level of dormitories and houses, or classrooms, or departments, or across the entire university? One can imagine a diverse student body that subsequently self-selects into tight and insulated homogeneous groups—defeating some of the aims of educational diversity.

Should we look at numbers of proportions? To have a football team, we need fifty to seventy-five players, whether we are a small college or a huge one. So, too, for a symphony orchestra, or a humor magazine, or a minimum-sized undergraduate major in astronomy, numbers of students with certain attributes may matter, rather than percentages. If members of a certain group happen to perform better or feel more comfortable with others of that group around, we might ask whether the absolute numbers or relative proportions are what operationally make the difference. If students educate each other best in certain mixes, then proportions may be the right measure.

We might call this the problem of the *optimal composition of the student body.* It is difficult, perhaps insoluble, for several reasons:

1. The student body is only one of many sources of diversity. A student raised in a diverse socioeconomic community presumably would gain less from a socioeconomically diverse student body than a student from a homogeneous socioeconomic community. One learns not only "outside the classroom," but also outside the university. The educational value added of various kinds of homogeneity and diversity will therefore vary depending not only on the interests of each student but on his or her other available sources of diversity. Obviously, the curriculum's diversity also matters.

2. The benefits of having others like oneself, or different from oneself, will probably not increase in a linear fashion. Physicists, for example, may learn more or feel more comfortable the greater the number of physicists —indeed, there may be some analogy to a "critical mass." But conceptually, as the number or proportion of physicists becomes very large, the educational benefits to physicists of an additional physicist may diminish or even become negative.[26]

3. Even within a single educational institution, "treatments" such as living quarters, majors, clubs, and activities, vary. Homogeneity in levels of academic achievement may be valuable for students pursuing higher mathematics; it may be relatively unimportant in other fields or at other levels of study. Diversity in backgrounds and opinions may be educationally important in a department of government, but not in a department of biochemistry. If students can select different "treatments," they may exploit the benefits of homogeneity in the midst of diversity or, as noted above, vitiate the benefits of diversity. An optimal admissions policy would need to take account of the various available treatments and patterns of self-selection.

4. We may judge that some benefits of diversity or homogeneity

should not be taken into account. If rich students said they felt uncomfortable having too few rich students, and poor students were found not to care one way or the other, we might nonetheless feel uncomfortable in giving rich students preference in the admissions process. We might not wish to recognize the need for a critical mass of religious fundamentalists, whatever the evidence might show. We might not desire to give greater weight to physical beauty even if the beautiful students' classmates were thereby made happier. Then again, we might.

Columbia University struggled with a related problem in the first decades of this century. President Nicholas Butler asked Virgil Prettyman, the headmaster of Horace Mann School, which was housed and staffed at Columbia, why Columbia was receiving ever fewer of the school's graduates. Prettyman's report in 1908 noted the prevalent view of the parents of private school students that Columbia's "undergraduate body contains a prepondering element of students who have had few social advantages and that in consequence, there is little opportunity of making friendships of permanent value among them." He was referring, of course, to the large proportion of academically able but socially undistinguished Jewish students who were being admitted on the basis of academic criteria. Columbia decided to limit Jewish enrollment, in our terms for the sake of "diversity" and "maximizing the social value-added of the education." The fascinating and troubling history of Columbia's efforts to admit a more socially desirable student body during Butler's years as president has often given me pause as I think about "leadership" and "diversity" as criteria for selection.[27]

5. Students who finish at the bottom of the class may undergo psychological pressures that should be taken into account in the composition of the class. Harvard College's notion of "the happy bottom quarter" meant that those predicted to perform academically less well should have compensating nonacademic strengths and tough hides. If many of the low performers are readily identifiable as members of particular groups, other side effects may occur, which the admissions process may wish to anticipate.

These complications probably preclude an analytical solution to the problem of the optimal composition of the student body. Notice that they argue against simple weighting schemes or quotas. My inquiries to leading educational authorities have failed to turn up existing models of the optimal composition problem. Typical was the response of one of the deans of selection theory, Stanford's Lee J. Cronbach:

I worried in the 1950s with some problems that are tangential to yours, and I learned that an attempt to reason rigorously about diversity is doomed to failure. You can think about preferring a more diverse set of graduates to a less diverse set or, more shortsightedly, preferring a more diverse set of incoming students. But when you try to formulate an index of diversity you have to speak of diversity on specified dimensions and have to assign weights so that you can combine the scatter on the several dimensions properly. If you don't do that, you kid yourself; weights determined by various artifacts such as the numbers on the score scales subtly take over decisions that should be made from a high philosophic perch.[28]

We may not be able to construct an ideal model of diversity, but our often primitive thinking about this issue could be enhanced. We might try to formulate an explicit justification for certain types of diversity and homogeneity. In a simulation exercise, we might compose a wide variety of admitted classes and ask what difference it makes to have more, or less, students with particular characteristics. We might also study existing procedures to see how much weight is actually being given to various sorts of diversity. In my experience, the results are often surprising (see chapter 2, pages 28–46).

C. The Effects of Admissions Policies on Incentives

In theory, selection improves productivity in two ways. One way, which we have just been discussing, involves *allocation effects*. Here, how applicants are allocated to educational opportunities affects the social value added or efficiency of the educational system. We have had a taste of how difficult and complex calculations of social value added would be.

There are also the *incentives* created by the selection process. Incentive effects can be important, and a complete examination of the objectives of an admissions system should take them into account. Several kinds can be distinguished.

First, admissions criteria change the way potential applicants behave. If Greek is a prerequisite, some potential candidates will not apply; others will decide to study Greek when otherwise they would not have done so. If extracurricular activities are highly valued in the admissions process, students may "invest" in them to a greater extent than they ordinarily would. (Some admissions officers call this "leaf gathering.") If high grades in science are essential for admission into top medical schools, premeds may earn the awe, or disapprobation, of their peers and teachers through their devotion to grade-getting.

Second, admissions criteria also create incentives for the institutions that prepare potential applicants. The level and scope of high-school and college curricula are shaped in part by the requirements and desiderata of the next level of the educational system.

Arguably the most important issue in turn-of-the-century debates over college admissions was their effects on high schools—what Harvard's President Eliot called "articulation." Harvard routinely expected applicants to complete up to eleven separate entrance examinations, such as Latin (with separate tests for grammar, reading ability, and comprehension), history, literature, and so forth. Many secondary schools were forced to teach such required subjects and, as a result, were tightly constrained in their curricula. Furthermore, those students not going on to college—the vast majority—were denied the most relevant preparation. President Eliot's *Report of the Committee of Ten* (1893) advocated more flexible admissions requirements for the sake of the high schools. In the decades to follow, several changes in admissions were motivated in part by a consideration of such incentive effects—including the development of fewer and more general tests, an increased emphasis on "ability" rather than "achievement," and the acceptance without examinations of students who finished in the top seventh, say, of their class at accredited high schools.

There is now interest at Harvard and elsewhere in substituting standardized achievement tests for the more usual aptitude tests. One argument for doing so is that "achievement" will thereby be stimulated in high schools. (Given all the furor over "aptitude" and IQ, using "achievement" tests also has public relations benefits.) It turns out statistically that scores on standardized achievement tests capture all the predictive power of "aptitude" tests, in terms of forecasting academic success in college. A worry that has not yet surfaced, however, is one President Eliot had—that achievement tests may have a constraining effect on high school curricula.

Third, admissions criteria may also have incentive effects on the university's faculty. Although I have found no studies of this phenomenon, it is widely believed that the best professors are attracted by able students. Admissions criteria help determine the kinds and levels of courses that faculty are able to teach. Both the average level and the distribution of academic talent matter. David Riesman cites the work of Martin Trow on the student body at Berkeley, where the freshman class includes students of equal ability to Harvard's and students "who are the equal of the freshman class of an undistinguished teachers college." As a result, "a faculty member there faces a constituency which appears less inviting to all but missionaries than the numerically smaller constituency of able students at a selective private university college such as Harvard."[29] Also, professors may not like the prospect of having to fail students. Faculty members may value students' diversity in nonacademic terms, as indicated in a survey at Harvard College in the 1960s.

The choice of admissions criteria may create incentives for alumni and potential employers of Harvard graduates. The choice of entering students in part affects the value and informational significance of the resulting degree, especially if few students fail, and this in turn may affect alumni and employers.

Finally, the incentives of admissions committees may be affected. The exclusive use of quantitative measures of academic achievement allows committee members little leeway. But when "diversity," "character," and other vague criteria are applied by a group with a high degree of discretionary power and a low degree of accountability there will be suspicions, if not the reality, of whim and subjectivity, and even of bias and unfairness.

In earlier days, it has been argued, "character" and "diversity" were used as means to limit Jewish enrollments at Columbia and elsewhere.[30] In the context of that debate, the "liberal" position was to favor admissions solely on the basis of academic merit. Some people apparently believe that admissions committees disproportionately exclude activists and "trouble makers." A recent mystery novel contains this conversation at Harvard between a visitor and an assistant professor:

> "Harvard and Yale and Princeton take a lot of care to see that they avoid trouble. The best way to avoid it is to be careful whom you have around, and in what numbers."
>
> "Lots of people think they pick their students on that basis, among others," Andy said.[31]

Vague criteria can be used to cover for selection based on attributes that would be embarrassing to acknowledge publicly. For example, in the 1920s, a number of colleges that disavowed athletic scholarships nevertheless subsidized their athletes. A 1929 report on college sports by the Carnegie Foundation explained:

> Certain American institutions (for example, Dartmouth, Rutgers, Swarthmore) award scholarships upon what is termed an "all-round" basis, including, besides scholastic excellence, qualities of "leadership," interest in undergraduate activities, usually physical vigor, and, perhaps, value to the student body. Obviously, all of these qualifications except the first may be interpreted as athletic ability. When, in awards, intellectual achievement is underrated and qualities of character and "leadership" thereby are given undue emphasis, an "all-round" scholarship is in reality granted on the basis of athletic skill and attainment . . . . When examination of a list of scholarship-holders reveals that practically

every important athlete at the institution enjoys a scholarship, the fact points to the use of general scholarship aid as an athletic subsidy.[32]

The existence of incentive effects transforms the selection problem from a static to a dynamic framework. The classic selection problem is static—given an applicant pool with certain characteristics, choose those most likely to succeed along certain criteria of later performance.[33] The dynamic problem is richer. The choice of this particular class of students must take account of the effects of the choice on applicant pools in the future, as well as its effects on the faculty and the value of the degree as a credential or signal for alumni and potential employers.

This much more complicated problem has, to my knowledge, received little attention in the literature—although the existence of these effects has long been noted, and acted upon, by admissions officers and university officials.[34] A thorough treatment would take us too far afield, but several interesting features of the expanded problem are worth noting.

The incentives created for students are presumably productive in most cases. In several countries, the creation of open admissions at the university level has been said to have had disastrous effects on secondary schools, since students have a greatly reduced incentive to achieve.[35] Occasionally students may "over-invest" in the criteria valued by the selection process. Officials at Harvard's Schools of Medicine and Law have expressed the worry that stringent academic requirements lead students to over-invest in narrowly academic pursuits while in college. I have uncovered no empirical studies of these positive or negative effects in the United States.[36]

Admissions criteria vary in their incentive-creative effects. Grades are presumably more a function of student effort than are test scores. Students can "invest" in test-taking; witness the existence of specialized schools to prepare students for standardized tests. The gains from coaching courses may be on the order of an additional 20 points on the SAT verbal test.[37] But compared to some other criteria for admissions, aptitude scores are less a function of student effort and therefore, for better or worse, provide a weaker incentive effect.[38] The weighting of admissions criteria can be altered to create different mixes of desirable and undesirable incentives.

In a dynamic setting, an imperfect measure may be preferable to a perfect measure. (This result cannot occur in the static selection problem.) Suppose a university rejected all students below a certain level of achievement and accepted all those above that level, and suppose achievement could be measured by a "perfect" test. Students who knew they would perform well above, or well below, that level on the test would not have an incentive to study hard because their probability of admission would not be affected. But if the test were imperfect, even very capable students would not be assured of passing, so they would have an incentive to try harder, to raise the probability of passing. A similar effect might be imagined for students with low achievement, who would then perceive a small probability of being accepted that could be increased by studying harder.

In this fashion, a mysterious admissions process with vague criteria may create stronger incentives than a perfectly clear set of criteria. The optimally imperfect measure—or optimally mysterious admissions criteria—would trade off the benefits of increased incentives against the costs of less efficient static selection.[39]

How should we factor in incentive effects as we design an admissions policy? Notice that the incentives facing prospective students depend not only on a university's policy but also the policies of other institutions. When Bowdoin College stopped requiring SAT scores, 70 percent of Bowdoin's applicants still submitted SAT scores. Why? Because most candidates applied to other colleges that required SATs. The history of college admissions around the turn of the century displays the need for action by more than one university. Occasionally, one college could push others into a change in policy—as when Harvard, in the 1870s, allowed students to take examinations at several sites away from Cambridge, which threatened Williams College's geographical monopoly. Harvard's action forced Williams into adopting a certificate system for admission.[40] Similarly, premeds respond to the entire industry of medical schools and not just to Harvard's standards and criteria.

It is true that a university like Harvard can occasionally play a leadership role, as it did in stressing diversity in the 1950s and does today in affirmative action. If Harvard College allowed applicants to take five standard achievement tests in lieu of the usual aptitude tests, other colleges might follow. "If Harvard makes the SAT optional, it will be like Chase lowering the prime," said Arthur Levine, president of Bradford College. "If Podunk College does it, most people assume you're lowering standards. If Harvard does it, I think a lot of colleges will move in that direction."[41]

Yet for the most part, if we are setting the admissions policy for only one of many hundreds of institutions, what we do will probably not create strong incentives for high schools and aspiring students. It is a different matter, of course, if we are designing a selection policy for a state college system, or for a civil service system. Then, incentive effects may be of first-order importance.[42]

D. The Intrinsic Value of Certain Kinds of Students

An institution may wish to select some people because their attributes have intrinsic value. For example, some universities with religious affiliations look for students of demonstrated religious dedication. In the summer of 1983, Iran's universities reopened after three-and-a-half years, and applicants now must pass a religious test for admission as well as a general qualifying exam.[43] In some countries, political criteria have been paramount. During the Cultural Revolution in the People's Republic of China, local groups of workers, peasants, and soldiers became the university admissions committees, selecting those "whose proletarian stand is firm and who are active in the great socialist cultural revolution."[44] A similar criterion has been applied in Cuba since 1962.[45]

Less dramatically, Brown University has declared that preference in undergraduate admissions will be given to those who have served their communities. Most medical schools examine students' motives for entering the profession, preferring those with "altruistic" aims. Would a law school be a better place if similar questions were given greater weight than at present? Or, as several high officials have suggested, might the Harvard Law School strive to select "nice" people, perhaps to alleviate the fact that:

> Harvard Law School students today—to the extent one can accurately generalize —are more intense, more driven, and more diligent than their predecessors. Many have defined their lives in terms of success in the artificial environment of classroom participation, periodic essays, and final examinations.[46]

These character preferences may be defended in terms of social value added or educationally beneficial diversity. But this may not be necessary. It may just be that a university wishes to declare itself for certain traits of character, just as it does for certain traits of mind. Religious strength and tolerance, honesty, temperance, freedom from racial or sexual bias, demonstrated concern for the disadvantaged, and a nonmaterialistic outlook are some of the qualities which, if we had perfect information, we might wish to select.

A university may also declare preferential policies to compensate groups for past discrimination, or because the university values greater social mobility. An institution may declare that the "appropriate" representation of various subgroups in its student body is of intrinsic value. The Harvard Medical School has stated: "The minimal goal should be a representation of minority groups in the student body at least equal to the proportion of these minority groups in the population of the U.S.A.

at large."[47] Malaysia and China have seats reserved for members of certain ethnic groups; India reserves some positions for applicants of lower-caste origin. Poland has quotas based on social class: "Political directives —formulated in laws, acts, and regulations—provide for a stable percentage of students from manual workers' and peasant families in institutions of higher education."[48]

In theory, to the extent group preferences are explicitly justified, they are usually based on arguments of social value added, students' contributions to the university and to other students, and the effects admissions decisions have on incentives.[49] But in practice, in my experience American admissions committees behave as if the "appropriate" representation of various groups were a separate objective. In my consulting work in several developing countries, I have found that policymakers prefer to treat appropriate representation as a goal distinct from efficient selection (in the sense of social value added) and the creation of beneficial incentives.[50]

Summary

"Whatever else may be problematic," writes economist Susan Rose-Ackerman, "Societies obviously do not use a single, consistent method to make allocative decisions." She continues:

> A good or service may be allocated through a market system in which wide inequalities of income are taken for granted; dispensed through a democratic political system that grants a formal equality to each citizen's vote [; or] assigned by administrative rule, by random selection, or on the basis of "worthiness." Mixed systems are common, and many allocative mechanisms do not easily fit under one or another simple rubric.[51]

An admissions policy is a method for allocating a scarce resource, namely places in a selective university. Admissions is what Rose-Ackerman calls "a mixed system." Market forces matter, even when auctions are out of the question—when we set the university's tuition, we affect who will apply and therefore who can be admitted. Admissions decisions are seldom made by a democratic vote of all the university's "citizens," but there are analogues to political constituencies that we may wish to, or have to, appease. But among all the allocative mechanisms found in society, selection policies for universities and many entry-level jobs are perhaps the most extreme example of allocation on the basis of "worthiness." In theory if not always in practice, universities attempt to select the most meritorious students, disdaining auctions or random selection or political processes.

Who, then, are the most meritorious applicants? It depends. The worthiest students for a medical school that trains researchers probably differ from the worthiest for a medical school that produces general practitioners. One business school may decide to focus on entrepreneurs, another on business analysts—their admissions objectives should differ. So, in all likelihood, should their curricula—and maybe their faculty, academic standards, and a host of other educational policies. In principle, admissions policies should be chosen simultaneously with many other university policies.

As a consequence, there is no one "right" admissions policy. But perhaps a single framework for thinking about the aims of a selection system may be applicable across a wide range of institutions and circumstances and philosophical positions. The framework I have propose in this chapter contains two economic (or utilitarian) models, with various places for nonutilitarian considerations to enter.

The first model treats places in the university as just another commodity on the market. It asks, "Why not auction the commodity?" Answering this question helps us identify the nonfinancial values (or mission) that we want an educational institution to serve.

The second model goes one step further. "All right, if you won't auction the scarce places, then define the applicants' 'worthiness' according to a calculation of the social value added that selecting them will create. Use your values in calculating value added." There are several ways that choosing one student over another creates value. We may or may not, according to our values, include all those ways, and we may not give each way the same weight in our assessment. The ways are:

- The education provided students will have a different value added in terms of their later social contributions, depending on their attributes and what other universities offer.
- Students will vary in the value they add to the university, in terms of their contributions to its financial, academic, and social well-being and how they affect the education obtained by other students.
- When we make an admissions policy, we create incentives that may have social costs and benefits.
- We may attribute intrinsic value to the selection of certain people or groups— apart from the utilitarian considerations of the foregoing points.

I have tried to summarize this framework in exhibit 3.1. It is by no means a "solution" to the problem of choosing objectives, even in the rarefied world of perfect information that we have been inhabiting in this chapter.

EXHIBIT 3.1

A Framework for Discussing the Objectives of Selection

I. Why do you need to be selective?
   A. Is the price of your education too low? Why not raise tuition?
   B. Do you have too few slots? Why not expand your enrollments?
   C. Why not use a lottery?
   D. Could you use a "try out" policy? Why not admit more students and assess them at the university?

II. If you are selective, choose students to maximize social value added. This has four components.
   A. What is the social value added of the education for students' later life?
      1. How does this depend on both students' academic and nonacademic characteristics?
      2. Have you properly accounted for your institution's comparative advantage, calculating value added relative to what students would obtain at other institutions?
      3. How should you assess social value added in an imperfect society?
         a) Adjusting for injustices in society's definitions of value and success
         b) Adjusting for injustices in the system that prepares students for the university
         c) Weighting "irrelevant" or "offensive" characteristics that affect success (appearance, for example)
         d) Rewarding "effort" versus "inborn talent"
   B. What is the value of various students' contributions to the university?
      1. How should you weight students' financial contributions (tuition, later donations, etc.)?
      2. How should you weight students' contributions to the academic values of your institution?
      3. What other contributions (athletic, social, cultural) should matter and how much?
      4. What composition of the student body produces the best learning experience, in the broad sense?
         a) How do the educational effects of "diversity" depend on the prior experiences of students, other sources of diversity available to them, and opportunities for homogeneity within the institution?
         b) Should you count all educationally beneficial dimensions of diversity or sameness, or should should some dimensions be "irrelevant"?
   C. What positive and negative incentives will your admissions policy create?
      1. How should you weight the incentives created for potential applicants, institutions that prepare applicants, your faculty, alumni and employers, and your admissions committee?
      2. In terms of incentives, what are the benefits and costs of clear-cut versus "mysterious" admissions policies?
   D. To what attributes of students do you assign "intrinsic value," and how much?
      1. Personal, moral, and political traits or behaviors
      2. The representation in the student body of certain groups

---

But I hope that such a framework may have heuristic value in resolving disputes over what one should be trying to accomplish in choosing an elite. When we disagree about selection policies, as we often do, a framework like this one may help us sort out exactly where and how we disagree.

This discussion of objectives has been long and complicated. But I am sorry to say that the complexities of our problem are not yet exhausted. We need to relax the fantastic assumption that we have perfect information on the past and future accomplishments of those who apply to our institution. In reality, we do not.

4

Prediction and Selection

IN THE preceding chapter, we concentrated on the ideal objectives of a selection policy. To clarify conceptual issues, we imagined that we had perfect information about applicants—about their future attainments as well as their present attributes. We ignored the palpable facts that some objectives and some attributes are easier to measure than others, that we may be unable to tell which candidates have, or will develop, the qualities we desire.

But real selection policies must be made and managed with predictions, not certainties. With incomplete and unreliable information, we try to predict which applicants will fulfill our objectives. The policy we would choose under conditions of perfect information may be undesirable when the information is incomplete, inexact, or nonexistent.

How imperfect is the information that selection boards and admissions committees have or could have? How well can we predict (using which predictors) the various kinds of social value added, or "later-life success," or academic performance, or the educational benefits of diversity? As these predictions are imperfect to various degrees, what does this imply about our choice of admissions policies?

These issues are difficult for two reasons. First, enormous bodies of literature address various parts of each question. Much of the literature in applied psychology, for example, concerns the value of various tests and measures to predict various things about the people tested. More narrowly, the literature on the prediction of academic performance includes literally thousands of articles and monographs. I have uncovered hundreds of studies of the determinants of future earnings, to name one partial, and debatable, indicator of social value added. Then there are separate literatures about interviews, assessment centers, intelligence tests, the effects of various student characteristics on individual and group learning, measures of academic success such as grades, the analogous problem of personnel selection in business, and so on.

Second, much of the literature may be misleading or irrelevant to our problem of choosing elites. We must predict at the right tail. The fact that IQ scores successfully discriminate between truck drivers and surgeons is of little use within an applicant pool of would-be surgeons. Moreover, many results and arguments are confined to the fact that a predictor is statistically significant, or that the percentage of variance explained is low, neither of which addresses the operational issues we face. Many popular ways of assessing the strength of a predictor are misleading for our purposes. Indeed, much of the current debate over the value of standardized test scores to predict academic performance can be understood as disagreement, or confusion, over how to think about prediction.

Consequently, before we begin to assess the evidence on prediction, we need guidelines for correctly thinking about it. The aim of this chapter is primarily conceptual. I will talk a lot about one particular example, the prediction of academic performance, but only as a vehicle for understanding more general issues about prediction. Please avoid an assumption that academic performance is the main topic of interest for admissions; the preceding and subsequent chapters make clear that this is not the case.[1] My aim is to show how the answer to "How valuable is it to use this variable in making admissions decisions?" depends on:

1. How well we can measure our objectives
2. The particular composition of our applicant pool
3. How selective we are
4. What other predictors we have
5. How we value various-sized improvements in our objective

Correlations and Beyond

First some statistical preliminaries. We will be interested in measuring the typical level of performance among a group of people, and to do so we can use statistics like the mean or the median. We will also be interested in variations in performance within the group. A popular statistic for measuring such variations is the standard deviation. For most types of data we will be examining, one standard deviation is the amount that must be added to the middle score, or 50th percentile amount, to make a score or amount just higher than the 84th percentile of the group we are studying. Thus, in a group of one hundred people, the difference between the person ranked 50th and the person ranked 84th is about one standard deviation. About two-thirds of the people are found within one standard deviation each way from the average. About 95 percent fall within two standard deviations each way from the average.

As an example, figure 4.1 shows the approximate distribution of scores on the verbal portion of the Scholastic Aptitude Test in 1983. The mean score was 425, and the standard deviation was 109. If a student could move from 425 to 534—one standard deviation above the mean—he or she would move from the 50th to about the 84th percentile among college-bound high-school seniors who took the SAT in 1983.[2]

In this chapter, we will also be interested in assessing statistically how

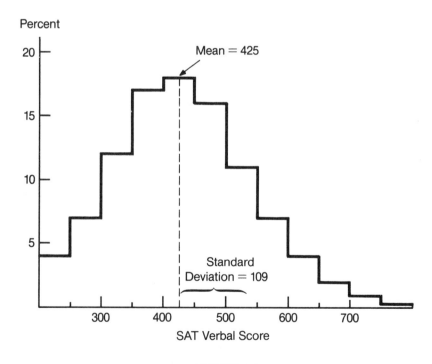

FIGURE 4.1
Distribution of SAT Verbal Scores in 1983

changes in one variable are associated with changes in another variable. For example, we want to know how changes in SAT scores correspond to changes in academic performance at the university. If there is a strong association between two variables, then knowing one helps a lot in predicting the other. But when there is a weak association, information about one variable does not help much in guessing the other.

To gauge the strength of the association between two variables, a popular statistic is the correlation coefficient. It can take values ranging from one to minus one, where one indicates a perfectly positive relationship, zero indicates no linear relationship, and minus one indicates a perfectly negative relationship. Suppose SAT verbal scores and college grades are correlated 0.4—this indicates a positive but hardly perfect association.

A convenient starting point for interpreting a correlation like 0.4 is this: If the correlation is 0.4, it means that a one-standard deviation increase in the SAT verbal score is associated with a 0.4-standard deviation increase in college grades. This 0.4-standard deviation increase corresponds to moving from the 50th to about the 66th percentile in college grades.

Notice the use of words like "association" and "relationship." Correlation does not entail causation. It is incorrect to say that a one-standard deviation gain in the SAT verbal score "caused" an 0.4 standard deviation gain in college grades. What is correct is to say that if the correlation coefficient between these two variables is 0.4, we would predict that two students differing by one standard deviation in SAT scores would on average differ by 0.4 standard deviations in college grades.

Another way of getting a feel for correlations is to look at some interesting examples:

- The correlation coefficient is 0.77 between the Scholastic Aptitude Test verbal score and the total score on the English Placement Test of Basic Skills, used by many colleges.[3]
- The correlation is about 0.6–0.7 between a student's college grade-point averages in the fall semester and in the spring semester.
- "Taking all jobs as a whole . . . it can be stated that by and large the maximal power of tests to predict success in training is of the order of .50, and to predict success on the job itself is of the order of .35. . . ."[4]
- The correlation is about 0.4 between scores on a standardized reading comprehension test in eleventh grade and hourly earnings twelve years later.[5]
- The correlation is about 0.4 between years of education and adult earnings.
- The correlation is about 0.4 between doctors' diagnoses of the same patient.[6]
- The correlation is 0.38 between the grades given to the same essays by two different graders.[7]
- " . . . the near maximum criterion validity coefficients for personality measures [that is, correlations between a psychological test and any criterion of performance) fall around 0.30."[8]

- The correlation is 0.25 between oddsmakers' point spreads in professional football and the actual differences in scores.[9]
- The correlation is about 0.15–0.25 between one's father's occupation and one's own later earnings.[10]
- The correlation is about 0.12–0.28 between the incomes of two brothers.[11]

As we shall see, if we use several variables as predictors, the best combination of them may correlate 0.6 with grades at the university. The best combination of variables for predicting income may lead to a correlation of 0.5. Is this a lot or a little? How do such numbers help us decide whether and how to use a predictor for purposes of selection?

I believe many current discussions founder on these statistical questions. One can interpret the same statistical association in ways that sound quite different. For example, one can make a correlation of 0.4 seem unimportant by stating—correctly—that only $(0.4)^2 = 0.16$ or one-sixth of the variance in the college grades is "statistically explained" by SAT verbal scores. On the other hand, one can make it seem important by saying—correctly— that such a result is "highly statistically significant," in the sense that one can confidently reject the hypothesis that the predictor has no relationship with the outcome. Some "anti-testers" emphasize the first point, while some advocates of test scores stress the second. We needn't go into the details of their debate. My purpose instead is to show how, for the problem of selection at the right tail, we should go beyond these two interpretations —how the interpretations of a statistical study of prediction depends on five specific features of the selection problem.

1. Imperfect Measures of Our Objectives

In the last chapter, many possible objectives were highlighted: the social value added of the education our institution provides; students' contributions to the institution's "academic values"; the diversity of the student body, both to enhance education and perhaps as a means of accelerating equal opportunity; and several other objectives. The first practical problem we face in choosing an elite is how to measure the successful fulfillment of such objectives.

The outcomes we are trying to predict in admissions decisions are imperfectly measured. This fact is glaringly apparent when we think about various sorts of social value added. For example, how can we gauge achievement after graduation? Proxies for achievement, such as income, social status, and professional attainments, are highly imperfect even in their own terms, and even if we could perfectly measure them, would we call them "social value added"? Academic objectives are also imperfectly measured by such widely used indicators as grades and honors.

The incompleteness and unreliability of the usual measures of later-life success—income, social status, and various sorts of professional achievements—are obvious. (Chapter 6 reviews research on various measures of later-life contributions within and across professions.) Popular measures include such interesting but obviously imperfect indicators as salary; subjective ratings of performance, as by supervisors, peers, or experts in the field; appearance in *Who's Who;* membership or office in professional societies; the number of publications or citations to one's publications (for academics); ratings based on time it took to get tenure or partnership or some other rank; prestige of one's employer; and scores on qualifying examinations for entry into the profession. Almost no studies attempt to combine these various indicators; to their credit, almost all researchers include strong caveats against interpreting their chosen measures as "success" or "social value added." We may call this the problem of *incompleteness in measurement.*

Even if one were to accept a measure like income as a proxy for social contribution, reported income figures are unreliable. In other words, they contain various errors of measurement. The size of these errors is indicated by the reliability coefficient, which can be thought of as the correlation coefficient between two independent measurements of the same outcome taken at the same time. A reliability coefficient of 1.0 would indicate perfect agreement and no measuring error, 0 would indicate pure measurement error and no agreement. Sociologist Christopher Jencks and his colleagues estimate the following approximate reliabilities based on longitudinal studies: total income, 0.8; earnings, 0.8 to 0.9; social status as measured by the Duncan scale, 0.86 to 0.96; and years of education, 0.9.[12] Thus, for total income, some of the differences among people are due to measurement error and cannot possibly be explained by any predictor variables. We may call this the problem of *unreliability in measurement.*

Measures of academic performance are also incomplete and unreliable. Consider university grades. This is the most popular measure of academic performance, and the reason is easy to understand. A grade represents a teacher's estimate of how well a student has mastered what was taught in the course. As students presumably do not take courses whose subject matter they have already covered, grades are a measure of how much students have learned. However, grades are incomplete. They may measure learning relative to other students in the class, rather than absolute mastery. And grades are not usually designed to assess progress toward other educational goals, such as creativity, aesthetic and ethical sensitivity, and so forth. Finally, even if we accept that grades measure how much is learned in a course, they do not estimate academic value added or a student's contribution toward the university's own academic objectives. The level of academic achievement is one thing, and the amount of academic progress a student makes may be quite another.

Grades are also unreliable measures. One authority estimates the average reliability of a college test as 0.45.[13] Within a given course, grades are often quite unreliable, in the sense that two section leaders might give different grades for the same work. Grade-point averages (GPA) are more reliable. But even when students take the same courses, much of the variation among student grade averages can be attributed to measurement error rather than real differences in achievement. One study of grades in the first semester of freshman year estimated that "GPA in this study can be conceptualized as approximately 80% true variance and 20% error."[14] Grade averages are difficult to compare across students. Some courses and departments grade equivalent students more stringently than others. Because students self-select into courses, aggregating across courses and fields make grade averages less meaningful indicators and predictors. Two of the most careful researchers of academic prediction have shown how the systematic self-allocation of academically weaker students into easier courses seriously distorts the meaning of grade-point averages, even within the same institution: "As long as there are radical differences in grading standards, and students are able to choose most of their classes, then no predictor will have more than moderate validity for predicting GPA."[15]

Moreover, high schools, colleges and universities vary widely in their grading standards. For one thing, they calculate grade averages in different ways, as table 4.1 shows. More important, different institutions vary widely in the academic talent of their students. A given grade average obviously means different things at different institutions (More on this in chapter 5).

Grades may sometimes be systematically biased. Several studies have shown what many teachers suspect from anecdotes: grades are sometimes unduly unfluenced by gregariousness or gender.[16]

Measuring academic success in graduate school may be especially hard. Two authors conducted an exhaustive review and concluded " . . . that while grades serve several useful functions in graduate education, the one served least well is that of providing an understandable criterion of graduate student performance."[17] The authors also examined and found wanting such proxies for performance as degree attainment, time to the degree, comprehensive examinations, dissertation quality, and others.

TABLE 4.1

Composing the Grade-Point Average[18]

Practice	Number of Colleges with Practice
All grades in all courses at any institution are counted	159
Only grades in courses counting toward the degree are used	43
Only grades from the institution doing the computing are counted	246
When a course is repeated, all grades are counted	136
When a course is repeated, only the last grade received is counted	266

Most predictors we might use are also unreliable. The standardized tests used by colleges and graduate schools fare well in this regard. Such aptitude tests are closely related to intelligence tests. *The Eighth Mental Measurements Yearbook* (1978) classifies the Scholastic Aptitude Test as a group intelligence test. Former Educational Testing Service President Henry Chauncey and a co-author equated Scholastic Aptitude Test scores with scores on an intelligence test.[19] Scores by the same students on the various admissions tests—SAT, American College Testing Program tests, Graduate Record Examinations, Graduate Management Admission Test, Law School Admission Test, Medical College Admission Test, and so forth—are highly correlated, almost as highly as two scores by the same student on any one of the tests.[20] These tests usually have reliability coefficients of around .90.

Most other predictors are less reliable. We have seen that grades, which are often used as predictors as well as measures of later performance, contain a considerable amount of measurement error. In chapters 6 and 7, we will review various psychological tests and predictors such as interviews and recommendations. These contain a large amount of measurement error, reducing their ability to predict later outcomes of interest.

What do these imperfect measures imply for judgments about predictive power? *Part of the problem of inaccurate predictions resides in outcome measures, rather than in the predictors themselves.* If indicators of success are incomplete, it is impossible to tell how well predictors would correlate with valid and complete outcome measures.[21] If measures of outcomes are unreliable, correlations between predictors and outcomes are lower than if there were perfectly reliable measures. Predictors will look worse than they really are.

In the case of unreliability, statistical adjustments can be made that yield more meaningful correlations. A standard technique, which depends on simplifying assumptions and accurate measures of reliability,[22] is to divide the observed correlation by the square root of the reliability coefficient of the outcome measure. For example, if the reliability of grades is 0.7 and the observed correlation between test scores and grades is 0.4, the correlation adjusted for "criterion unreliability" is 0.48.

The logic behind this adjustment is that, in most cases, we are really interested in predicting the underlying outcome or behavior being unreliably measured. We care about the "true" academic performance that grades try to measure, not the unreliable grades in themselves. If we have a good estimate of the unreliability of the outcome measure, we should adjust the correlations accordingly. After all, the individual's actual achievements are not limited by the errors inherent in the methods used to measure the criterion, nor should judgment of the power of the predictor to forecast the actual achievements be undervalued because of criterion unreliability. (Of course, such adjustments do not help with the problem of incomplete objectives.)[23]

Available outcome measures are incomplete and controversial. Even when we can specify certain outcome measures—such as income, status within a profession, or academic performance—measurements are unreliable. This unreliability means that unadjusted correlation coefficients *underestimate* the power of predictors.

2. Assessing Prediction in a Highly Selected Sample

Selecting at the right tail creates special problems of prediction. The major pitfall involves erroneous extrapolations from findings about prediction at the right tail to the broader population, and vice versa. There are two reasons why such extrapolations often err. First, those admitted tend to be the more able, which restricts the range of the predictor. In the case of test scores and later grades, this restriction of range reduces the correlation between test scores and grades, compared to how large that correlation would be over the larger distribution of the applicant pool or the population as a whole.

A football example helps to capture this point. Suppose we wanted to assess the importance of running speed in predicting performance as a wide receiver in the National Football League. We might correlate speed as measured in the forty-yard dash with a measure of performance such as coaches' rankings of NFL wide receivers. Those wide receivers now in the league are fast—way out on the right tail of running speed. Among wide receivers now playing, variations in speed might be weakly correlated with differences in performance, but it would be foolish to infer that speed is unimportant for succeeding as a wide receiver.

For example, thirty-six wide receivers were selected by NFL teams in the 1982 college football draft. Using their forty-yard dash times, I calculated a correlation of 0.35 between running speed and the order in which they were selected. This "low" correlation coefficient might lead some naive observers to conclude that speed was not particularly important for playing this position. Yet, all wide receivers selected ran the forty yards in 4.8 or under, which is fast even in the population of college football players. If we expanded the pool to include people of widely varying speed afoot, we might well discover that slow men should not apply—and perhaps that speed was the best single predictor of performance in the broader population.[24]

A similar lesson might hold for predictions of academic performance and later-life success at highly selective institutions. We need to be very careful that the sample *from* which correlations and regressions are derived, and the sample *to* which we wish to apply them, are similar.

If we make certain simplifying assumptions about extrapolations, correlations can be adjusted depending on the population of interest.[25] The technicalities of these adjustments might divert our attention from the central points.[26] A correlation derived from a sample with restricted range will usually underestimate the same correlation calculated for a broader range of the population. Conversely, it is risky to extrapolate findings from the general population—or from the majority of institutions—to institutions at the right tail.

Second, students with low scores on the predictors, who are nonetheless accepted, are likely to be chosen because they are high on other dimensions. This in turn affects the correlation between the predictor and later performance. The process of selection reduces the simple correlation between test scores and later grades.[27] We may be led once more to underestimate a predictor's power, as measured by correlations.

Again, a sports example may help. Suppose that players under 6' tall in the National Basketball Association turned out to score as many points per game as players over 6'5". It would be unwise to conclude that height makes no difference to basketball scoring in the broader population of aspiring basketball players. The few "short" players in the league have extraordinary capabilities along other lines. (It is correct to say that restrictions according to height would eliminate some excellent players.)

These same methodological problems are also prevalent in other areas of research. The ideal solution would be an experiment with random selection, but in practice this is usually infeasible.[28] Because of the selection process, correlations are usually biased downward by these problems. Correlations based on the selected group look weaker than they would be for the entire applicant pool or the broader population.

3. Selectivity and the Usefulness of a Predictor

We have been discussing several specific features of the selection problem that can affect the interpretation of a correlation between a predictor and an outcome—the incompleteness and unreliability of outcome measures and the fact that we are working within a highly selected sample. We now turn to a third specific feature: the degree of "selectivity."

The usual measure of selectivity is the ratio of admits to applicants. This can be misleading, because applicants self-select partly on their perceived probability of being admitted. But the ratio will be helpful heuristically as we consider how the usefulness of a predictor depends on selectivity.

Suppose a law school admits 10 percent of those who apply and that 80 percent of the applicant pool would pass if admitted. Over the entire applicant pool, an admissions test is correlated 0.4 with passing.[29] By assumption, if applicants were admitted randomly, 20 percent would fail. If, instead, admission were on the basis of the test, calculations show that only 5 percent would fail—even though the correlation is only 0.4 and the percentage of variance explained is only 0.16[30] (see table 4.2).

Suppose the law school is also interested in some level of superb academic performance, and suppose superb performance is correlated 0.5 with the test score. Suppose that 5 percent of the applicants are thought to be

TABLE 4.2

Value of a Predictor

Class Chosen by:	Percent Failing	Percent Performing Superbly	Grade-point Average
Random selection	20	5	2.0 (C)
Admission with test score	5	19	2.7 (B−)
Perfect prediction	0	50	3.76 (A−)

NOTE: The calculations for this table assume correlations of 0.4 between the test score and passing, 0.5 between the test score and superb performance, and 0.4 with average grade. It is also assumed that, by some objective standards, 80 percent of applicants would pass if admitted, 5 percent would perform superbly, and the expected distribution of grades among all applicants would be normally distributed with a mean of 2.0 and a standard deviation of 1.0. The ratio of admits to applicants is 1:10.

able to give a superb performance if admitted and, as before, only 10 percent of all applicants are admitted. With random admissions, 5 percent of the class would perform superbly. Using the test score for selection, calculations show that this figure would rise to 19 percent. This seems to be a large and important gain.

Suppose that we knew that the grade distribution of a randomly admitted class would be a normal distribution with an average grade of C and a standard deviation equal to one grade. Suppose the test correlates 0.4 with grades and 10 percent of the applicants are admitted. With random admission, the average grade would be C. Using the test, the average grade would be B—. (With perfect prediction, the average grade would be A—.)[31]

Thus, in highly selective admissions processes, a predictor may have a "low" correlation coefficient and still be very useful. On the other hand, if two out of every three applicants are being selected, a predictor with an 0.4 correlation may be of little value. The usefulness will be greater the higher the correlation, the lower the percentage of applicants admitted, and the more diverse the applicant pool, other things equal.[32]

4. Considering Information Already Possessed

The analyses just presented of the value of a predictor are steps in the right direction. But for admissions policymaking, different questions may come to mind. Consider this question about the use of test scores in college admissions: "How much do test scores add to the predictions we can make with information we already have? And how do we interpret the importance of, say a one-hundred-point increase in a test score?" The real question is not: "How well do we do, compared to chance, when we use test scores alone?" The answer to this last question usually overstates the usefulness of test scores because other information used in admissions will already be capturing some of the test's predictive power. (As the point is general, these statements could be rephrased in terms of other predictors, such as letters of recommendation and measures of leadership, and other outcomes, such as various forms of later-life success.)

For example, when grades or class rank in high school (or college) are used to predict first-year college (or graduate school) grades, typical correlations, as reported in the literature, would be those in the first column of the following table. The correlations rise when test scores are added to the grades as predictors, as shown in the second column:

Grades in:	Correlations between Later Grades and:	
	Previous Grades	Previous Grades and Test Scores
College	0.55	0.62
Medical School	0.41	0.52
Law School	0.30	0.50
Graduate School	0.30	0.45
Business School	0.25	0.40

Expressed in some statistical formulas, these increases would seem small to many people. The major statistical interpretation used in a Ralph Nader-sponsored critique of testing was based on small increases in the "index of forecasting efficiency" due to test scores. The report refers to tests predicting "five percent of nothing," the "five percent" being a low estimate of the increase in predictive power thus measured and the "nothing" being grades, which, the report argues, matter little to later-life success.[33]

More helpful is an analysis along the lines of the law school examples above. Suppose that previous grades correlate 0.3 with passing and 0.4 with superb performance and that using test scores raises these correlations to 0.5 and 0.6, respectively, (adding 0.20 to each correlation). Again, one of every ten applicants is accepted. Then some of the additional benefits of using test scores can be crudely gauged from this table:[34]

	Percent Failing	Percent Performing Superbly
Random selection	20	5
Admissions with college grades only	8	16
Admissions with college grades and test scores	3	24

The increase is not as marked as table 4.2 indicated. Nonetheless, in light of these results, it is easy to see why most admissions committees in a highly selective situation would make use of grades and test scores in choosing a class, even though it remains true that the correlation between grades and scores and future academic performance may seem low.

Such tables help assess the value of using a predictor as opposed to not using it. Now we turn to a slightly different question, also of great importance in admissions decision making: "Suppose we have decided to use a predictor like test scores. How do we interpret the importance of, say, a one-hundred-point increase in a test score?" (Again, the same sort of question can be asked about interpreting athletic ratings or personality tests or interview results; I use test scores and grades simply as a convenient example of a general methodological issue.)

To answer this question, *regression analysis* is helpful. This statistical technique combines several predictors, so that the effect of changes in one predictor can be estimated with the other predictors "held constant," or "controlled for." For example, suppose we wish to predict college grade averages using a series of predictors, such as test scores, previous grade averages, and interview ratings. Regression analysis combines these three predictors linearly in such a way that errors of prediction are at a minimum. The resulting equation is of the form:

College grade average = a mathematical constant *plus*
$\beta_1 \times$ test score *plus*
$\beta_2 \times$ previous grade average *plus*
$\beta_3 \times$ interview rating

The estimated *regression coefficient* β_1 indicates roughly how large a change in college grade average is associated with a one-unit change in the test score, with previous grade average and interview rating statistically held constant.[35] Thus, the regression coefficient β_1 gives us the answer we are seeking.

An example is helpful at this point. To illustrate what may be learned from regression coefficients, I have reanalyzed one of the most famous studies of academic prediction, T. Anne Cleary's study of test bias.[36] Her question was: "Do test scores give different predictions for the grades of black and white students at the same colleges?" She analyzed correlation coefficients and obtained the results in table 4.3.

We may ask, "After statistically controlling for high-school grades, how much difference does a one-hundred-point increase in a test score make

TABLE 4.3
*Correlations between Test Scores and College Grades for
Blacks and Whites at Two Colleges*

	College X	College Y
Blacks		
SAT verbal	0.26	0.47
SAT math	0.17	0.47
Whites		
SAT verbal	0.38	0.47
SAT math	0.30	0.39

to college grades?" For this question, the correlations in table 4.3 by themselves provide little help. But regression coefficients can help.

Table 4.4 presents Cleary's regression coefficient results. In the first line of table 4.4, the coefficient of SAT verbal of 0.0048 means that, holding constant the SAT math scores and high school rank (HSR), a one-point increase in a black student's SAT verbal score is associated with a 0.0048 increase in grades at College X. Thus, a hundred-point increase in SATV is associated with a 0.48 increase in college grades, after statistically controlling for SATM and HSR. This is an increase of about 0.70 of a standard deviation in college grades.[37]

Consider the average black student in College X. He or she has an SATV of 484, an SATM of 468, and an HSR of 60. His or her college grade average is 1.80, or about the 50th percentile of black students. Suppose there is another black student with an SATV 100 points higher, but with the same SATM and HSR. What does that 100-point increase mean?

One way to answer is to calculate the student's predicted grade average. Plugging the numbers into the equation in the first line of table 4.4 yields the answer: the second student is predicted to get a college grade average of 2.28. This 2.28 average corresponds to the 76th percentile of black students in College X. So, the one-hundred-point increase in the SATV score is predicted to correspond to moving from the 50th to the 76th percentile among black students in College X, in terms of their college grades. Table 4.5 presents similar calculations that assess the effects of

TABLE 4.4

Results from Cleary's Study of Grade Prediction[38]

School X:	Black	GPA = −1.41 + 0.0048 SATV + 0.0015 SATM + 0.0031 HSR
	White	GPA = 0.741 + 0.0027 SATV + 0.0014 SATM + 0.0103 HSR
School Y:	Black	GPA = −0.592 + 0.0018 SATV + 0.0018 SATM + 0.1104 A
	White	GPA = 0.110 + 0.0014 SATV + 0.0004 SATM + 0.1571 A

School X		Mean	Standard Deviation	School Y		Mean	Standard Deviation
Black	GPA	1.80	0.69	Black	GPA	1.81	0.56
	SATV	486	67		SATV	338	71
	SATM	468	68		SATM	371	66
	HSR	60	20		A	9.9	1.8
White	GPA	1.94	0.80	White	GPA	2.38	0.70
	SATV	502	80		SATV	436	100
	SATM	517	85		SATM	461	101
	HSR	57	22		A	9.0	2.3

NOTE: GPA = college grade average on a 1–4 scale with 4 = A; SATV = SAT verbal score; SATM = SAT math score; HSR = high-school class rank; A = high-school grade average on a 1–14 scale with 14 = A+.

one-hundred-point increases in both verbal and math scores, after controlling for high-school rank. It tells how much effect a one-hundred-point difference in those scores makes in terms of grades in college.

As we shall see in chapter 5, regression results can also be used to show how uncertain these predictions can be for any individual student. Unfortunately, Cleary's paper does not provide information which would enable this point to be illustrated here.

5. Utility Functions for Outcomes

Before we can decide how much using a predictor helps, measures of success have to be appropriately scaled. How much do various-sized increases in the predicted outcomes matter? In economics parlance, is the utility function over outcomes linear—or should the available measures be transformed in some nonlinear way?

For example, grade-point averages are usually scaled so that the difference between a C and a B counts the same as the difference between a B and an A. Is this what we believe? And if income is used as one index of later-life success, is a $10,000 increase valued the same whether income goes from $20,000 to $30,000, or from $100,000 to $110,000?

These questions ask us to provide a utility function for measures of outcomes. Most of us do not have linear utility functions for measures of success, such as grades or income or status within a profession. For example, economic models often assume the decreasing marginal utility of income, where each additional dollar is not quite as important to us as the last.[39] The importance of various degrees of eminence within a profession varies across professions and probably is nonlinear, too. Educator James

TABLE 4.5

*Gains from a 100-Point Increase in SAT Verbal and Math Scores,
Controlling for High-School Rank*

		Gain in GPA	Gain in Standard Deviations of GPA	From 50th Percentile to this Percentile in College Class
School X	Black	0.63	0.91	82nd
	White	0.41	0.51	70th
School Y	Black	0.36	0.64	74th
	White	0.18	0.26	60th

March studied the careers of secondary school administrators and argued that differences in performance among the top half were relatively unimportant. This contrasts sharply with findings in academia, where the top 2 percent of researchers are often found to publish 25 percent of the research.

> Unlike some other areas of advanced education (e.g., pure mathematics, theoretical sociology) in which the primary concern should probably be addressed to increasing the average quality of the top 1 percent of a cohort, national strategies for developing programs in educational administration probably should be more concerned with the average quality of the top 50–75 percent.[40]

Thus, being able to predict whether a student will end up in the top 1 percent or the top 25 percent matters much more in academic research than in educational administration.

As a heuristic device, however, it is useful to assume linearity and ask, "How much would a one standard deviation increase in academic performance (or some outcome measure) be worth with a given utility function?" In my work in developing countries, I have found that such questions help to focus policymakers' thoughts. John E. Hunter and Frank L. Schmidt reviewed estimates of supervisors' evaluations of the dollar value of a one-standard deviation difference in the performance of people in the same job. The authors concluded that it ranged from 40 to 70 percent of the annual salary on that job. They go on to calculate how much it would be worth to improve the personnel selection process by adding or improving predictors of performance.[41] I have used similar methods to estimate the benefits of Pakistan's testing system and to analyze the benefits and costs of alternative selection systems in Indonesia.[42]

In this book, judgments about utility are left to you; I do not try to estimate the utility of a one-standard deviation gain in performance. But I will stress that the answer to the question, "How good a predictor of outcome Y is variable X?" does not just depend on statistical significance or on the size of a correlation coefficient or a regression coefficient. Nor should the answer be driven by an arbitrary scale of measuring the outcome, such as grade-point averages or some metric of "professional success." The answer also depends on how much such changes are valued.[43]

Summary

The statistical issues in this chapter are crucial. At the heart of selection policies are predictions about applicants—predictions based on various brands of imperfect information. Seldom will we encounter a policy issue that hinges more on statistical interpretation.

For example, my reading of the current debate on test scores leads me to conclude that most of it concerns the interpretation of agreed-upon facts. One side tends to cite a "low" percentage of variation explained by test scores. Another side is fond of alluding to the "statistical significance" of test scores as predictors, or draws flattering comparisons to other predictors.

One conclusion is that neither interpretation helps us much with the problem of choosing an elite. We want to know how much difference using a particular predictor makes to something we care about. We want to know how much a certain-sized increase in a predictor—say, a one-hundred-point increase in a test score—will matter. To answer our questions, we need to take account of particular features of an admissions problem, such as:

1. How completely and reliably the outcomes we care about can be measured
2. How a sample at the right tail of the distribution has been chosen
3. How selective we are
4. What other information we have
5. The "utility" of increases in the outcome measures

Because of these complications, it is not enough to discuss predictive power simply in terms of correlation coefficients, the percentage of variation explained, or statistical significance, as the literature usually does. We have seen, for example, that in some circumstances a predictor with a "low" correlation can nonetheless be highly useful in selective admission (see table 4.2). On the other hand, in different circumstances a predictor with a "high" correlation may not help. The numbers must be interpreted in a specific decision-making context.

A second conclusion also emerges from this statistical foray. We must be careful that the sample *from* which we have derived certain conclusions about prediction and the sample *to* which we wish to apply those conclusions are similar. Universities at the right tail select within highly able—and atypical—applicant pools. Studies done at other institutions or across the entire population are therefore difficult to extrapolate to these situations. The reverse is also true—studies of prediction among those already selected, or among those who have graduated, cannot simply be assumed to hold for the larger applicant pool or the broader population of potential applicants.

A third point is commonly forgotten. A certain piece of information may help if it is the only information available—that is, if the alternative is random selection. But it may be of no additional help, if we already make admissions decisions on the basis of other information. As we shall see, predictors such as creativity tests and letters of recommendation can be criticized, not because by themselves they would not give some useful information, but because they do not add much to the already available information such as test scores, grades, and biographical information.

Furthermore, the value of a predictor depends on how selective an institution is. At highly selective universities, even "weak" predictors can lead to great improvements in the class chosen. If the information is free, the more selective we are, the more valuable the predictor is. A mathematical formula can be used to quantify the gains of utility as a function of several features of a given situation.[44]

We have seen some examples of how to evaluate the usefulness of a predictor. Our examples went beyond the simple reporting of correlation coefficients and tests of statistical significance. In the context of choosing an elite, unadjusted correlations often understate predictive power; on the other hand, statistical significance may lead many people to overestimate predictive power. Multiple regression analysis can help to judge how much a certain-sized increase in a predictor really matters. But judging what "matters" is a value judgment—in economics jargon, it depends on the utility function. Although this point retrogresses to the topic of chapter 3, it is also a useful epilogue to a discussion of statistical methodology. If we fail to understand the statistics, we may easily be misled in the chapters that follow. Even if our interpretations are methodologically impeccable, however, our final judgments about the importance of the evidence transcends statistics.

5

Predicting Academic Performance

I N chapter 3, we saw that one—but probably only one—of the ideal objectives in admissions is to select those students who will further an institution's "academic values." Academic achievement may matter for its own sake, in addition to whatever value added it creates through the later social contributions of an institution's graduates.

No theme is more popular in university speechmaking than the value of academic excellence. But measuring it is another matter. How would we know whether one student did more for our academic values than another? How well could we predict this, given the imperfect information available at admissions time?

The most commonly used measures of academic success in a university are grades. Grades reflect teachers' assessments of how much students have learned and the degree of academic excellence students have achieved. But grades are incomplete and unreliable measures of academic performance. They do not necessarily measure progress toward subtler educational goals, such as creativity, aesthetic and ethical sensitivity, and so forth. They are full of measurement error, in part because students self-select into harder and easier courses and majors, and in part because course grades themselves are unreliable.

Are other measures available besides grades? As I have repeatedly posed this question during the course of this research, I have been surprised by how little effort universities have devoted to developing and evaluating measures of how well students do in terms of the institutions' academic values. Three authors recently surveyed "competence assessment" at a variety of educational institutions. They sadly concluded that "only a few programs spend much effort developing explicit manuals and checking agreement among evaluators. Very rarely is research on the relationship between competence measures and real-life performance carried out."[1]

We can look beyond grade-point averages to the extremes of academic achievement—performing unsatisfactorily or brilliantly, not completing the degree or completing it rapidly, and so forth. We might also use standardized tests to measure academic mastery or professional readiness. Some studies have used Graduate Record Examination achievement scores as outcome measures. Others have looked at scores on the examinations administered by the National Board of Medical Examiners.

A few researchers are pursuing another path, which seems full of promise. They have attempted to create new indicators of educational progress, to measure objectives like those described by Harvard's Dean K. Whitla:

> . . . an ability to communicate in writing with clarity and style, a capacity to analyze problems by collecting relevant data and marshalling pertinent arguments, an ability to master new concepts and materials across major disciplines, critical appreciation for the ways we gain an understanding of the universe, society, and ourselves, a sensitivity to ethical considerations and a capacity to make relationships, broadening intellectual and aesthetic interests, and the extent to which life's experiences are viewed in a wider context.[2]

These objectives go beyond grades in assessing more general progress in learning. But even proponents of this path admit that proposed new measures, such as stories written for a Thematic Apperception Test or indicators of nonverbal sensitivity, are not yet demonstrably better than grades:

> . . . while the competency-based education movement has contributed fresh ideas and valuable perspectives on the goals of liberal education, its assessment procedures do not necessarily offer an improvement on either traditional grading or "objective" tests.[3]

The new measures of educational progress are in an experimental stage. Although they are promising, pending their further refinement and implementation, we are limited to the analysis of grades, scores on standardized examinations, high honors, "persistence" and "attrition," and time to degree. In short, we cannot yet precisely measure the ideal objective of how well a student serves a university's academic values, partly because this objective has not been carefully specified and partly because, even for clearly defined aims, proven measures are usually not available.

Consequently, the task of this chapter should not be misunderstood. We will address certain questions that would likely interest those who are choosing an elite. We have several sources of information on aspiring students at a particular university. We wonder how we should use this information and want to calibrate the data we have. How, for example, can we interpret a one-hundred-point difference in a test score? How much does it help to use test scores if we already have information about a student's previous grades?

Thousands of studies have examined academic prediction. Yet, most of them are difficult to apply to selection at the right tail. This is true for several reasons. First, most studies do not address academic prediction from the point of view of admissions policymaking. This is not the result of scientific sloppiness or a desire to hide information, although these factors are sometimes present. In part, it is an artifact of the correlational methods so popular in psychology and of the propensity of some test makers to ask less useful questions, such as, "Do test scores significantly correlate with academic performance?"

Second, as we shall see, universities differ greatly in their grading standards. The grade of B in one institution does not necessarily correspond to a B at another school. Often, studies of the impact of grades on later performance, or of the prediction of grades at various universities, overlook this obvious fact, acting instead as if there were a universal grading standard across universities. Simply pooling different institutions in studies of prediction is a bad idea; by doing so, estimates of predictive relationships are biased toward zero.

Third, universities at the right tail encounter unique statistical problems in estimating predictive power. Should we expect predictive power to be higher or lower at the right tail? Considerations cut both ways. Some factors lead us to expect less predictive power at the right tail. Predictors are restricted in range, which lowers correlations between the predictors and academic outcomes. Moreover, many predictors are less accurate at the right tail. Test scores are an interesting case in point. In equating scores on different versions of the same test, larger errors are made in the upper range of scores than around the middle. The confidence interval on the "true" score given the observed score is wider at the right tail. It is hard to say exactly how much worse tests are at the right tail; this seems a topic worth more research.[4] But the SAT and similar tests are not designed to distinguish among those who apply to universities like Harvard. Instead, the SATs mostly include items that best discriminate between the top and bottom halves of the test takers.[5] Analyses of a recent SAT math test shows that most questions were answered correctly by the majority of test takers; few questions were very difficult (see table 5.1). A recent SAT verbal test has proportionally even fewer very difficult items. It would be misleading to conclude that only three questions on the SAT math test help sort out the top 10 percent of test takers. Even very smart students sometimes miss easy questions. But tests constructed with more difficult items would be better for measuring differences at the right tail.[6]

On the other hand, several factors lead to more predictive power at the right tail. The very able sometimes display greater variation than equal numbers of those of roughly average ability. Since the work of Francis Galton in the nineteenth century, studies have revealed large variations in achievement among the top-ranked few. To see why, think of a normal distribution sliced into groups of, say, one thousand people. The highest-scoring thousand will show more variability than the next highest thousand and much more than the middle-thousand scorers.[7] This greater variation might lead to higher correlations than expected based on the average college.

Furthermore, there is a phenomenon that might be called "imposed variation in the criterion." The selected group of students at an elite university will probably have greater variability in their grades than they would if they attended universities with less able students. As these students are in the top 5 percent of their cohort, they might achieve A averages at many other institutions. Even though an elite university typically gives fewer Ds and Es, or even Cs, than other universities, it probably imposes greater variability in grades than would occur among its students

TABLE 5.1

Why the SAT Math Test Discriminates Better at the Middle Than at the Right Tail

Type of Question	Correct Answers (%)	Number of Questions	Percentage of Total Questions
Difficult	under 10	3	5
↑	10–20	6	10
	20–30	6	10
	30–40	4	7
	40–60	8	14
↓	60–80	19	31
Easy	over 80	14	24

were they to enroll elsewhere. This phenomenon could lead to greater predictability of grades than would be expected based on extrapolations from typical universities.

As a result of these conflicting tendencies, it is hard to say in advance whether academic performance at highly selective universities should be more or less predictable than grades at other institutions. We must be wary of extrapolating results from the average institution to the right tail.

Predicting Academic Performance

At the end of a recent review of the literature available, educational researcher Hunter M. Breland concluded that high-school grades and test scores were the best predictors of undergraduate grades. Other material used in admissions decisions—such as letters of recommendation, biodata, essays, and so forth—added a slight amount to predictive power.

> Often, however, adequate cross-validation was not conducted, and consequently the demonstrations are not altogether convincing. One doubts, moreover, whether the small increments shown offer sufficient justification in and of themselves for the use of these procedures. Better arguments can be made, it seems, for the use of biodata and interests as a source of diversity, as means for promoting exchanges of information useful to both students and institutions and as ways which broader objectives of students and institutions can be realized.[8]

More generally, psychologist Robyn Dawes and his colleagues have demonstrated that subjective judgments of admissions officers do not predict students' later grades as well as a combination of the students' prior grades and test scores. And, if you know the students' prior grades and test scores, then subjective judgments add nothing to your ability to predict undergraduate grades.[9]

Is this also true at the right tail? Few published data exist. In a recent study of nine private colleges, Breland and Warren W. Willingham showed that the median correlation between first-year college grades and a combination of SAT scores and prior grades was 0.51. Adding twenty-three different "background measures" raised the correlation by only 0.04. The academic ratings of applicants made by admissions officers had less predictive power than the combination of SAT scores and prior grades and, when added to that combination, did not significantly improve the prediction of grades.

Evidently, in attempting to improve on objective measures, expert raters often overcompensate for aspects of an applicant's record that merit only slight consideration, or they make spurious adjustments for other aspects that are actually not relevant to subsequent performance. . . . The result is frequently a rating less valid than the information on which it is largely based . . . . [10]

It may be that the prediction of some other academic outcomes could be improved by using these other sources of information.[11] But to predict undergraduate grades, we have to rely on high-school grades and test scores.[12]

Calibrating Predictors

How can we estimate the academic importance of different high-school grades and test scores? For instance, if there were two students whose high-school grades were identical but whose SAT verbal plus math scores differed by 200 points, what would that mean in terms of predicting their later grades? How should differences in test scores among applicants be compared to differences in their high-school grades? If we knew students' high-school records, how much would it be worth to know their scores on standardized examinations? There are several ways to address these questions (appendix 1 analyzes them in detail, for colleges and various kinds of graduate schools).

Scores and grades compared to the pool of eligible applicants. We might calibrate test scores and previous grades by looking at the distribution of those predictors in the entire applicant pool. For example, in a recent year the mean score among college-bound seniors on the SAT verbal plus math (V +M) was 894, with a standard deviation of 207. A 200-point difference in SAT V+M corresponds to the difference between a student at the 50th percentile of test scores and another student at the 83rd percentile. In terms of where students are in the distribution of college-bound seniors, a change of 200 points on the SAT V+M is equivalent to about a 5.6-point change on the American College Testing Program test (ACT) and about an 0.58 change in high-school grade average. Figure 5.1 shows the distribution of SAT V+M scores.

Scores and grades compared to students at other institutions. Universities vary greatly in the academic characteristics of their student bodies. We might see how various test scores and prior grades correspond to students at various institutions we know—and to differences among the average stu-

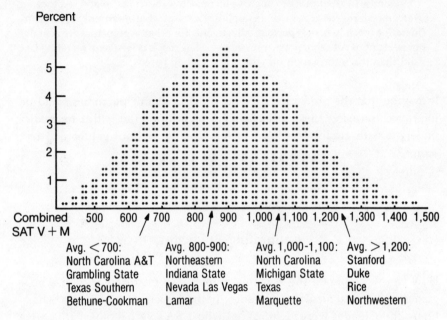

FIGURE 5.1

1983 Distribution of SAT V+M Scores

NOTE: Based on black and white students in a random sample of 100,000 college-bound seniors who took the SAT in 1983. Below the histogram are the approximate SAT V+M averages of various undergraduate institutions.

dents at those institutions. For example, a student with a 1,060 SAT V+M score would be at about the 10th percentile of students at college with SAT V+M averages over 1,200, a group that includes Stanford, Duke, Rice, and U.C. Santa Cruz. The same student would be at about the 98th percentile at a college with an SAT V+M average between 700 and 800; sample institutions in that category are Prairie View, Texas El Paso, and Delaware State. And the same student would be at about the 84th percentile at the modal college, with an SAT V+M average of 900.

A 200-point increrase in SAT V+M—or about 0.4 in high-school grade point average (HSGPA)—corresponds roughly to the difference between the average student at Stanford/Rice/Duke/U.C. Santa Cruz and the average student at Texas/Michigan State/Pittsburgh/Marquette. Those are also the approximate differences between the average student at the latter schools and the average student at Northeastern/Indiana State/Lamar/Morehouse.

Scores and grades compared to students at an elite institution. In a highly selective institution, students' academic qualifications will be higher than at most other schools, and distributions of students' qualifications will be tighter.

110

For example, a selective college with an SAT V+M average above 1,200 will have a standard deviation of SAT V+M only about two thirds as large as the standard deviation across all SAT test takers. At such a college, a 200-point difference in SAT V+M will correspond roughly to the difference between a student at the 50th percentile of test scores and another student at the 93rd percentile.

Scores and grades compared to other educational inputs. We might assess how much a 200-point increase in SAT V+M meant to later learning, compared to variations in how much students studied or in the quality of their instructors. Economist Elisabeth Allison carried out one of the only studies to address such questions.[13] Looking at Harvard's survey course in economics and using a complicated set of simultaneous equations, she estimated how a host of variables—what students did with their time, students' tastes and abilities, teachers' characteristics, and the way the course was taught in different sections (pass/fail, programmed instruction, and so forth)—affected how much economics students learned and their satisfaction with the course. How much they learned was estimated via an objective examination given at the end of each semester. With all these variables ingeniously and extensively measured over a number of years, Allison made the following discoveries:

- With other variables held constant, a measure of "academic ability" that combined high-school records and SAT test scores was about ten times as important as a measure of "student effort" (study time and so forth), in terms of how much was learned.
- Other things equal, a hundred-point increase in both the SAT verbal and math scores made a slightly greater difference to how much more students learned than did the difference between the best and the worst instructors in the course.
- Students' ratings of the competence and personality of their teachers had absolutely no relationship with how much the students learned. But the teachers' grades in graduate school did.
- A twenty-five-point increase in both SAT verbal and math scores had about the same effect on how much economics was learned as an increase in study time of ten hours per week for this course.[14]

These discoveries are helpful ways of calibrating predictors. But they stop short of telling us how much, say, a 200-point difference in SAT V+M means in terms of predicted academic performance at an institution. They do not tell how confident we can be about the prediction of a given student's later grades. Nor do they tell how much it is worth to use test scores, say, in addition to previous grades, in the selection process. To address these questions, multiple regression analyses of the kind discussed in chapter 4 are needed.

I have carried out a number of such studies and reviewed many others. Appendix 1 contains a variety of important and interesting results for a broad range of colleges and types of graduate schools. Let me summarize some of the major findings.

1. *Colleges and graduate schools at the right tail give high grades, and their grade distribution is tight.* Very few students flunk out, and few receive grades below C. In selective graduate and professional schools, grades below B are relatively rare. To assess academic performance, it is probably more informative for decision makers to talk about where in the distribution of an institution's grades a student is likely to fall—the 10th or the 50th or the 90th percentile—rather than to talk about grade averages per se.

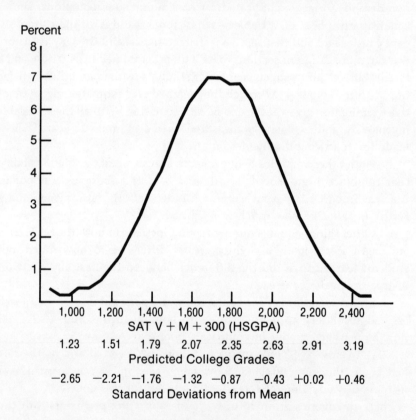

FIGURE 5.2

How 1983 High-School Seniors Would Do at Top Universities

NOTE: Based on a random sample of 83,464 black and white college-bound high school seniors who took the SAT in 1983. Predicted grades are based on the nine institutions studied in appendix 1 that had average SAT V+M scores greater than 1,100. As an example: a high-school senior with a 3.33 high-school GPA and a combined SAT V+M score of 1,200 would score 2,200 on the index, which would predict a 2.91 freshman grade-point average at a college in which students' average SAT V+M was above 1100. A 2.91 average would be just above the mean at such colleges; a 3.19 average would be 0.46 standard deviation above the mean freshman grade-point average at those schools.

2. *Even at the right tail, substantial increases in test scores and prior grades usually correspond to substantial increases in later academic performance.* Holding constant high-school grades, a 200-point increase in SAT V+M corresponds to an increase in grades at a selective college of about four-tenths of a standard deviation. This is roughly the difference between a student at the 33rd percentile and another student at the 50th percentile of the college class. At right-tail institutions, test scores tend to be relatively stronger predictors than prior grades. Roughly similar conclusions about graduate and professional schools are detailed in Appendix 1.

For colleges with SAT V+M averages above 1,100, the best combination of test scores and high-school grades in terms of predicting freshman grades is approximately SAT V+M plus 300 times the high-school grade-point average. Figure 5.2 shows the approximate distribution of this com-

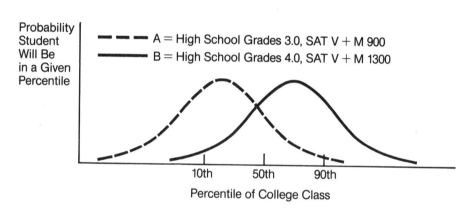

	Candidate A 3.0; 900	Candidate B 3.5; 1,300
Predicted Percentile Rank in Class	18	73
50 Percent Confidence Interval	7–37	51–89
95 Percent Confidence Interval	<1–79	14–>99
Probability in Top 10 Percent of Class	<1	22
Probability in Bottom 10 Percent of Class	34	1

FIGURE 5.3

Uncertainty of Academic Prediction

NOTE: The figure shows the probabilities that indicate that two students, at a college with an average SAT V+M greater than 1,100, will end up at various grade percentiles of the freshman class. One student has a 3.0 high-school grade average and a 900 SAT V+M score—both about the national average for college-bound high-school seniors—and is predicted to be at the 18th percentile of freshman grades. The other student has straight-A high-school grades and a 1,300 SAT V+M score and is predicted to end up at the 73rd percentile of freshman grades. The difference between the 18th and 73rd percentiles is considerable. But notice the range of uncertainty surrounding those predictions. With information like this, selection committees can be made aware of both a candidate's predicted performance and the uncertainty surrounding that prediction.

bination among college-bound seniors who took the SAT in 1983. It also shows the expected grades students would be expected to receive at selective colleges with SAT V+M averages above 1,100.[15]

Institutions do show substantial variation, however, in the strength of various predictors. Grades at one university may be quite predictable, grades at another rather unpredictable. Grades at highly selective institutions are usually less predictable than grades at less selective ones. Some of the variations across institutions are due to statistical artifacts, such as sampling error, differences in the reliability of grading, and differences in restriction of range.[16] But because universities differ, it would still be advisable for an institution to carry out its own predictive studies, preferably over a number of years.

3.   *The predictions made for any individual student are imperfect.* As science historian Derek de Solla Price said after a series of breathtaking generalizations about distinguished scientists, "Just as one cannot measure the individual velocities of all molecules in a gas, one cannot actually measure the degrees

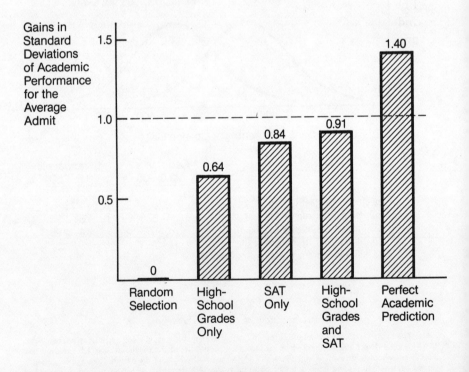

FIGURE 5.4

Gains in Academic Performance from Alternative Selection Policies

NOTE: For a typical college at the right tail, the figure shows the gains in academic performance of the average admit that accrue from using various admissions criteria. [For details, see appendix 1.]

of eminence of all scientists.[17] This is also true in academic prediction—predictions about any individual student are imprecise.

For example, at a typical college with SAT V+M averages over 1,100, a student with a 3.0 high-school grade average and a 900 SAT V+M score would be predicted to fall at about the 18th percentile of freshman grades. A student with a 4.0 high-school grade average and a 1,300 SAT V+M score would be predicted to end up at the 73rd percentile in grades at that college. This is a substantial difference. But as figure 5.3 shows, there is a wide margin of uncertainty about each of these predictions.

4. *In most situations involving selective universities, using both test scores and prior grades as admissions criteria will lead to what seem to be important gains in the later academic performance of the student body as a whole.* Of course, an assessment of the value of using various predictors depends on how much one thinks increases in later grades matter. In appendix 1, I demonstrate how the usefulness of using test scores and prior grades in an admissions process might be evaluated. The answer depends on how much a standard deviation's increase in academic performance is valued and how many students will be enrolled. Figure 5.4 displays one result from appendix 1.

Understanding that points 3 and 4 are simultaneously true is, I think, the beginning of wisdom about academic prediction at the right tail.

6

Academic Performance and Later-Life Contributions

AN EARLY WRITER on the general subject of choosing elites pointed out that being smart and well educated were not all that mattered for success in life:

> And do not suppose that there will be many of them; for the gifts which were deemed by us to be essential rarely grow together; they are mostly found in shreds and patches.
>
> What do you mean? he said.
>
> You are aware, I replied, that quick intelligence, memory, sagacity, cleverness, and similar qualities, do not often grow together, and that persons who possess them and are at the same time high-spirited and magnanimous are not so constituted by nature as to live orderly and in a peaceful and settled manner; they are driven any way by their impulses, and all solid principle goes out of them.
>
> Very true, he said.
>
> On the other hand, those steadfast natures which can better be depended upon, which in a battle are impregnable to fear and immovable, are equally immovable when there is anything to be learned; they are always in a torpid state, and are apt to yawn and go to sleep over any intellectual toil.
>
> Quite true.
>
> And yet we were saying that both qualities were necessary in those to whom

the higher education is to be imparted, and who are to share in any office or command.

Certainly.

And will they be a class which is rarely found?

Yes, indeed.[1]

Like Plato, we may believe that a person's social contributions do not depend solely on his or her academic characteristics and achievements. So, if we selected a class solely on academic grounds, we might not select the class that would contribute the most to society. We would like to know which students, with which characteristics, will enable an institution's education to have, through its graduates, the greatest social value added.

Chapter 3 reviewed some of the complications attending this objective, even in a world of perfect information. Now we face further difficulties:

1. Not only do we have the conceptual problem of defining "social value added," we now have to measure it and describe a utility function for the measures we choose.

2. Somehow we have to estimate how much the education contributes to that social utility measure compared to other universities. Very crudely, we might think of the difference in social utility between a student attending one institution and the student attending an alternative university.

3. Then we have to estimate how this difference depends on various student characteristics.

4. In making the empirical estimation, we face fierce statistical problems (as reviewed in chapter 4).

5. We may not want to use some of the student characteristics in admissions because they reflect ascriptive characteristics, such as social class, sex, race, and so forth.

These are serious problems. Despite a truly voluminous body of literature on the value of higher education, most of them have not been resolved.

For one thing, available measures of later-life success are unreliable and incomplete. They show unreliability, in the sense that they contain random error of various kinds. This is especially so with measures like status and publications. More important, these measures are at best incomplete proxies for ill-defined variables like social or academic productivity. As Nietzsche wrote, "Success has always been the greatest liar."[2]

Some of the imperfections in measurement reduce the predictability of later-life success by introducing random noise. Others are fundamental conceptual shortcomings. We cannot tell how well we can predict something we cannot define and measure.

Even with a given measure of "success" like income or professional status, many experts point out that estimating which personal characteristics affect the value added of higher education is a statistical nightmare. At the outset of a review article on the returns from schooling, econometrician Zvi Griliches listed the statistical problems involved and noted that they would comprise a good outline for a course in advanced econometrics.[3] Economist Douglas Windham began an excellent review of recent literature pessimistically:

> There is no more consistent social science finding than that of the correlation between educational attainment and higher personal income. . . . Such consistency in research findings and expectations would seem to imply that there exists a consensus on higher education's value to the individual. Unfortunately, such is not the case. The causal mechanism behind the correlation of higher educational attainment and higher income is only slightly better understood now than at the beginning of the 1950's, when research on the economics of education became a legitimate part of the social science agenda.
>
> Most of what has been gained in the last three decades relates more to taxonomic than theoretical clarification. Economists and their fellow social scientists have devised several alternative classifications to explain the phenomenon of correlation, but empirical research has done little to clarify even the relative importance of the various explanations. The major contribution of this research has been to convince nearly all scholars that the causal process which transforms education into higher income is a complex one and that simple ideological or methodological explanations will no longer suffice.[4]

An example of the complexity of estimating the value added of education for different prospective students concerns education's role as a "signal." Education may be associated with higher earnings or greater success because it is a credential, not just because it is socially productive. This criticism is especially popular in regard to elite schools and universities. And in many professions, of course, certain educational credentials are prerequisites for practice. Critics argue that credentials are overvalued from a social view. Economists have constructed admittedly extreme models with self-reinforcing credentialing in which each individual finds an education beneficial but, in social terms, there is no social benefit from the education at all.[5]

From the perspective of this chapter, this work in signaling suggests that the perceived "value" of a Harvard education cannot directly be attributed to the university's educational value added or to characteristics of candidates. The point about signaling is that, to *some* extent, anyone with such a credential would receive an added boost in life, no matter what they learned here or who they were before they came.[6]

The actual importance of this phenomenon remains in doubt. As Harvard Dean Michael Spence said, "What we take to be the signal and later success are highly correlated, but the data don't tell you, and are not likely to tell you, whether this is because of a credential effect or a productive effect of the education. In principle, it could be tested, but in practice what we're left with is intuition."[7]

John Riley of UCLA, a leading expert on credentialing and signaling, concurred. "Just how big the social costs of educational signaling are, no one has any feeling for. Who knows? The problem is really that we can't disentangle signaling effects from the other effects of education." Empirically, it is hard to separate the productive effects of education from its signaling effects or from the individual's underlying characteristics.[8] Credentialing is not all bad, either; it may allow employers to allocate employees efficiently, when the former are unsure about the later's working productivity. "If, as we have suggested," wrote economist Joseph Stiglitz, "education provides information as well as skills, then it is providing a 'commodity' for which it is well known that the market 'fails' . . ."[9]

The signaling literature implies that we cannot assume that the effects of education on later-life success all represent social benefits. If social benefits are our objective, we therefore face further difficulties in predicting which applicants will make the greatest social contributions.

Because of these abundant methodological problems, we do not have the kinds of predictive studies we would like to have. Moreover, existing studies are not focused on the right tail of the distribution of academic achievement, so extending their findings to our samples is perilous. "The kind of research we did," said sociologist Christopher Jencks, author of numerous studies on the determinants of later-life success, "is almost irrelevant to your problem. Not only do you have severe truncation of the sample, but in the case of the professional schools, careers are much more homogeneous than in our work. Nobody has done the right sort of study for your purposes, to my knowledge. And I would be skeptical of our ability to do it if we set out to do such research."[10]

Hints and Suggestions

The voluminous literature on academic variables and later-life success is not worthless. There are hints about the upper bounds of predictive relationships and about the types of future research likely to prove useful.

The basic message of the available literature is this: Defining them as we will, "later-life contributions" are very difficult to forecast. Many are surprised to learn how little of the variation in common measures of "later-life success" can be explained by the usual predictors. For example, think about the difference in annual earnings between two randomly selected, economically active men between the ages of twenty-five and sixty-four. Now consider two brothers. Suppose that they have identical intelligence text scores, the same years of education, and the same years of work experience. How large would you guess the difference between the two brothers' earnings compared to the difference between the two randomly selected men to be? From Jencks's research, the surprising answer is that it is from 84 to 89 percent as large.[11]

Earnings is only one partial measure of later life success.[12] If, instead, we looked at a measure of "occupational status," the hypothetical brothers with equal test scores, years of education, and years of work experience would have a "status differential" 70 to 78 percent as great as the corresponding differential between the two randomly selected men.[13]

Occupational status may still not be what we mean by "later-life contributions." Before turning to studies of "professional success" and other criteria, it will be worthwhile to summarize my findings on the academic characteristics associated with earnings and social status (see appendix 2 for more details).

Most of the variance in earnings or in occupational status cannot be statistically explained by academic variables. The weight of the evidence seems to show that IQ and educational achievement each correlate about 0.3 with income. These correlations are slightly higher with later occupational status. If years of education are held constant, there are still substantial correlations between measures of academic ability and later income or later social status. The evidence on grades is mixed, as we shall see.

Academic variables explain relatively little of the variance in income or social status. But there is another central finding—neither do other predictors.

> Parental income only seems to account for about 4 percent of the variance in incomes. If one also takes account of race, ethnicity, father's occupation, father's and mother's education, region of birth, whether the family remained intact while the sons were growing up, errors in measurement, and errors in measuring income, one can explain 13 to 19 percent of the variance. This leaves much of the resemblance between brothers unexplained.[14]

Moreover:

> We were not able to identify most of the background characteristics that affect earnings independent of cognitive skills and education. The only demographic characteristics with such effects are race, religion, region of birth, father's occupation, and whether the respondent grew up on a farm.[15]

Chapter 4 argued that correlation coefficients and the percentage of variance explained by these can be misleading measures of predictive power. One step forward is to look at regression coefficients. I would summarize the literature on these as saying that a one-standard deviation increase in IQ corresponds to a 10-to 30-percent increase in average income, or a 7-to 25-percent increase for those with equal schooling (notice the use of "corresponds," rather than "causes"). A slightly higher coefficient holds with occupational status as the dependent variable. Obviously, the size of the regression coefficient will vary according to what other variables are in the regression equation and the nature of the sample. Generalizations are therefore risky.

Academic Performance and Professional Attainments

How well do academic variables predict "success" within a given job or profession? Again, the outcome measure is problematic. Most studies have used one or more of the following:

- Salary or earnings
- Subjective ratings of performance by supervisors, peers, or other experts in the field
- Appearance in *Who's Who*
- Membership or holding office in professional societies
- For academics, number of publications or number of citations to one's publications
- Scores on qualifying examinations for entrance to a profession, which are presumed to measure ability to practice the profession

I have reviewed dozens of studies that look at what predicts "general occupational success" in law, business, engineering, medicine, and academic science. Some of these are summarized in appendix 2. Generalization is difficult, not least because the studies vary in outcome measures, predictors, samples, place, and time. Typical, however, is the result obtained in a recent government review of all studies on grades and occupational success from 1964 to 1979. The pooling of the correlations is shown in table 6.1.

As grades are not a perfect forecaster of job success, all the statistical difficulties of chapter 4 reemerge here, making the application of such results problematic:

1. Grading standards across universities vary greatly. Not taking ac-

TABLE 6.1

Average Correlation Between GPA and Job Success[16]

Occupation	Total N	Number of Correlations	Average Correlation	Standard Deviation
Military Officers	1,788	6	.14	.10
Teaching	524	5	.05	.09
Retail Sales	168	2	−.02	.04
Engineers	693	7	.08	.07
Managerial	2,723	4	.26	.07
Federal Workers	886	7	.10	.11
TOTAL	6,782	31	AVERAGE .17	AVERAGE .12

count of the different standards will bias the estimate of the predictive power of grades toward zero.

2. On the other hand, grades may mask the true causal variables. Thus, the correlations may overstate the "independent" predictive power of grades.

3. Self-selected samples and the use of thresholds of academic performance in hiring will tend to reduce the correlations, leading to an understatement of the value of the predictor in an unselected sample. In some occupations, relatively few people are found below certain thresholds of academic attainment, which again restricts the range of the predictor and thereby attenuates correlations.

4. The results for an average university, or across the range of universities, may not hold at the right tail.

Studies within the various professions are also full of statistical problems. After reading many of them, I conclude that grades and test scores have a modest predictive power for "success" among lawyers, doctors, Ph.D.s, and other professions, with correlations on the order of 0.1 to 0.5. So, for example, a one-standard deviation change in the test score of a member of the professions would be associated with a 0.1 to 0.5-standard deviation change in measures of professional success. Grades and test scores are better predictors of performance on professional examinations than of performance on the job. I would venture to say that the better the study methodologically, the stronger the predictive relationship tends to be between grades and test scores and various measures of later professional success.

As an example of this last point, the careful articles by my colleague David Wise are helpful.[17] He studied white male college graduates in the Ford Motor Company, using salaries, rates of salary increase, and frequency of promotions as performance measures. His study held constant years employed and various other variables—socioeconomic status, indices of leadership, ability, need for job security, initial job, and supervisor experience.

In regard to salaries, academic variables—namely college GPA, college selectivity, and whether or not the employee received a master's degree—accounted for about 20 percent of the variance in salaries, and for about 12 percent if other variables were held constant. This doesn't sound like much, but by examining regression coefficients the importance of academic variables comes into clearer focus. A one-point increase in college GPA was associated with between a .84 and 1.6 percent increase in the annual rate of salary growth, depending on the selectivity of the college.

Promotions were also much more frequent among those with higher grades:

College GPA	Annual Probability of Promotion
3.5–4.0	0.526
3.0–3.5	0.458
2.5–3.0	0.420
under 2.5	0.383

Aggregated over a number of years, these differences would seem even larger. Despite "low" percentages of variance explained, academic performance seems to have an important effect on career success.

Prediction to the Right Tail

As in the case of predicting academic performance, we must worry that findings elsewhere may not hold for highly selected samples at the right tail. What evidence is there for applicant pools like Harvard's?

Unfortunately but understandably, given the cost and difficulty of conducting such studies, little research has been carried out about the predictors of later-life contributions of graduates of highly selective universities.

We do know that the alumni of some universities are unusually successful. In an eccentric but affectionate book, Yale Professor of History George W. Pierson amply documented that graduates of elite universities are found in disproportionate numbers among the eminent in almost every profession. Pierson and a platoon of research assistants worked for more than twenty-five years compiling historical lists of eminent people. A total of eighty-five different tables were prepared for colleges and eighty-nine for professional schools, covering statesmen, lawyers, doctors, Protestant ministers, eminent members in the fields of business and finance, philanthropy, science, engineering, literature and the arts, education, scholarship, and "over-all indices of achievement." Harvard College finished first, with a comfortable margin over Yale, and Pierson's tables for graduate and professional schools show "the unquestionable preeminence of Harvard," with Columbia second.[18]

Pierson had several ways of generalizing about the relationship of success to where one studied. For example:

> All of which is to say that in a "normal" group of distinguished elder statesmen [in any of the professions or in scholarship, politics, and business], 1 man in every 6 was likely to have studied in some school at Harvard; 1 in every 11 might have lived for a time in New Haven; 1 in every 13 had attended Columbia; 1 in every 16 was probably from Princeton; and every 25th man was likely to have had a Michigan connection of some sort; while no other alumni constituency could be counted on to contribute more than 1 leader in 30, on the average, throughout the profession.[19]

After adjusting the figures to reflect the number of graduates of each institution, Pierson suggested another comparison:

> Thus 1 alumnus for every 25 (approximately) of the undergraduates at H-Y-P in the years 1920–49 had achieved recognition in *Who's Who*. This compares with 1 in 36 for Williams, 1 in 48 for Dartmouth, 1 in 82 for Michigan, 1 in 87 for North Carolina, 1 in 89 for Wisconsin, and 1 in 145 as a median figure for the state universities as a group.[20]

Or, considering a combined category of "leaders," he creates a comparison of "chances to become a leader":

> Translating these ratios one may conclude that for every 100 chances the men of Harvard College have had, the undergraduates of Yale have had in the neighborhood of 89; the men of Princeton, 89; of Dartmouth, 48; of Williams, 42; and the men and women of Stanford, 18.[21]

Pierson acknowledges the incompleteness of his measures of eminence. Moreover, he understands the difficulty of attributing causation. Is the university's education responsible for its graduates' success, or the prior characteristics of students, or a credential effect? Or if, as is likely, it is a combination of the three, what is their relative importance? He does not address these questions statistically, nor does he explore the characteristics of eminent graduates. Thus, it is impossible to conclude from his work which sorts of students had or would most have their chances for eminence enhanced by attending Harvard.

A few other studies have looked at later-life success among graduates of selective universities. Louis Bevier developed lists of "eminent" and "highly successful" graduates of the Rutgers classes of 1862 through 1905. The classification was performed independently, by four men with information about the alumni but not about their grades, on the basis of "reasonable judgment." Of the 1,326 male graduates, 54 were considered eminent, and 480 highly successful. Analysis of college grades revealed that both lists were drawn disproportionately from the top of the classes. Of the eminent, 67 percent graduated in the top third of their classes, 30 percent in the middle third, and 3 percent in the bottom third. Of the highly successful, 45 percent graduated in the top third, 35 percent in the middle, and 20 percent in the bottom third. "It is quite clear that undergraduate scholarship has a very important relation to future success, not necessarily in regard to an individual, but unmistakably when the whole membership of classes is considered."[22]

In an article published in 1957, R. W. Husband studied graduates and nongraduates of the Dartmouth class of 1926. In one analysis, he found that median incomes of those with GPAs in five intervals between 1.7 and 3.1 ranged from $13,125 to $15,000. But those with GPAs over 3.3 had a median income of more than $20,000, and for those with GPAs of 1.5 to 1.7, the median income was only $10,625. With regard to test scores, Husband found that those with the lowest scores had not fared as well as those with scores in the middle, and those with the highest scores did not earn as much either, because they pursued academic careers in disproportionate numbers. Of 32 "outstanding successes" in later life, 16 had "superior" GPAs, 10 "average" GPAs, and 6 "fair" GPAs. Of 7 graduates who had experienced "poor success," 6 had "below average" GPAs and 1 an "average" GPA.[23]

A study of the very early career successes of Woodrow Wilson fellows at Princeton found that measures of academic ability were not helpful in predicting earnings.[24] This result is typical of many studies of the first few years after graduation.[25] Measures such as test scores have little predictive power for earnings in the first decade of work, but are more important over a twenty- or thirty-year period.[26]

Another study of Yale Phi Beta Kappas from 1931–1950 related their later-life achievements to their SAT scores. It is interesting that average test scores of this elite sample were not all that high: the SAT verbal mean was 619, and the average SAT math score was 601. In contrast, in the entire Yale class of 1967, the average scores were SAT verbal 676, SAT math 624. The authors note that "many of these [Phi Beta Kappa] individuals might not qualify for admission to Yale at the present time."[27] Without knowing their SAT scores, subjective ratings "about the level of achievement reached by each individual in most of the occupational groups" were made by Albert B. Crawford, editor of the Men of Yale Series; he also labeled 20 of the 1,087 men as "eminent." For the Phi Beta Kappas of 1931–1934, a search was made in *Who's Who, American Men of Science,* and the *Dictionary of American Scholars* to see if their names appeared.

The average "levels of achievement," measured on a nine-point (1 to 9) scale, for different SAT verbal and SAT math scores are:

	Test Score			
	< 600	600–700	700–750	750–800
SAT verbal	5.92	6.03	6.04	6.21
SAT math	5.80	6.08	5.99	6.56

Higher occupational ratings had higher SAT scores, but again the differences was not pronounced. Those judged eminent averaged perhaps 50 points higher on the SAT verbal test than the rest of the Phi Beta Kappas (no information is given for the SAT math test). Those listed in *Who's Who* and so forth, scored about 15 points higher on the SAT verbal than the others (no information on math results). No correlations or other analyses were reported.

Educator Evrard Nicholson examined the predictors of academic and later-life success of Brown students of the 1950s.[28] Using the data available to admissions officers, he constructed indices of socioeconomic status, personal ratings by counselors and principals, and two indices of high-school extracurricular activities—one for "leadership and social" activities, the other for "literary, artistic, and scientific" activities. He also used SAT scores and high-school grades as predictors.

For later-life success, Nicholson eschewed measures like income and "executive status." "We believed these were not good measures," he said in an interview. "They would not pick up the good minister or the successful teacher." Instead, "literally hundreds" of active Brown alumni rated their colleagues' careers as "successful" or "not successful." Nicholson added objective indicators such as appearance in *Who's Who.*

Nicholson's findings were interesting. "SAT scores predicted academic success in college," he said, "but not necessarily real-life success." Moreover, "academic success in college was not necessarily predictive of later success." The best predictor of career success was the socioeconomic index, based on parents' occupations, income, and other information. "This was a somewhat sad finding," Nicholson recalled. "Regardless of abilities, a student's home environment before coming to college was the strongest predictor of our measure of career success."[29]

Later-Life Studies for Harvard

As noted in chapter 2, faculty reviews of admissions processes at Harvard have often lamented the lack of knowledge about the later careers of graduates. These committees have usually recommended studies that would link admissions data with information about career choice and later contributions. However, little such research has been carried out.

In an early study, R. M. Knapp examined Harvard College graduates from 1851 to 1900. He discovered that 50 percent of those who were graduated *summa cum laude* were listed in *Who's Who*, compared to 17 percent of *cum laude* graduates and 10 percent of those who graduated without honors.[30]

The remarkable, unpublished research conducted by Dean K. Whitla and his colleagues provides valuable insights into the prediction of early career success at the right tail. The authors caution again generalizing "much beyond the current status of Harvard classes from the mid-60s."[31] Their sample comprises 1,035 of the 1964–65 Harvard graduates ten years out of college. The response rate was only 43 percent, but the sample does seem to be representative of the 2,400 members of the 1964–65 classes based on a comparison of the SAT verbal and math scores and high-school type.

Whitla and his associates examined the influence of various measures of academic ability and achievement—SAT verbal and math scores, the Predicted Rank List (PRL, a measure of predicted Harvard undergraduate grades), graduate school prestige, college grades and honors, career aspirations, and social background (measured on a 1 to 5 scale based on parents' occupations)—on the "career success" and income of 930 graduates in their mid-thirties. The analyses focused on differences within the four mainstream occupations chosen by a majority of Harvard graduates: law, 18.7 percent; medicine, 17.3 percent; academia, 18.7 percent; and business, 19.2 percent.

Income was one measure. The authors also ingeniously constructed performance criteria of "success" for law, medicine, and academia. These criteria were rather subjective and no doubt contained a considerable amount of unreliability.[32] The results generally showed that college performance played a crucial role for admission to graduate schools within each profession. Surprisingly, the measure of social background was an insignificant predictor in every case. College grades had a small direct influence on success in law and an even smaller effect on later success in academia, and grades were negatively related to later success in medicine. Test scores had insignificant direct influences, with the exception of SAT math scores on medical success. But the major lesson of all the analyses was that within this highly able sample *none of the variables—including career aspirations expressed before college and parents' occupation—had much power to predict later-life success.* This probably reflects both the unreliability of measures of success and the lack of predictive power of academic and background variables within a "right tail" sample.

Let us examine these results by profession:

Lawyers. "Success" was determined by a ranking of the current positions on a 1 to 5 scale by a practicing lawyer and two third-year law students (each rating was usually done by one of the three and was not usually cross-checked). These raters considered and evaluated (1) the size, location, and name of firm; (2) the position within a firm balanced against time spent in firm; (3) legal specialties of lawyer and firm; (4) income level; (5) organizational affiliations; and (6) career plans, along with other considerations relating to a respondent's description of his position and responsibilities.

The results showed that only college achievement and law school prestige exercised a statistically significant, though modest, direct influence on "success." The effects of SAT test scores were "marginal."

The authors concluded:

> First, the skills and attitudes which make for high college performance are also modestly important for success in the legal profession, and second, they are very important indeed for admission to the nation's two most prestigious law schools.[33]

About half of the influence of school prestige on success was attributed to college grades. The other half suggested "a marginal discrimination on the part of employers in favor of Harvard and Yale [law] graduates," which could be a result of a credential effect or the fact that these graduates might be more productive or desirable in ways grades do not measure. Moreover, all background variables only accounted for 11 percent of success variance, suggesting that substantial differences in jobs, skills, and preferences, were simply unrelated to individuals' academic histories and family backgrounds.[34]

Professors. Success was measured on a 1 to 10 scale based on prestige of department where respondent taught, academic rank, tenure status, and in rare cases, major administrative responsibilities. Of those entering academic careers, 43 percent attended one of the three top-ranked graduate departments in their respective field. A surprising finding was "the meager size of all paths to success."[35] College performance made the most difference, but the correlation was only 0.20 and its net effect was barely statistically significant. The authors also examined three small samples of sixty professors in natural science, social science, and humanities. Again, the predictive power of the variables was small.

The basic lesson may be this: within this highly selected sample, career success in academia could not be predicted with much accuracy.

Physicians.   Criteria for measuring successful performance among doctors were perhaps the most difficult to formulate. The "prestige" of a person's post was finally measured on a complex scale from 1 to 6.

Unlike the other careers, pre-college aspirations exercised a significant influence on success. College grades appeared to influence success only through medical school prestige, which in turn may have affected success in part because of the incorporation of prestige into the criteria of success. The statistical relationship between undergraduate honors and the prestige of the medical school attended "has exactly the same size as analogous paths for lawyers, social scientists, and natural scientists (despite the vagaries of differing means and prestige scales). Thus with the exception of humanities scholars, college performance plays an equally crucial role for admission to graduate schools *within* each of the major professions . . . ."[36]

Test scores did have a positive direct effect on success, although it was small. All of these models only explained a small percentage of the variance in "success."

Income as a success measure.   As might be expected, there were substantial differences in income across professions. "Time on the job" was the best predictor of income within occupations. Apart from that, the simple correlations were not large, although they were often statistically significant, as table 6.2 shows. The authors constructed complicated models based on a sample of those in law, business, and "other technical and non-technical professions." Apart from "time on the job," almost none of the variables were significantly related to later income. The exceptions: differences in graduate school prestige made a difference among the incomes of some businessmen and among non-technical professionals; graduate honors were statistically significant predictors of variations in income among non-technical professionals. But the basic picture "adds to our impression that even the most inclusive predictors of college performance say little about post-college outcomes."[37]

Summary

Two classic studies have disputed the notion that university grades or test scores independently and importantly affect later-life success. Donald P.

TABLE 6.2

Correlations of Various Predictors with Income within Professions[38]

Predictor	Law	Bus.	MBA Bus.	Med.	Acad.	Tech.	Non-tech.
						Profession	
SAT verbal	—	−.07	−.05	−.13	.09	.17	−.12
SAT math	—	.07	.07	−.11	−.12	.21	−.13
PRL	—	—	−.08	−.14	—	.07	−.10
Undergrad. honors	.10	—	.14	—	—	.09	.22
Grad. school prestige	.13	.16	.11	−.10	—	.07	.31
Time on job	.44	.17	.30	—	.20	.32	.23
"Success"	.35	NA	NA	.13	.31	NA	NA
Number of graduates	186	166	96	152	184	61	66

NOTE: All correlations shown are statistically significant at (two-sided) $\alpha = 0.05$. MBA Bus. = businessmen with MBA degrees. "Tech" = "other technical professionals "Non-tech" = "other non-technical professionals." NA = not applicable.

Hoyt's review of the literature from 1902 to 1965 concluded, "Evidence strongly suggests that college grades bear little or no relationship to any measures of adult accomplishment."[39] Psychologist David McClelland argued that neither test scores nor college grades were related to on-the-job performance, even in "highly intellectual" jobs.[40] In an interview, Professor McClelland said that differences in test scores under about 650 on the SAT verbal or math tests may matter, but beyond such a threshold—where many, if not most, Harvard applicants fall—he believes that differences in scores do not matter for later performance.[41]

Statistical fallacies are easy to commit here, and we have few studies that tell us what we wish to know. It also merits recalling that discussing "later-life contributions," or, more broadly, "social value added," involves values as well as facts. But I would be less pessimistic than Hoyt or McClelland, although when I began this research, I favored their conclusion. Across a rather large spectrum of the population, both test scores and grades tend to have modest predictive power for many kinds of "later-life contributions." Without corrections for unreliability and restriction of range, correlations between aptitude tests and performance on the job average about 0.2, with higher figures for managerial and professional occupations and lower figures for service and sales jobs.[42] Correlations between grades and "professional success" typically range between 0.1 and 0.3. An A student is likely to earn more, have a higher occupational status, and achieve more success within his or her chosen profession than a C student.

But this is not where the action is in admissions decisions. The difficult choices are usually not between a potential A student and a potential C student, but between a B+ and a B; they are not between a student with a combined 1,400 GRE and a combined 1,000 GRE, but between 1,350 and 1,275. In this narrower range I would agree that research suggests that such differences tell us little about various kinds of "later-life success."

But then what might tell us about it? We have seen that many commonly used proxies for later-life success are extraordinarily unpredictable —at least when intuitively appealing predictors are used. Are there other variables that might be used in admissions to identify these applicants who will make the greatest social contributions? We turn to this question in the next chapter.

7

Nonacademic Predictors of Later-Life Contributions

WHEN LEADING doctors or lawyers or businessmen are polled about the personal qualities important in their professions, their answers reflect interesting similarities. "Intelligence" and "specialized knowledge" are nearly always near the tops of their lists. Also prominent are traits like honesty, ability to work well with people, diligence, and reliability. That elusive label, "leadership," is often listed as well. For each profession, the desired traits are usually those of a perfect Everyman—the classic virtues praised by scoutmasters and coaches, clergymen and editorial writers, principals, and, indeed, admissions officers at selective universities.[1]

I speak of "traits," but this common usage may beg a key question. Are such characteristics stable over time? Does the generous, forthright socially committed boy of seventeen turn into the same sort of man? More generally, can we take a group of young men and women applying to a university and predict from their "personal characteristics" those who will contribute most in later life? What measures and methods might enable us to do such forecasting, and how well? And how should an admissions process make use of them?

These queries are vast in scope, encompassing much of applied psychology. Large, separate bodies of literatures cover such relevant topics as personnel selection in business, psychological testing, college admissions, and the importance of many variables to career success. There are also an abundance of hunches and impassioned beliefs on such questions. We all have ideas about which characteristics are truly valuable, and we tend to have considerable confidence in our own (if not in others') abilities to discern those characteristics accurately and without bias. A mass of unrelated research combined with a variety of strongly held personal opinions are preconditions for controversy; it is perilous for any one chapter, or one book, to attempt conclusions.

Nevertheless, I have tried to pull together facts about three categories of nonacademic predictors of later-life success. First, there are the personal data admissions officers customarily use: biodata, letters of recommendation, essays, interviews, and the like. Second, there are psychological tests and personality inventories. Third, there is what seems to me the most interesting and promising of the devices used by businesses and government to identify top future professionals, the so-called "assessment center." Here are some principal findings:

1. As in the preceding chapter on academic predictors, few of the studies on nonacademic predictors are completely adequate to our task. Not many look at long-term performance with samples at the right tail and with appropriate consideration of other predictors, such as academic variables.

2. Among current information in use, biodata are probably the best. Past attainments in particular areas—leadership, music, athletics, entrepreneurship—are the best predictors of similar attainments in the university and, to a lesser extent, in later life; but even here, predictive power seems quite limited. Studies of interviews and letters of recommendation almost invariably show low reliability and very weak predictive power in terms of later achievements.

3. Psychological tests purport to measure many of the personal characteristics that we intuitively associate with success. But two problems emerge. First, among relatively normal individuals, I find virtually no persuasive evidence that differences in such measures predict later-life success. Second, if used in selection, most tests would present grave practical difficulties associated with unreliability and the possibility of coaching.

4. Assessment centers are promising in terms of identifying future organizational leaders. Even here, however, their independent predictive power—that is, apart from the usual predictors—is controversial. They deserve more study, even though in my estimation they are now practically infeasible in most admissions processes.

The Importance of Nonacademic Variables

By "nonacademic," I mean characteristics other than those measured by admissions tests and academic performance. Naturally, test scores and grades may themselves be a function of some nonacademic variables. But we are particularly interested in what we can learn apart from whatever is captured by test scores and academic performance—what additional predictive power we might obtain by adding other variables to the usual academic measures. And unlike most studies of nonacademic predictors in admissions, the outcomes we are focusing on are not measures of performance at the university, but various kinds of later-life success.[2]

As we have seen, most of the variance in certain aspects of later-life success, such as income and occupational status, is not statistically explained by test scores, grades, the selectivity of one's college, or even the level of education attained. This has led some critics to argue that other variables should be taken into account in admissions and hiring. Some have pointed to such attributes as social competence, leadership capability, or, in a redistributive vein, socioeconomic status or ethnic group membership as alternative grounds for selection.

This argument sounds attractive. If the desire is to select along these lines on the grounds that it is right to do so, then the argument should be taken seriously on its merits. But sometimes a different goal is implicit: "If we based selections on nonacademic variables, we could do a better job in training those for whom the social value added would be greatest." In this case, we need to learn exactly which variables predict social value added; we need a positive agenda, not simply a negative critique. Here the task of this chapter begins, and it is a hard one.

First, later income and occupational status seem to be even more weakly associated with some of the personal characteristics we can measure than they are with academic variables. Christopher Jencks and his colleagues looked at how well various personal characteristics measured in high school predicted later-life income and occupational status. Among the personality dimensions measured were "sociability, social sensitivity, impulsiveness, vigor, calmness, tidiness, culture, leadership, self-confidence, and mature personality." The results were not impressive. For example, in a regression equation predicting occupational status twelve years later, with "social background," cognitive test scores, and grades held constant, only one of the ten personality dimensions was statistically significant. Adding all ten personality variables to the three variables just mentioned raised the percentage of variance explained from 27.1 to 27.5. Slightly larger effects were found with earnings as the dependent variable.[3]

Adding indirect measures of personality and ratings by teachers helped:

> With [family] background and [cognitive] test performance controlled, a one standard-deviation advantage in our combined measure of personality traits is associated with one-third of a standard-deviation advantage in occupational status twelve years later.[4]

But this composite personality measure was the authors' *ad hoc* combination of disparate sources of information that happened to have the largest predictive success; almost surely, therefore, the coefficient is biased upwards. Moreover:

> We found little support for the idea that any single personality trait is of critical importance in determining individual success. . . . Only when the effects of numerous measures of personality are considered together do they explain even a moderate portion of the observed variation in individual achievement.[5]

Among brothers, all personality measures explained only 1.5 percent of the variation in later occupational status after cognitive test scores and education were held constant.[6]

In an ingenious paper, economist Joop Hartog estimated the relative importance of "intellectual, social, and manual capabilities" in determining earnings in a sample of 239 job types. "Intellectual capability comes out as the capability with the highest price; social capability, as reflected in PEOPLE and SALES, comes next; manual capability appears to carry the lowest price."[7] Other things equal, a one-standard-deviation increase in the intellectual factor is associated with a 0.41-standard-deviation increase in earnings; this was more than twice as large as the corresponding figure for a social capability factor, and about seven times the size of the manual ability factor. No interaction effects were found among these "capabilities."

Other studies support this general point that nonacademic, personal characteristics seem weakly related to measures of later success like income and status.

A second, related point pertains to how well we can measure those characteristics. How accurately do the categories of information available, or potentially available, to admissions officers gauge the traits we care about? Suppose, for example, that we want to measure "leadership." What measures can we use that are reliable, fair to candidates of different backgrounds, and so forth? How might we identify other characteristics, such as social commitment, perseverance, or independence?

A third point relates to the dynamic or incentive effects of admissions policies. Might the use of personality measures in admissions create incentives for distortion, faking, and so forth? With self-reported achievements and personality tests, these can be grave problems as we will see. They pose insurmountable obstacles for the practical use in admissions of many psychological measures—even if these measures were reliable and could be shown to have predictive power.

That "nonacademic characteristics" are valuable to later-life contributions, not to mention simply to being a good person, is evident. But it is a long leap from truism to application: Which characteristics, measured in which ways, and how are they to be used?

Information Admissions Committees Use Now

Biographical information.   In terms of predicting some sorts of success at the university—in leadership activities, athletic endeavors, music—biographical information works fairly well, with correlations in the 0.1 to 0.4 area.[8] For this reason, among all the nonacademic predictors recently evaluated by Hunter Breland, biodata seemed the best, albeit with qualifications:

> This summary would indicate that biodata offer some promise for use in admissions. With the exception of interest measures, the other predictors seem less promising. . . . One doubts, moreover, whether the small increments [in predictive power] offer sufficient justification in and of themselves for the use of these procedures. Better arguments can be made, it seems, for the use of biodata and interests as sources of diversity, as means for promoting exchanges of information useful to both students and institutions, and as ways in which broader objectives of students and institutions can be realized.[9]

Although some researchers are rigorously investigating how students' biographical data are related to later managerial success—for example, Rensselaer Polytechnic Institute's "Early Identification of Management Talent" program—such longitudinal work has not been underway long enough to assess predictive power.[10]

At a later age, however, biographical information of various sorts has been shown to predict success in employment. A study of managers at Standard Oil of New Jersey (now Exxon) found correlations of about 0.5 between biographical items and later salary history, performance ratings, rank, and a combined "criterion of overall success." For reasons of confidentiality, their biographical categories have never been disclosed.[11] And therein lies a problem with biodata—the term indicates many kinds of information. Should one use demographic factors such as race, sex, and social class if such variables do indeed predict career success in our present, imperfect society? Or should one only use "job-related" biodata? Many studies of the predictive validity of biodata do not make this distinction, which leaves one wondering what the predictive power would be if only "job-related" biographical information were used.

The U.S. government has recently published a review of how well biodata predict later-life success. The application blanks used in university admissions—as contrasted with multiple-choice biographical questionnaires—are widely used in personnel selection, especially "for management, professional, technical, and trades and craft occupations . . ." Several conclusions emerge from this survey:

> Despite their wide use, evaluations of application blanks have not been systematically researched and are the object of considerable dissatisfaction.
>
> Without a careful job analysis, ratings of application blanks tend to rely on irrelevant information and tend to be relatively unreliable.
>
> Even when the validity estimates are corrected for criterion unreliability and restriction of range, the validity of these application blank rating procedures remains lower than the validities of most written employment tests.[12]

Biographical information is obviously also susceptible to dissimulation, particularly, it would seem, if it is not verified or cross-checked.

Essays by applicants. It is sometimes believed that persistence and commitment can be gauged through essays. I have found little useful research on this subject. Autobiographical and topical essays are often required, in the hope that they will reveal character, personality, and maturity. In cases of woeful or wonderful writing, admissions officers find essays useful as a measure of literacy. But even in admissions processes where essays are heavily employed, some officers worry that, in most cases, little of value is conveyed. Many people think that statements of purpose are unreliable and susceptible to dissimulation. Intuitively, some readers may think they can learn a lot about candidates from essays, but studies do not support the predictive power of such measures, and again one worries about dissimulation.[13]

Interviews. As described in chapter 2, admissions committees at Harvard have no uniform policy with regard to interviews. Most do not use them. The Medical School interviews a subset of applicants, and Harvard College obtains alumni interviews for almost all candidates. The Business and Divinity Schools interview a few applicants on the understanding that the interviews will play no role in the admissions process. Some graduate departments find interviews useful for eliminating nonserious applicants and for increasing yield rates.

I have examined more than thirty studies and review articles about the predictive validity of interviews and to my surprise, on the average, interviews have almost no predictive power for either academic or on-the-job success. (I hasten to add my now customary warning that the studies do not usually use the best statistical methods, the most appropriate outcome measures, or the most relevant samples in terms of ages and abilities, from the point of view of selection at the right tail.)[14]

I have found no information about how well interview data improve the prediction of later-life success at universities like Harvard. There are tantalizing hints, however, that interviews may help distinguish among those with high test scores. Edgar Antsey published a thirty-year followup of candidates selected for the British Civil Service. Written exams including measures of intelligence, biographical information, a two-day assessment center session, and three personal interviews were used to select entry-level civil servants in the mid-1940s. Combined ratings from these techniques correlated 0.35 with rank achieved after thirty years in the civil service. "These figures are probably the highest validity coefficients that have ever been obtained for high-grade selection in any country."[15] Antsey does not report how much interviews added to the other predictors,[16] but he does conclude:

> Interviews have greater predictive validity at the higher end of the scale. If the Board thinks very highly of a person, they are probably right, far more often than by chance. . . . Those graded by the Interview Board as fliers [the top rating] fared very well . . . but those graded as 'borderliners' fared rather better than those in the middle (fully acceptable) range of Interview Board marks.[17]

Such a result whets one's appetite. But the dominant message of the literature on interviews is discouraging. Interviewers' ratings contain much random error, with reliability coefficients often down around 0.4 to 0.5. This problem is exacerbated when different interviewers, untrained for that task, conduct unstructured interviews—conditions that often hold in the case of university admissions. Although the literature is contradictory on this point, many experts believe that interviews are biased by irrelevant characteristics of both parties.[18] Interviews are also costly—imagine the expense involved with two interviews each for a thousand of the applicants to the Harvard Medical School.

But it is difficult to know what to make of the torrent of pessimistic conclusions about interviews, and not only because of the usual methodological complexities. After all, interviews are widely used in hiring and selection. This seems anomalous, in light of the evidence of their poor predictive power. Upon further examination, however, the paradox abates. Interviews have several other purposes, especially in hiring a co-worker. They are a vehicle to provide information, to persuade, to see if first impressions are positive, to obtain a quick idea of verbal facility, to establish the interviewer's authority in the hiring process, and so forth. Personnel expert Marvin D. Dunnette has remarked that the continued use of the interview "had best be rationalized on the basis of its utility as a public relations device rather than as a personnel predictor."[19] Interviewing applicant may be a kind of reward to recruiters or admissions committee members—a way to keep them involved in the enterprise.[20]

These are valid points: interviews can be useful. They may help to find people who speak readily and well, which is an explicit purpose of interviews in admissions to the Grandes Écoles of France; they may be used to identify people who make "a good impression" or have certain qualities deemed worthwhile no matter what the predictive power for future success. But contrary to popular intuition (including my own), studies discourage the belief that interviews will help admissions committees to identify those applicants who will make the greatest later-life contributions.[21]

Letters of recommendation.   Opinions vary at Harvard concerning the usefulness of letter recommendations. In a few cases, they contain unusually positive or negative information and are helpful, but most admissions people worry that, on average, letters of recommendation are unenlightening. A dean of admissions at a law school recently remarked:

> Letters of recommendation have become so devoid of meaningful information that rarely can an admissions officer put any faith in them. The pattern reveals an inflation of praise, an overstatement of merit, a conspicuous avoidance of anything negative, and a boiler plate of sanctimony that is reminiscent of Victorian poetry.[22]

Good research on the use of letters of recommendations to predict later-life success is limited. What is known is not encouraging. For example, a study of teachers found a correlation of -0.03 between recommendations written by "professors of practice teaching" and later first-year teaching performance.[23] In a large survey, members of medical school admissions committees said they found recommendations most useful for appraising scholastic achievement and least useful in both assessing motivation and judging the suitability of the applicant as a potential physician.[24] As a recent flurry of letters in the *New England Journal of Medicine* indicates, many experienced admissions officers at medical schools find that reading recommendations is like entering "fantasy land."[25] The most relevant study I have found is Evrard Nicholson's 1970 work on later-life success of Brown University undergraduates. Nicholson's index, based on personal ratings by counselors and principals, was a significant predictor of later success, even with other predictors statistically held constant. As he said in an interview, "When push comes to shove and a counselor or principal says, 'I don't care about his scores, I know this guy's going to be a success,' he turns out to be a success. If they check the right-most box on every dimension, it's something an admissions committee should take seriously." He added, "This was my major recommendation."[26]

Like Antsey's study about interviews, this is a tantalizing finding. It is entirely possible that neither interviews nor recommendations will be good predictors across the entire population, but that both might be useful at the right tail. And yet, the weight of the evidence available seems to go against this theoretical point. As a review of the literature concluded:

> The major drawback to the use of references is that they are almost universally positive, containing almost no negative information about an applicant. This bias toward favorable responses, or positive leniency, reduces the variance in scores to the point where discrimination between applicants cannot occur.[27]

According to another expert, "These predictive validity studies tend to paint a rather bleak picture for the utility of recommendations as they are normally used."[28]

Despite these negative results about their predictive power, letters of recommendation are widely used. They must be of some value, one would hypothesize. As in the case of interviews, recommendations may serve other ends besides adding to predictive validity. They may provide a kind of check on students' self-reported biodata—without recommendations, biodata may be more likely to be misrepresented. They may give teachers, principals, and counselors a certain hold over students—because the latter know they need at least a good recommendation.

But recommendations engender large costs, although not primarily to admissions committees. I asked a Harvard Law School professor about his current research and writing, and he cited as his major output his "Annual Volume of Letters of Recommendation." A dean and teacher at an independent day school, contemplating 129 letters of recommendation, sounded despondent:

> It depresses me to think that those efforts may not count for much, and even more to wrestle with the question of what constitutes honest disclosure. The colleges encourage "candid" statements, yet I have acquired sufficient distrust

of admissions committees to wonder what they would do with a fully candid statement.[29]

The costs of recommendations may be offset by the benefits, but they do not seem justifiable in terms of greater ability to predict later-life success. It might be different if, as in China a thousand years ago, recommenders could be held responsible for the later performance of those they recommended. Sponsorship by a high official was needed for medium- and high-level official appointments. If the person recommended or sponsored did poorly later, the recommender himself could be demoted or even corporally punished. Apparently the system worked:

> The method of competitive examination offered a way of testing abstract reasoning powers and skills that could be formally taught, but it could not foretell how a man would meet the practical challenges that faced an official. Merit ratings attempted to measure energy, zeal, and ability in the actual performance of duties, but were almost inevitably deficient in objectivity. Sponsorship, however, gave greater emphasis to the act of appraising merit, and strengthened the incentives to perform it objectively and responsibly. Thus sponsorship seemed particularly suited to supply the deficiencies of the examination method.[30]

With the much weaker incentives facing the typical recommender today, however, our verdict must be that recommendations have little predictive validity.

Personality Measures

Beyond the indicators now used in university admissions are a host of psychological instruments which, in principle, seem highly relevant. For example, consider table 7.1, which lists some of the chapters in the *Encyclopedia of Clinical Assessment.*[31] Aren't many of these traits of interest either for their own sake or, in line with this chapter's focus, as predictors of later-life contributions to society? How well can such characteristics be defined and measured? And what do they predict?

Obviously these are vast questions, which exceed both my powers and the scope of a single book, but I have enjoyed looking into them. It has been fascinating to learn, for example, how handwriting analysis is used "in business and industry. . . where graphoanalysts assist personnel specialists in job application selection based on specific aptitudes, in job place-

TABLE 7.1

Some Chapter Headings, Encyclopedia of Clinical Assessment

Temperament	Decisiveness	Guilt (2 chapters)
Ego strength	Altruism	Classroom motivation
Ego delay	Interpersonal distance	Leadership potential
Moral development	preference	Authoritarianism
Moral reasoning	Associative elaboration	Psychosexual development
Personal needs system	Behavioral levels	Sex-role orientation
Personal responsibility	Graphoanalytic clues	Intelligence
Risk taking	Nonverbal cues	Genius
Self-disclosure	Dominance	Creative thinking
Tolerance for ambiguity	Disturbed thinking	Social conformity
Object relations	Information-processing	Conservatism
Assessment of the others	deficit	Nonauthoritarianism
concept	Primacy process ideation	Dangerousness
Aggression (2 chapters)	Anxiety (2 chapters)	

ment and promotion, and of the determination of character in credit risks."[32] (I am not, however, prepared to suggest that henceforth applicants' essays be handwritten—and not solely because the handwriting sample "is desirably a full page or more of spontaneous writing made with a ball-point pen or pencil on unruled paper without the subject's knowing that it is for analysis"[33]). Seemingly frivolous examples aside, it is the case that businesses, governments, and the military occasionally use psychological tests in selection. What is known about the predictive power of such measures?

Surprising to me, this question seldom receives an answer in such collections as the *Encyclopedia of Clinical Assessment,* the revised edition of Rapaport, Gill, and Schafer's *Diagnostic Psychological Testing,* and McReynolds' collection of *Advances in Psychological Testing Assessment.*[34] My interviews have largely but not always confirmed the judgment that in virtually every case, among samples at the right tail, *there is no persuasive evidence that differences in various personality measures predict academic or later-life success of various kinds.* This is not to say that no predictive power exists, nor is it necessarily a criticism of these measures, which were usually developed with other purposes in mind than selection or our sorts of prediction.

An example is cognitive style, which refers to the way people think and learn. Fifteen or twenty models of cognitive style may be found in psychological literature. One distinction is "field-dependent" versus "field independent." Field dependency can be measured via tests of people's reactions to visual fields, such as a simple figure embedded in a complex design. "Field-dependent" individuals are more attentive to people around them, are perceived as "warm, tactful, considerate, socially outgoing and affectionate . . . Altogether, field-dependent persons may be characterized as having an 'interpersonal' orientation to the world."[35] Field-independent people have been described as "insensitive to social undercurrents, cold and distant with others, unaware of their own social stimulus value and individualistic. Their interests are likely to be in the theoretical and abstract."[36]

It turns out that field dependent people tend to enter the humanities and the soft sciences, whereas field independent people are happier in the hard sciences and abstract disciplines. Other dimensions of cognitive style have been shown to differentiate among various kinds of business managers.[37]

Nonetheless, few studies have assessed the ability of various measures of cognitive style to predict later-life success. A recent, exhaustive review concludes simply: "Finally, the relationships between measures of cognitive style and measures of performance have not been consistently explored in the various approaches to the study of cognitive style."[38] This is not, of course, to say that there is no predictive power.

Another example of a potentially important psychological measure for predicting later-life success concerns achievement, affiliation, and power motivation, measures of which have been developed and applied by David McClelland and others. The various kinds of motivation are measured by the Thematic Apperception Test, where test takers write stories about pictures supplied in the test. Some (in my view, weak) evidence indicates that successful managers evince higher power motivation, lower affiliation motivation, and higher self-control. Outstanding entrepreneurs tend to have higher achievement motivation. Ethnic groups differ significantly in their motivational patterns, even after accounting for differences in social class.

Tests of creativity have also been developed. Various efforts have been made to test what might be called "divergent thinking," or the fluency, flexibility, and originality of responses to open-ended questions. Unfortunately, to the extent that tests of creativity are not measuring "intelligence," they do not seem to predict future performance of interest.[39]

Another example involves tests of scientific thinking. These attempt to gauge problem-solving ability of the sort needed in scientific research. Studies show that these tests correlate with certain self-reported bits of "scientific behavior" by graduate students, such as subscribing to journals and attending professional meetings, but they have not been shown to predict later scientific achievements.[40]

Howard Gardner's recent book on "multiple intelligences" has rekindled interest in the idea of identifying specific aptitudes and both selecting and training students accordingly. Like the psychological measures just discussed, this idea intuitively seems right, and Gardner's description of current research is intriguing. However, "there does not yet exist a technology explicitly designed to test an individual's intellectual profile."[41] Moreover, even if we could measure different intelligences, it is not certain what would be gained pedagogically:

> Of course, the idea of matching individuals with particular subject matters and/or teaching styles is familiar and has implicitly guided much instruction since Classical times. It is therefore disappointing to note that attempts to document significant improvements as a result of matching students with appropriate teaching techniques have not met with much success.[42]

Gardner advocates more research before application. "Even good ideas have been ruined by premature attempts at implementation, and we are not yet certain of the goodness of the idea of multiple intelligences."[43]

Many other psychological measures are possible: interest tests, Rorschach tests, nonverbal communication, and so forth. One eminent psychologist even suggested to me the possible usefulness of data on the body types of applicants. The *Encyclopedia of Clinical Assessment* reviews the evidence on many such measures and predictors, usually citing few adequate studies and, in such studies, very weak predictive power for outcomes like ours. The other evidence I have reviewed seems to lead to an agnostic conclusion.

Therefore, the first major problem with personality measures in admissions—for outcome measures we value and in samples at the right tail—is the lack of evidence of predictive validity.

A second major problem with most personality measures is their unreliability. Whatever they measure is measured with a considerable amount of random error. Statistically unimpressive reliabilities of 0.6 to 0.7 are considered excellent by personality testers. Many measures have much lower reliabilities. As David McClelland notes:

> Unreliability is a fatal defect if the goal of testing is to *select* people, let us say, with a high *n* Achievement [achievement motivation]. For rejected applicants could argue that they had been excluded improperly or that they might have high scores the next time they took the test, and the psychologist would have no good defense. One could just imagine beleaguered psychologists trying to defend themselves against irate parents whose children had not gotten into a preferred college because their *n* Achievement scores were too low.[44]

Third, the vast majority of available measures can be faked or coached. There is a distinction between the two. Faking refers to the candidate's ability to alter answers in what he or she believes to be desirable directions. Coaching alludes to the possibility of training by sophisticated professionals who understand both the personality test and the objectives of the institutions administering the test. If personality measures were used in highly competitive admissions, one could anticipate that both faking and coaching would take place.

Most psychological measures were not developed to be used in situations where faking and coaching could be involved. Most have been validated in experimental contexts. Often those taking the tests have an interest in answering sincerely—for example, when personality measures are used in counseling. But if important decisions are based in part on the results, candidates have an incentive to dissimulate and to "mug up" the test. Lois Crooks of the Educational Testing Service, author of such works as "The Selection and Development of Performance Measures for Assessment Center Programs," noted in an interview, "If you know a lot about personality characteristics, you can answer so that those characteristics you want come out on the test."[45] Psychologist Robert Rosenthal made the same point:

> Once you understand how a personality test works, you can easily say the right things on it. For admissions purposes, they're hopeless. Someone in the profession would show their kids or their friends how to give the "right" answers. You couldn't trust the profession, because the questions on the tests are not confidential.[46]

Even on tests of skills, such as Rosenthal's own test of nonverbal sensitivity, a person can raise his or her score by a half a standard deviation with an hour-and-a-half of practice.[47]

Thus, even in personality measures where indices of faking have been developed or where faking is minimized by the careful construction of questions, coaching presents difficulties for their widespread use in admissions.[48] For example, with the widely used Strong Vocational Interest Blank (SVIB), which helps people see how their preferences match those of people employed in various jobs and professions, ample research has shown that the patterns of preferences in particular jobs are relatively similar, and the patterns differ across jobs. Thus, it might be considered desirable to use the SVIB to select candidates for certain kinds of jobs. Indeed, this is done in a variety of industrial settings, some medical and engineering applications, and in the military service (for example, in selecting pilots for the Air Force).[49]

But on the SVIB, dissimulation is easy. "If one wishes to modify his SVIB answers, that is, to fake them, to affect his resulting scores, that is certainly possible. When investigators have asked students to sway their responses in specified directions, the scores always reflect this."[50] A review of the literature on SVIB faking established the following conclusions:

1. Test takers can raise their SVIB scores on specific scales when in-

structed to try to do so. The increases are roughly one to two standard deviations.

2.   When instructed to fake in specific directions—say, telling a woman to answer "like a man"—the answers are exaggerated. In a sense, the women answer much more "like a man" than does the average man.

3.   In real-life situations, people alter their answers when applying for a job or advanced training, compared to when they are seeking counseling; typical differences are one-third of a standard deviation.[51]

Studies of the SVIB have examined "uncoached faking." If the SVIB were widely used in university selection and students knew in advance which profiles of interests were most valued by the admissions committee, a minimal acquaintance with the published literature about the test would enable students to reproduce the desired profiles.

My remarks are certainly not intended to deny the value of all personality tests. It may well be that further research will show that current measures do have an important ability to predict various forms of later-life success. But even if they do, practical problems of coachability will still exist.

Assessment Centers

I was looking for something that worked as a predictor of later-life success. I asked experts in personnel management what devices large organizations used to select people who would make a difference, and I read a wide sampling of the personnel literature. Most personnel managers do not think much of personality tests, although there are vigorous dissenters. Most are not fond of interviews as predictors, although they recognize that interviews have other useful organizational functions—motivating candidates to accept an offer, establishing an authority relationship, providing rather than receiving information, and so forth.

Letters of recommendation are generally discounted by personnel managers. As Nancy Badore of Ford Motor Company put it, "Letters of reference can be all over the map, since different people have different ideas about what merits the praise 'outstanding.' "[52] Intelligence tests and academic records are employed, but often for prescreening candidates rather than as the key dimension in the final hiring decision. Biodata—the candidate's "track record"—are of course a key piece of information, but they are less useful for entry-level employees (who are more like entering students) than for promotion decisions.

What does seem to work is the assessment center. Over a thousand large organizations use assessment centers for screening candidates, especially for promotions and high-level hiring. I found that assessment centers are widely lauded not only by their developers, but by over twenty users of their services who were interviewed for this book and by many scholars who have studied their predictive power.

What an assessment center does is give applicants simulated problems on which performance is rated by a team of assessors. The assessors are usually chosen from within the firm or agency and given careful training on assessing various behaviors. Although the centers may include pencil-and-paper tests and personality inventories, their distinguishing feature is the use of "situational exercises" and simulations. An assessment center is the closest thing to a job trial without being a job trial.

Simulated problems in assessment center testing vary according to the job and profession.[53] Typically, they include:

- In-basket exercises, where applicants must quickly work through a range of typical problems, deciding what to expedite and what to delay and making decisions when appropriate.
- Leaderless group discussions, where decisions must be made by the group but candidates are rated individually on their contributions.
- Individual tasks, such as impromptu talks, written reports, and the candidate's conducting a mock interview.

Assessors rate the candidates along a number of dimensions, or "behaviors" or "competencies," such as their ability to analyze and solve problems, interpersonal sensitivity, leadership, resistance to stress, planning and organizing skills, and thoroughness. One review has catalogued 103 "behavioral dimensions" that have been assessed in such centers.[54] Usually, a global, or overall, rating is also given to each candidate.

Psychologist Henry Murray was a pioneer of assessment centers. In 1943 he helped apply assessment techniques in the Office of Strategic Services. Murray used simulated "cloak-and-dagger" situations to test for personality traits and behavioral skills necessary for an effective secret agent (the CIA still uses such techniques in its hiring). In the mid-1950s, assessment centers were revived in industry by psychologist Douglas Bray. The management exercises that Murray and Bray developed are models for most of the assessment centers in operation today.[55] Here is a description of the routine in a typical one:

A walk through the assessment center will illustrate the way in which the exercises develop. Twelve individuals are assessed in a two and one-half day program. After orientation in the first afternoon, they take the in-basket test in a group (two and one-half hours). When this is completed, they are told that they will retain the role they assumed in the in-basket throughout the program. They are given a folder and the opportunity to make notes on any in-basket problems or situations "they may wish to follow up." They also each receive a memo from the President, their superior in the simulated organization, setting up a personal meeting "to discuss problems and to offer assistance." Prior to this, they are instructed that they are to have a meeting with their staff (five division heads introduced in the in-basket), who will brief them for the meeting with the President.

Beginning the following morning, the assessees are divided into two groups of six. Three assessors, senior executives who have undergone a week of intensive training in all aspects of the assessment program, are assigned to each group of six, and these two modules proceed concurrently and separately through the center.

Each assessee meets with his staff in turn. This is a live meeting. The staff members are played by actors who have been carefully briefed and rehearsed in a prepared script, according to the personalities and roles described for them in the in-basket. The assessee is handed materials, is asked questions and to make decisions by his staff, and can thus take the leadership role prescribed for him according to his ability to understand and adjust to the situation. This meeting lasts an hour. The assessee then has a period to prepare for his meeting with the President. This meeting then takes place, also live, with the role of the President played by an actor. The President has an abbreviated script with prepared questions. He is a supportive senior person of stature as described in the in-basket. An assessor, present at the meeting, is introduced as an assistant.

The two assessors, one present at the staff meeting and one at the President's meeting, then write separate reports on the process they observed and describe behavior on dimensions they were to have been observing. Since they are both familiar with in-basket content and the staff meeting script, they can report synthesis of this information in the two meetings. The dimensions to be observed in these two exercises are Oral Communication, Stress Tolerance, Quality of Judgment, Interpersonal Awareness, Leadership, and Analysis and Synthesis.

The next exercise is a meeting with representatives of the agency responsible for reviewing and approving budget allocations. This meeting is set up to occur immediately upon the return of the assessee from a hypothetical business trip. His staff has prepared a file of information which he has to assimilate and organize for a presentation of his preliminary budget forecast. The file includes a lengthy proposal from one of this five division heads, estimates of staff and other expenses for the next three years from each division, and supporting memos from each division head. In order to prepare an adequate presentation, he also has to incorporate information gathered from previous exercises. Time is set aside for the assessee to prepare for this presentation. Two assessors play the roles of the program planning officers of the agency to whom the presentation is made. They have an abbreviated script and prepared questions, as needed.

In the final exercise, the President, in a memo which each assessee receives individually, sets up a task force of the six assessees in their role as the Director General of Personnel and Administration to work on problems in the organization first emerging in the in-basket, reinforced and enlarged upon in the Staff

Meeting, the meeting with the President, and in the budget presentation. The assessees are given a period of time to prepare for this meeting and come to it prepared to present and back up their individual points of view. They do appear to find it unusual to be in a meeting of five others in the same role. They are asked to reach consensus on a plan of action in a two-hour discussion and to prepare a written document for the President's consideration. The three assessors in this module are present, with each one responsible for observing the recording behavioral data on two assessees on the dimensions being measured in this exercise.[56]

Almost every personnel officer interviewed for this book was pleased with assessment centers. For example, Mick Sheppeck at Honeywell said that the results have been basically "positive"—bosses find those promoted because of their assessment center scores to be competent, the candidates feel the system is fair, and assessors believe that the process has given them the chance to measure important characteristics. Linda Pittari said that Merrill Lynch had experienced very few "disasters" from using assessment center ratings, and those had resulted from bad placements. Barbara Tokar at Owens-Illinois, while admitting that the assessment center process meant more work, claimed that it got "super results."[57]

How well do assessment centers predict later success? Although methodological problems are not absent, studies have shown remarkably good results, at least compared to other predictors. Several reviews of the literature on the centers are available.[58] "Assessment centers do predict future performance," concluded a government review, "and they do it well, with *predictive* validities in the .50's and .60's not uncommon."[59] Researchers Barry M. Cohen, Joseph L. Moses, and William C. Byham conclude that the global rating is "highly valid" with median correlations across studies of 0.63 with "job potential" and 0.40 with "job performance."[60] Another review on the validity of the centers concurs with this favorable verdict, although it is noted that ratings on individual competencies often contain a lot of measurement error.[61] But the global rating for each candidate turns out to be quite reliable and valid.[62]

In the studies on assessment centers, as elsewhere, methodological problems plague the appraisal of predictive power. Some of the studies, particularly those at AT&T,[63] are technically excellent. But others suffer from "criterion contamination." For example, if we use an assessment rating to predict later success, but promotion decisions are made in part on the basis of that same assessment rating, it is difficult to say that the rating "predicted" the success. Correlations may, therefore, be artificially inflated.[64]

There is also what might be called "predictor contamination" in appraisals of assessment centers. The raters at the centers often have access to other predictors, such as a candidate's previous performance ratings, various traditional paper-and-pencil tests, interview reports, academic records, and so forth. Information from these goes beyond the results of the center's own simulations. Thus, a significant correlation between the raters' overall score for candidates and later success may not be entirely, or even partly, attributable to the assessment center itself.

Predictor contamination is a virulent form of a disease we have encountered in previous chapters. It is hard to judge predictive power with simple correlations; it is necessary to see something like a multivariate regression analysis. Unfortunately, few studies explicitly address the increase in predictive power that is obtained from assessment centers compared to traditional techniques, and the question remains in need of further research. Studies by AT&T seem to show that assessment centers do have independent predictive power. However, an article by Richard Klimoski and William Strickland is methodologically the best study of this problem I have seen, and it reaches a pessimistic conclusion.[65]

The authors examined one particular assessment center, and they found that the simple correlation of ratings on simulations in the center and later promotions was rather large (0.34), similar to correlations reported elsewhere. But in a regression equation with other predictors such as IQ tests and pre-assessment ratings, the assessment center *added* almost no predictive power (see table 7.2). As we saw in chapter 4, the simple correlation can be a misleading answer to the question, "How much better do we do by adding this predictor to the others we now have?"

For other reasons, it is difficult to be sure how well assessment centers would work with students. True, assessment centers are sometimes used to screen entry-level managerial personnel of the ages of most applicants to Harvard graduate schools. Yet:

TABLE 7.2
Predicting Job Success with and without Assessment Centers[66]

	Success Measures				
	Recent Performance	Recent Potential	Level Attained	Level Changes	Number of Salary Changes
Multiple correlation without assessment center rating	0.51	0.70	0.43	0.40	0.43
Multiple correlation with assessment center rating added	0.51	0.72	0.51	0.42	0.46

NOTE: Other predictors included IQ test scores, personality test scores, and pre-assessment ratings.

Little research is available regarding the use of the assessment center as a selection technique for entry-level professional occupations when the applicant pool consists largely of recent college graduates with little or no relevant job experience. Most assessment center research has focused on the selection of managers into upper-level positions, and in selection for initial entry into an organization.[67]

Interviews with a few personnel officers who use assessment centers for entry-level positions—and for the fast-track Presidential Management Intern Program—found them to be uniformly positive about the technique. But no one had any hard data to estimate predictive power for such candidates.

To my knowledge, no university has used assessment centers in admissions; there is no direct experience to build upon. On the other hand, several colleges use assessment techniques for other purposes:

· To help place students in classes[68]
· To "chart academic careers"[69]
· To give career guidance[70]
· To assess whether college credit should be given for "life experience"[71]
· To determine whether students will be allowed to graduate.[72]

Despite the lack of experience with assessment centers in university admissions, most experts interviewed for this book were positive about the idea. Designers and users of assessment centers were asked what such techniques would add to our current predictors of academic performance and later-life success (test scores, grades, interviews, essays, letters of recommendation, and so forth). They mentioned a number of possibilities. For undergraduates, assessment techniques might give insight into leadership, creativity, and maturity. For professional schools, the uses seemed even clearer. Future doctors could be assessed for their ability to relate to people and their nonverbal sensitivity. Assessments of future lawyers could give an indication about oral and written communication skills, leadership, interpersonal skills, and thoroughness. Aspiring business students could be rated on these same skills plus their ability in situations of group decision making.

But why would assessment centers help find these elusive traits any better than the usual devices? Those interviewed gave several answers. First, assessors would be able to see whether the candidates possessed these traits, rather than relying on the candidate's self-description in background essays and interviews. Nancy Badore, who developed Ford Motor Company's assessment center, believes that with an assessment center universities would "get new and different information that is not subject to a person's ability to fake," and "you would find out whether or not the person were capable of performing that particular skill."[73] Second, an assessment process standardizes information. Letters of recommendation and interviews are notoriously unstandardized.

I confess that I am intrigued by the prospects of assessment centers for selective universities, but some inherent problems are daunting. Coaching may distort results, although I have found little hard evidence either way.[74] Another major issue is cost—development costs for a center begin at $50,000 and running one costs from $200 to $1,000 per person, not counting the cost to candidates of spending two or three days being assessed. A half-day assessment process might be feasible, perhaps as a substitute for interviews and given only to a set of "finalists" among the applicants. To date, however, there is no evidence on how well such a brief process would do; it remains an interesting topic for research. For the present, the costs of adopting a full-scale assessment center for university admissions seem prohibitive.

Nonetheless, I believe it would be worthwhile for selective universities to explore assessment centers more fully, using their psychologists, personnel experts, and admissions officers. Indeed, such an exploration could be an excellent vehicle for a general rethinking of admissions. If we were to have a good assessment center, what skills and competencies would we wish it to identify? How would we determine the specific characteristics of "success"? How would this information, if available, add to our current repertoire of essays, biodata, recommendations, and so forth? A series of seminars on assessment centers might be an excellent way to approach broad policies via a concrete example—even if the short-term prospects of adopting assessment techniques were minimal. Certainly more research is in order, and the practical payoffs could be large.

Concluding Thoughts

If life were like chess, we would have fewer problems of predicting successful careers. Psychoanalyst Reuben Fine, himself one of the world's great chess players in the 1930s and early 1940s, has observed:

> Today every prominent grandmaster alive has scored some notable success in his late teens, or at the most early twenties. One could almost safely say that if a chess player has not reached the national championship class before he is

twenty-one he will never become world champion, and probably will never even become a grandmaster.[75]

Eminence in many other endeavors, however, is much less predictable than chess, at least with the measures we now possess. We have some confidence that those who do better academically will also do better in later life. But beyond this, current nonacademic information cannot be shown to help much in selecting among applicants at the right tail those through whom a top university will create the greatest social value.

A few months before his death in February 1981, Amherst's Dean of Admissions Eugene S. "Bill" Wilson wrote to the college's President Julian H. Gibbs. His enthusiasm for the problem of prediction at the right tail and his pessimistic conclusion about mastering it provide a fitting epitaph to this chapter:

> I had hoped that there would be some common denominator in the chosen students, something that would enable us to penetrate more accurately in the future the growers from the standstillers.
>
> The factor that kept me excited during my twenty-five years in admission was the mystery in human growth and development. When a young person leaves his protected and familiar acre he encounters a new set of forces which present new problems to him. My work for many years as Dean of Freshmen enabled me to test my selections. I had hoped to master the art of human assessment. I didn't.[76]

8

The Representation of Groups

ONE of the objectives in choosing an elite may well be to ensure an "appropriate" representation of certain groups. We may care about how many Kansans are selected, or want more or fewer women, or give preference to devout followers of a particular religion. In the United States and in this chapter, however, the main concern over group representation concerns members of ethnic minorities.

These are sensitive subjects. On the one hand, many believe that such characteristics as race, sex, and religion should not enter into decisions about whom to hire or admit. On the other hand, many advocate the allocation of public and private funds to help members of certain groups overcome past disadvantages and discrimination. The internal confusion or turbulence many of us experience from these conflicting ideas often erupt when choosing an elite.

Many selective universities act as though their regular criteria for admission do not provide a large enough representation of certain groups. Consequently, these institutions implicitly give minority group membership an additional weight. As an illustration, in a recent survey of four-year colleges, 41 percent of private and 46 percent of public colleges responded that some minority students were admitted with lower qualifications than some majority students who were rejected.[1] As a generalization, the more selective the college, the greater the preferential treatment for minorities. In chapter 2, table 2.4 presented three colleges where minority group status added about fifty percentage points to the chance of being admitted, other variables held equal.

Minorities, particularly blacks, have a similar edge at Harvard College, according to a publicly available analysis of the Harvard class of 1975. About two-thirds of the applicant pool for that class recieved academic ratings of 2 (likely to do "solid honors or magna work" at Harvard) or 3 (capable of honors work). Blacks classified in categories 2 or 3 had a 73 percent chance of being admitted, compared to 28.5 percent for whites in the same categories. If SAT verbal scores had been used to select students, the percentage of blacks in that class would have dropped from 7.1 percent to 1.1 percent.[2]

Most professional schools also give special weight to minority group membership. A careful study of ten medical schools showed that minority applicants with better than a 50–50 chance of being selected when evaluated by the minority admissions standards at these schools "would rarely have had better than a 1 in 20 chance of admission if evaluated by the same standards as majority applicants."[3] The average Medical College Admission Test (MCAT) scores of blacks and Chicanos accepted to medical schools were well below the average scores of whites who were rejected.[4]

In 1976–77, all 165 American law schools received a questionnaire asking, "How many minorities do you have in your present freshman class?" and, "Assuming that it were impossible to identify the racial background of applicants, how many of the above would have been admitted?" Of the 152 schools that responded, 15 did not answer the second question, one clearly misunderstood it, and 7 had no minorities. For the remaining 129 law schools, the answers are shown in table 8.1.[5]

As discussed in chapter 3, there are several possible justifications for such policies. Educating minority group members may be argued to have a higher social value added. Ethnic diversity in the student body may be

TABLE 8.1

Preferential Admission by Law Schools

	Number Enrolled	Number Admitted If Race Blind	Percentage Admitted If Race Blind
Blacks	1,539	285	18
Chicanos	462	126	27
Puerto Ricans	123	16	13
Other Hispanic	141	52	37
Asians	383	229	60
Native Americans	111	43	39
Others	51	23	45
Totals	2,810	774	28

thought to enhance the educational experience of all students. Admitting more minorities may be seen as compensating for past injustices or discrimination, or as part of a vision of a just society. Increasing the representation of minorities, however, may also create costs. If academic qualifications are lowered, there is a corresponding lowering of "academic values" (see chapter 5). If the lowered qualifications affect the social value added of the education, there will be a cost in that dimension, as well.

At the heart of this issue, then, is a trade-off between the benefits and costs of greater representation. Making the trade-off involves value judgments, but it also depends on matters of fact. For example, at the right tail what are the differences in academic qualifications among ethnic groups? Are qualifications like test scores and prior grades equally valid for minority groups? Or are such criteria biased against minorities? How important are the educational benefits of an ethnically diverse student body? In choosing an elite, how should one think about the trade-offs between group representation and other objectives?

I first became interested in these questions as a visiting professor at the University of Karachi in Pakistan in the mid-1970s. Several colleagues and I noticed the severe underrepresentation in universities of rural students and members of certain language groups. We conducted a study and concluded that the admissions system was biased against these students. We argued that their intellectual abilities and achievements were understated by their scores on examinations written in English, not their native tongues.

Later, when I became admissions chairman at Harvard's John F. Kennedy School of Government, a key issue was the underrepresentation of women and minorities in our student body. My colleagues and I carried out studies of the validity and possible biases of the criteria previous admissions committees had used. We instituted new efforts to recruit female and minority applicants. In 1980, I worked with the Sloan Foundation to design an evaluation of preparatory summer programs for minority undergraduates who might later study public policy in graduate school. A year later we inaugurated just such a program at the Kennedy School.

In 1982 I worked on a related problem of minority representation in Indonesia. There, 36 percent of the population live outside the island of Java, but only 20 percent of the applicant pool to the major universities and only 10 percent of those actually admitted are "outer islanders." I tried to help Indonesian policymakers think about ways to increase the enrollment of these students, who are often members of minority linguistic, religious, and cultural groups.[6] In 1984, I worked with the University of the Philippines to evaluate its efforts toward the "democratization of admissions," namely a program of preferential admission for students from poor and rural backgrounds.[7]

For the past several years, I have worked first with the American Council on Education and then with a group of historically black colleges on ways to strengthen academic standards in college sports without unduly harming historically black institutions. My research has analyzed alternatives to test score cut-offs in determining academic eligibility for intercollegiate athletics, especially for black students.

But these issues are not just my personal hobby horse. If we look at the most perplexing issues facing admissions people at selective universities or examine the topics receiving the most attention nationally, the representation of minorities is near the top of the list. "By 1979," a critique by Allan Nairn and other colleagues of Ralph Nader noted, "over a dozen national organizations concerned with education had expressed their opposition to standardized testing or supported the concept of Truth-in-Testing legislation with damage to minorities frequently cited as the reason."[8]

Should Minority Representation Be Openly Studied?

An admissions policy that ignored the issue of group representation would be subject to grave criticisms. So would a book on choosing elites. And yet, as I pursued this research at Harvard and other American universities, several colleagues and friends suggested that such issues were best left alone. They wondered whether it would be unpleasant or risky or even wrong to study group differences, bias, and representation. Some thought that studying bias and the performance of minorities could heighten racial sensitivities, with negative consequences. Minorities might feel hurt if they thought that as a group their test scores and grades and academic performance were being studied. Admissions officers and university administrators might worry that the results of an investigation of bias would cast them in a bad light. And those who studied such matters might find their integrity questioned.

Other colleagues suggested that these issues were not in need of study because the answer was already known: "Blacks do worse on standardized tests than whites, because the tests are culturally biased." But the existence of bias, or the existence of group differences in academic performance of various kinds, are not the only topics of interest. How strong the bias is and how it might be corrected are central questions for admissions policy.

As we shall see, the answers are by no means as evident as they may seem.

In an important article, civil rights activist David M. White urged that these understandable concerns be discounted. Indeed, he feared that they might represent "the unfortunate yet natural possibility of lingering subliminal prejudice."[9] He worried that universities had not investigated possible biases in the prediction of minority groups' academic performance because, deep down, many university people were themselves biased:

> The suggestion is unpleasant, and many may remain unconvinced that subliminal prejudice played any role in the University's failure to raise test bias in *Bakke.* Even the unconvinced, however, will recognize the need to retain heightened sensitivity to the possibility that subliminal prejudices and stereotypes will enter into their analysis of necessary adjustments and corrections for invalid admissions criteria.[10]

White also argued that the reticence of testing services and universities to assemble the facts and analyze them was part of the problem:

> The importance of the issues raised by invalid admissions criteria and culturally biased testing demands that litigators and courts collect all the available evidence and give their fullest consideration to the facts revealed by such evidence. An effort commensurate with that in *Brown v. Board of Education* should be made to bring the country's finest minds, from all the relevant sciences, to bear on the problem. And this effort should occur as a preparation for trial, not appeal, of the issues: Evidence of cultural bias must be adduced *on the record* to persuade appellate courts fully to consider the issues and, hopefully, to resolve them in favor of recognizing and correcting for predictive invalidity and cultural bias in standardized tests. . . .
>
> A successful attempt to build a record, win on the record, and implement the remedy awarded will require the full cooperation and support of the universities: They possess the necessary data and invaluable expertise.[11]

In short, White advocated more, not less, attention to the academic performance of minority groups and how well test scores and other criteria predicted that performance.

The arguments of White, Nader, and others are powerful: Issues of group representation and bias in testing deserve careful study. These issues are already on the table for discussion as major topics of concern both at selective universities and around the nation. Fair consideration of all applicants demands that we understand the criteria used and their possible biases. Most universities now have strong affirmative action policies. To implement these, sophisticated understanding is needed of the characteristics of the potential applicant pool, the predictive accuracy of admissions criteria for different groups, and the benefits and costs of an ethnically diverse student body. In choosing elites, we need to think hard about *how much* affirmative action is desirable, not simply whether affirmative action should exist.

Differences in Academic Qualifications

For many academic qualifications used in university admissions, the distributions of scores and grades differ across ethnic groups, and sometimes between the sexes. The differences are especially striking at the right tail. Standardized test scores are particularly suspect. Ethnic differences are pronounced, with whites generally scoring higher than Hispanics, who in turn score higher than blacks, although there are considerable overlaps among the groups. Figure 8.1 shows the distribution of SAT verbal plus math scores for a sample of test takers in 1983.

The patterns are similar for other tests. For example, in 1978–79, only

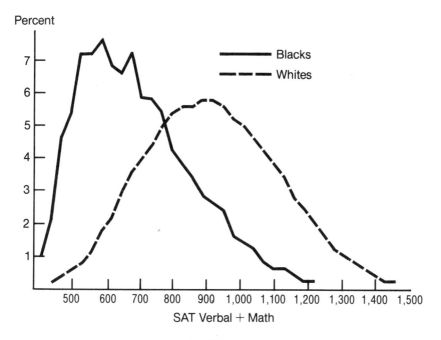

FIGURE 8.1

The Distributions of SAT Verbal Plus Math Scores for Blacks and Whites

NOTE: Based on a random sample of college-bound seniors taking the SAT in 1983. The number of blacks in the sample was 7,756; the number of whites, 75,708.

143 blacks scored above 650 on the GREQ, and only 50 scored above 700. Corresponding figures for whites were 27,470 above 650 and 14,540 above 700. For those entering law schools in the United States in the fall of 1976, the number of blacks with both undergraduate grades above 3.25 and LSAT scores above 600 (on the old scale) was only 39. The number of whites with those characteristics was 13,151.[12]

> The region bounded by LSAT at or above 600 and UGPA at or above 3.25 includes 20% of the white and unidentified candidates, but only 1% of the black, 4% of the Chicano, and 11% of the unidentified minority candidates.[13]

Similar results hold for other scholastic aptitude tests and the written ability test formerly used by the U.S. Government.[14]

Officials at several distinguished law schools have told me that a 600 LSAT score (on the old scale) and a 3.25 college GPA can be considered for most students the minimum needed for effective performance at their schools. The ratio of numbers of whites to blacks over that combined threshold in 1976 was 337 to 1. In 1978–79, the ratio was 260 to 1.[15] Similarly, if one finds that a 650 score on the GREQ is a rough threshold for success in a first-rate graduate school program in the physical or social sciences, the ratio of whites to blacks in 1978–79 was 192 to 1. For a 700 GREQ threshold, the ratio was 291 to 1. Above 650 on the SAT math test, the ratio is about 100 to 1. There are few blacks at the right tail of standardized test scores. Group differences also show up in high-school grades, although they are not as marked as those in test scores.

Women tend to do slightly worse than men on some standardized tests. For example, the average SAT verbal and math scores for them in 1981 were 420 and 445. For men, the corresponding figures were 430 and 492.[16] Above 700, the ratio of men to women was 1.19 to 1 on the verbal test and 3.39 to 1 on the math test, even though there were 1.07 times as many women taking the SATs. On the GRE quantitative test, about four times as many men as women scored above 700. In high school, however, women have higher grade averages than men. The College Board's data show a male high-school grade-point average of 3.00, compared to 3.11 for females.[17]

Bias in Academic Measures

These differences in educational qualifications among groups could have many possible causes—differences in the quality of prior schooling, socioeconomic factors, "culture," "effort," innate endowments, and biases in the qualifications themselves. It is difficult to untangle these causes statistically. We can, however, assess the extent to which tests (and other measures) are *predictively biased* against certain groups.

Suppose you had two candidates, one a black from a poor family and the other an affluent white. Suppose both scored 650 on the SAT verbal test. Who would you think would do better in college?

Some might speculate that the black student would, reasoning that the black student is on a "higher trajectory"; he or she has come up to a 650 despite a poor background and possible racial or class bias in the standardized test itself. The black would on average do better in college than a white with the same score. If so, the test would have *underpredicted* the later academic performance of the black student, compared to the white. Consequently, the test score would be predictively biased against the black student.

If predictive bias existed, we could have several options. We could drop the test, or, as White suggests, "add points to the test scores of minority groups so that the test has the same relative impact on groups as another more valid and less biased predictor."[18]

Bias in a test could be caused in several ways. The test might be in an unfamiliar format or language; it might be administered by uncongenial officials; it might be too "speeded" (that is, the test's time limit works to the disadvantage of minorities); it might be coachable and one group might have less access to coaching than another; or the test questions themselves might be culturally or racially loaded in ways irrelevant to the prediction of later performance. A large body of research indicates that these forms of bias cannot account for much of the difference in test scores between blacks and whites. For a particular individual, the causes just mentioned may make a sizable difference; but across racial groups, they do not.[19]

The best way to assess predictive bias is to see whether blacks and whites with the same scores do equally well later on at the university. If, for whatever type of test bias, blacks' test scores are "too low," then we should find that at the university blacks do better than their scores predicted.

Dozens of technical studies have addressed this question, and the results are surprising. On average, test scores overpredict the later performance of blacks compared to whites, especially at the right tail. This result holds for colleges, professional schools, and job performance. If a black and a white have the same test scores and prior grades, at right tail institutions the black will on average do about a third to two-thirds of a standard deviation worse in later academic performance than the white. In this sense, test scores are not predictively biased against blacks.

Let us look at some of the evidence most relevant to institutions at the right tail.

LAW SCHOOLS

How did black students fare when they arrived at ten top law schools, compared to what would be expected based on their test scores and prior grades? Figure 8.2 provides an answer. At these schools, on average, blacks made up 7 percent of the student body and had mean grades at the 8th percentile. The bottom of the class at these law schools was largely made up of black students.

On average, black students at these schools did worse than would have been predicted on the basis of their (lower) LSAT scores and college grades. Taking two students with identical LSAT and college grades, a white student obtained law school grades about a half-standard-deviation higher than a black student with the same scores and college grades.[20]

Let us explore this result in more detail. The average black at these ten top law schools had an LSAT score 144 points lower than the average white and college grades 0.5 grade points lower. On the basis of these differences, one would predict that, in law school grades, the average black would be about one standard deviation below the average white.[21] (This is shown by the dotted line in figure 8.2.) In fact, at these law schools the average

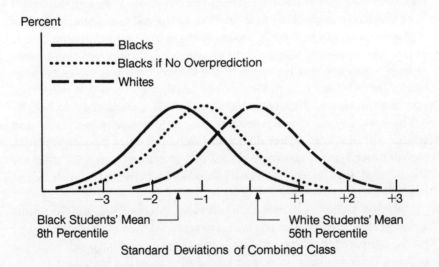

FIGURE 8.2

Where Black Students Fall in Distributions of Grades at Ten Top Law Schools.[22]

NOTE: The figures are normal approximations of average distributions of first-year grades at ten law schools with very high average LSAT scores. The dotted line indicates the expected distribution of black grades given the test scores and college grades of blacks—that is, without the overprediction that actually occurs.

black was a little over one-and-a-half standard deviations below the average white.[23] Thus, roughly two-thirds of the observed difference in average law school grades between blacks and whites is accounted for by the blacks' generally lower test scores and prior grades. The other third is due to overprediction—blacks on average do worse than predicted by their academic qualifications.

Another way to think about this difference is the following. To have unbiased predictions, how would we have to adjust the test scores and college grades of black students? To compensate for overprediction by half a standard deviation, we could subtract 50 points from blacks' LSAT scores (on the old scale) and about 0.4 from blacks' college GPA's—then we would have a roughly unbiased prediction of blacks' law school grades compared to white students. Or, we could leave college GPAs alone and subtract about 110 points from the LSAT scores of blacks.[24]

MEDICAL SCHOOLS

Rand Corporation researchers John Rolph, Albert Williams, and Lee Lanier carried out a methodologically strong study of what they called "majority" and "minority" group students at nine "representative" medical schools. They analyzed the extent of bias in the prediction of performance on the National Board of Medical Examiners tests. About 12 percent of the medical students were members of a minority group (not exclusively blacks). The average score for all minorities was at the 19th percentile of the distribution of majority scores on Part 1 of the National Boards, and at the 21st percentile on Part 2.[25]

The authors predicted National Board scores for minority and majority students separately, using variables such as MCAT scores, college grades, selectivity of college, which medical school the student attended, age, sex, and several others. The qualitative results paralleled figure 8.2. Minority students' scores on Part I were overpredicted by about a quarter of a standard deviation, and on Part II by about two-fifths of a standard deviation. The regression coefficients were about the same for the minority group and the majority group, but the intercepts differed.

Interpreting these results in another way, minorities on average scored about three quarters of a standard deviation lower than majority students on both Parts I and II.[26] A half to two-thirds of this difference was explicable in terms of the minority students' lower test scores, college grades, and so forth. The rest of the difference was due to overprediction.

To obtain unbiased predictions for minority students, one would have to subtract about 50 points from each of the four MCAT subtests (on the old scale). This is about 1.25 points from each score on the new scale.[27]

COLLEGES

Compared to white students with the same high-school grades and test scores, black students tend to get lower grades in college.[28] For students having test scores one standard deviation above the mean—that is, moving out toward the right tail—the overprediction of blacks' grades compared to whites' is about half a standard deviation.[29] For colleges whose average students are in this range, this overprediction corresponds to about 240 points on the combined SAT verbal plus math, holding high-school grades constant. In other words, to have unbiased prediction for blacks compared to whites, you would have to subtract about 240 points from the blacks' test scores.[30]

JOB PERFORMANCE

In 1973, a six-year study by the Civil Service Commission concluded:

> When work samples or job knowledge tests are used as criteria, there usually are differences in the regression lines between majority and minority groups. In these instances, a given test score is associated with higher job performance for the Caucasian group than for the other two groups.[31]

Moreover, "there is no substantial difference in background or experience variables for different ethnic groups." Similar findings have been made in careful industry studies, such as AT&T's.[32]

A 1982 review by the National Research Council concluded that overprediction of job performance is roughly the same as overprediction in the university:

> Results from studies in business and industrial settings, where regression systems for minority group employees have been compared to those for majority group employees have generally been similar to results in academic settings.[33]

And careful studies of twenty-four job areas in the U.S. Air Force found overprediction of the grades of black trainees compared to white trainees. The overprediction averaged a little less than half of one standard deviation.[34]

There are several possible explanations for this overprediction. Measurement error leads to the phenomenon called "regression toward the mean," and this mechanism may account for about one-third of the overprediction observed in universities at the right tail.[35] Affirmative action, coupled with missing variables in the usual prediction equation, might turn out in a complicated way to account for a small portion of overprediction.[36] "Floor" and "ceiling" effects in grading, and, in general, nonlinear reality imperfectly captured by linear prediction equations, could also play a role.[37] More research is needed on all of these possibilities.

Another explanation focuses on the environment at selective colleges and universities or the work environment. These institutions may have a racially hostile atmosphere that discourages minorities. One can conceive of an institutionally racist society so biased that test scores would turn out to be relatively less biased. A test might measure potential, but later racism would suppress performance. Therefore, the test would tend to overpredict the later performance of minorities. (This would be a curious twist on the usual argument that test scores understate later performance.)

A variant of this explanation says that the criterion of later performance —say, university grades—is systematically biased against blacks, which explains overprediction. I know of no hard data on these issues relating to selective universities like Harvard. One sometimes hears of the opposite phenomenon, "affirmative grading," where some minority students are graded more generously, or where higher grades are given in courses that minority students tend to take.[38] One also hears occasional complaints of grading biased against foreign students, those with divergent opinions, or those with "poor comportment" in class.

We therefore return to the old question of objectives and how to measure them. Are grades an appropriate criterion? What about National Board scores and the various measures of job performance? In the case of academic performance, I have emphasized how incomplete and unreliable grades are as measures. But if we do care about grades, then at the right time, we would be wise to expect test scores and prior grades to overpredict, not underpredict, the later performance of blacks compared to whites. If we do care about grades, we cannot wave away the ethnic differences in test scores by saying that the tests are predictively biased against blacks.

The Benefits of Group Representation

Grades are important, but we care about more than academic performance —or should. There are a variety of other reasons why preferential treatment for certain groups has been advocated (and opposed). Some of the reasons might be called philosophical. For example, some proponents think of preferential treatment as a kind of reparation for past discrimination and exclusion. It is only just, they say, to compensate groups for past injustices.

On the other side, opponents argue that it is unjust to utilize group membership as a criterion for allocating scarce opportunities. To do so, they say, is damaging to the principle of treating individuals equally.[39]

The ethical and political issues of group representation run deep. In my reading of the literature about them, I see little evidence of progress toward their resolution at the philosophical level. Increasingly, the debate over whether or not to have preferential treatment seems moot in practice. At most institutions that select elites, the issue is no longer whether to have it, but how much. How far should an institution go in the preferential treatment of various groups? This question demands that we balance the benefits of greater representation against the costs. Metaphorically, we can conceptualize the optimal degree of group representation for a particular institution. This ideal "how much" occurs when the benefits of representation are equal to the costs, as I will illustrate shortly. But what are the benefits and costs?

When discussing the objectives of selection in chapter 3, I used as a baseline the idea that we should select elites in order to maximize the social value added of our institution. This is also a useful idea for thinking about the benefits of the representation of groups. How might admitting more blacks to selective universities, for example, contribute to social value added?

There are several dimensions to the answer. First, the education that an institution provides may have a greater social value for members of disadvantaged minority groups. As part of a national policy to overcome racial inequalities, elite universities may be able to accelerate the advances of blacks and other groups into leadership positions in business, government, and the professions. This in turn may lead to a more just, stable, and ultimately more efficient society.

Second, greater group representation may contribute to the university's own health, to its own educational ends. Three possible categories of benefits can be distinguished here:

Broad educational benefits. It is likely that in a country where racial inequalities and misunderstandings are pronounced, students of different races will benefit from a chance to study together. In their interactions at the university, they will have a chance to learn—in the broadest sense—from each other. A racially representative student body may thereby foster tolerance and understanding, which would seem especially important in the training of future elites.

Learning in a narrower sense. It is sometimes argued that the representation of various groups affects how much students learn in the classroom. As noted in chapter 3, this is a difficult question to study empirically. My review of the literature on this subject and inquiries to its leading authorities uncovered no studies that addressed these issues empirically. There are indications that people of the same "learning style" learn better together than people of diverse "learning styles," but the evidence is weak and difficult to interpret.[40] Some evidence suggests that students from the same social class learn better together, but again, we would not want to rely on it. There are few data concerning if or how people learn more in classrooms or student bodies with more or fewer blacks, Kansans, preppies, athletes, Republicans, and so on. Nor is faculty or student opinion convergent on these issues.

Some say that blacks learn better in an integrated environment, or that there should be a "critical mass," or minimum percentage, of blacks. When these effects are measured, though, they are small and inconsistent.[41] As an example, consider the twenty-nine law schools studied by educational researcher Donald Powers.[42] The percentage of black students in these schools (compared to the number of blacks plus whites) ranged from 2 to 62 percent, with an average of 10 percent. I found no statistically significant relationship between the number ($r = 0.02$) or the percentage ($r = -0.07$) of blacks in each law school's class and the relative overprediction of blacks' grades. In other words, enrolling more or fewer blacks did not lead to better performance relative to these students' LSAT scores and college grades. This basic finding also seems to hold at the secondary school level, where it has been studied extensively.[43]

Noneducational values of diversity. Several studies show that both faculty and students like having different kinds of students around.[44] At Yale, detailed surveys revealed seven distinguishable categories of "successful students": "Leader, scholar, grind, artist, athlete, careerist, and socializer."[45] Students may also enjoy having classmates from various regions, ethnic groups, socioeconomic backgrounds, and so forth. For universities, the greater representation of certain groups may be a way to appease important constituencies.

There is a third category of possible benefits of group representations. Selection policies create incentives back through the educational system. Before policies of preferential admissions were introduced in the mid-1960s, the student bodies of elite colleges were typically 1 or 2 percent black, and top professional schools had similarly small percentages. It was difficult to encourage even the ablest black students to strive for those colleges and the professions because access seemed closed. With the introduction of preferential treatment, members of minority groups may have been motivated to study harder, to aim higher, and to perceive "the system" as at least partially open to them.

There are also possible costs to preferential policies. Those admitted under these policies may suffer a loss of self-esteem if their performance is worse than their classmates'. Because of preferential treatment, all members of the group may be stigmatized as second-rate or not up to the white standard. To some critics, promoting racial equality through preferential treatment leads to heightened racial consciousness and sensitivity, which they argue is not in the long-term interests of an individualistic society.

These possible social benefits and costs are, of course, difficult to measure. Few studies exist that would help us to assess their magnitude. Indeed, a prime motivation for my own research in international development is to see what we can learn about policies to overcome ethnic inequalities. I am studying countries like Malaysia, which has implemented an extraordinarily aggressive policy of preferential treatment for members of the majority Malay ethnic group, as opposed to the minority of Chinese Malays;[46] Brazil, which has no preferential policies and where recent data show the white-nonwhite income gap to be larger in percentage terms than in the United States;[47] and Zambia, where the issue is how fast to replace expatriate managers and technicians with Zambians. But in the absence of much more research in our own country and internationally, it is hard to estimate the various social benefits and costs of admitting more blacks to selective universities.

Even so, we can make some headway. I have found that policymakers in other countries have benefited from analyzing the academic side of the problem. It is an interesting fact that discussions of the many vague and controversial social benefits and costs of preferential treatment can be advanced through a detailed assessment of one admittedly partial dimension of the problem. For example, in my work with Indonesian policymakers, an important issue was preferential treatment for students from outside Java, who are greatly underrepresented in the nation's elite universities. Judging the social benefits of, say, an engineer or doctor from Java as opposed to Sumatra or Sulawesi is a matter on which no study can be precise, and endless debates can rage. But when I showed that the percentage of "outer islanders" could be doubled at the top universities with only a small cost in terms of academic performance, those debates seemed less relevant to many policymakers. The social benefits of regional representation, vague and unmeasured as they were, seemed worth it if the academic costs were small.[48]

I foresee no such dramatic implications ensuing from my analysis of blacks in American higher education, but that is not my aim. I hope to provide a framework for improving, but not resolving, discussions over how much preferential treatment should be given to various groups through an analysis of the academic costs of greater representation. I will show that even if two institutions have exactly the same estimates of the broader social benefits and costs of preferential treatment for a certain group, they should not in general select the same proportions of that group. This finding applies to a variety of selection problems and many sorts of groups; it is a qualitative result, not to be lost in the spurious precision of the numercial examples I will provide.

How Much Representation?

How strong should an affirmative action program be? To address this question, consider the following oversimplified and abstract approach. We care about the representation of blacks in an institution. We also care about the academic performance of the students admitted; we predict this, imperfectly, based on test scores and prior grades. Because blacks tend to have lower test scores and prior grades, if we were to select students on the basis of predicted academic performance, we would end up with disproportionately fewer blacks. We face a trade-off: As we admit more blacks than this, we reject non-blacks who would have performed better academically at our institution. How far should we go?

Economic reasoning suggests that we should decide the optimal representation of blacks by equating the benefits of greater representation with the costs. That is, we should accept more and more blacks up to the point where the benefits of an additional black student in terms of representation is equal to what we have to give up in terms of predicted academic performance. What we give up is the difference in predicted academic performance between the last black we accept and the last non-black we reject— this might be called the marginal cost in terms of academic performance.

This calculation obviously involves value judgments about what "representation" and "academic performance" mean and how much they matter. Although value judgments are inescapable, there are factual questions, too. I will present a framework to help analyze the facts. Amid the following graphs and specific examples, I try to convey a perspective. Increasing the representation of one or another group—Kansans, preppies, athletes, and so forth—may mean that something else of value must be given up. If so, the trade-off should be squarely faced. I want to show how that trade-off depends on a particular situation: not only on values, but on how selective we are, how well we can predict later performance, how different groups stack up on predictors, and the extent of over- or underprediction. Because these particulars vary, there is no "right" amount of representation that holds for all institutions.

I will illustrate the framework by analyzing a particular class of such

169

trade-offs—that between academic performance and the greater represen- tation of blacks. But the same methods could be applied to, say, the trade-off between job performance and regional representation, and to a host of other problems in selection. The principles are general.

There is a virtue to the specific problem I have chosen. By working it through, I hope to persuade you to recast the usual debate over affirmative action in higher education, which concerns whether or not affirmative action should exist. The issue is one of degree: How much affirmative action? Let me begin with an example based on a hypothetical selective college, but using real data. Then I will present a briefer example based on graduate schools.

For the college, suppose that whites make up 91 percent of the eligible pool of applicants and blacks 9 percent. (This is about the ratio of whites to blacks among a random sample of 100,000 college-bound seniors who took the SAT in 1983; the calculations below are based on this sample. Other ethnic groups are excluded for simplicity.) The college uses a com- bined predictor of academic performance: SAT V+M plus 300 times the high-school grade-point average. This is the best combined predictor for colleges with average SAT V+M scores over 1,100.[49] The distributions of this combined predictor for blacks and whites are shown in figure 8.3. The

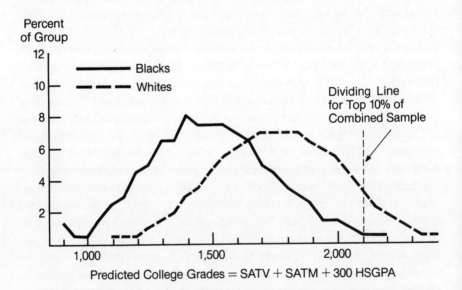

FIGURE 8.3

Distributions of Predicted First-Year Grades at Top Colleges

NOTE: Based on a sample of 7,756 black and 75,708 white college-bound seniors who took the SAT in 1983. About 10 percent of the combined group of blacks and whites scored above 2,100.

average white's score is about one standard deviation above the average black's.[50] The hypothetical college chooses the top 10 percent of this pool. This is roughly equivalent to admitting students with scores over 2,100 on the combined predictor. A 2,100 score can be obtained by scoring 600 on both SAT tests and having a 3.0 high-school grade-point average.

If the college based admissions solely on predicted academic performance, only 1.4 percent of its student body would be black. That is, among students with combined predictor scores above 2,100, only 1.4 percent are black. Suppose the college wanted more blacks. How much would it cost in terms of academic performance to raise the percentage of blacks?

To get more blacks, the college would have to admit some with scores below 2,100 and reject some whites with scores above 2,100. As more and more blacks were accepted, the gap between the lowest-scoring black admitted and the highest-scoring white rejected would grow larger. (That gap represents the "marginal cost" in predicted academic performance.) How do such costs grow as a function of the percentage of blacks admitted? Figure 8.4 graphs the answer.[51]

This figure looks complicated at first, but it conveys a lot of information. Suppose the hypothetical college wanted to know what would happen if it admitted 5 percent blacks, instead of 1.4 percent. The difference between the lowest-scoring black accepted and the highest-scoring white rejected would be 173 points in the combined predictor. This amounts to 0.62 standard deviations in terms of the distribution of the combined predictor among blacks and whites. If the college wanted 10 percent black, this difference would be 285 points of 1.03 standard deviations.

We want to translate these differences into grades at college. Suppose that after appropriate corrections following the methods described in chapter 4, the combined predictor is correlated about 0.58 with grades at institutions with SAT V+M averages above 1,100. This means that a one-standard deviation increase in the combined predictor corresponds to an 0.58 standard deviation increase in grades in college. Therefore, an 0.62 standard deviation marginal cost in the combined predictor, which is what the hypothetical college must pay if it wants 5 percent of its students to be black, corresponds to an 0.36 standard deviation cost in grades at that college. But this is without taking into account overprediction. Suppose that overprediction amounts to a third of a standard deviation. Then the whole curve in figure 8.4 shifts downward by a third of a standard deviation; I have indicated this shift by drawing two vertical scales at the right of figure 8.4—one with, and one without, allowing for overprediction. So the marginal cost of 5 percent of the institution's students being black increases from 0.36 to 0.69 standard deviations in college grades. The marginal cost of black students being 10 percent of the student body is

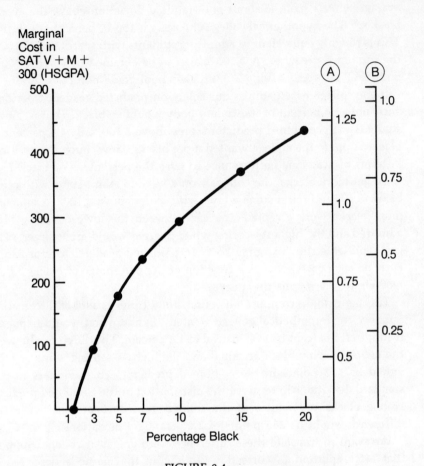

FIGURE 8.4

Marginal Cost of Minority Representation in Terms of Academic Performance

NOTE: Scale A shows the marginal cost in standard deviations of college academic performance including an overprediction factor for blacks of one-third of a standard deviation. Scale B leaves out overprediction.

actually 0.93 rather than 0.60 standard deviations in college grades, if one allows for overprediction.

In an internal discussion of admissions policies at our hypothetical college, one colleague might show figure 8.4 to another colleague and ask, "How much in terms of academic performance are we willing to give up?" The college should compare the marginal costs of additional black students with its assessment of the marginal benefits in terms of racial representation. The optimal degree of representation would be that percentage where the marginal cost equalled the marginal benefit.

It may also be useful to know the difference in academic performance between the *average* black and average white admitted under various preferential schemes. As the percentage of blacks increases, this difference becomes smaller than the marginal cost we have been calculating. For example, for 5 percent black the difference in average combined predictors is 158 points, whereas the difference between the marginal black and marginal white is 173 points. In the range of 5 to 20 percent blacks, the differences between blacks and whites in average predicted academic performance are roughly 85 to 90 percent as large as the marginal costs depicted in figure 8.4.[52]

These calculations are designed to illustrate a method of thinking, not to provide final or even approximate answers. Their main purpose is to show how the trade-off between representation and academic performance could be usefully analyzed. The institution has to supply its own utility function to say how much differences in grades matter. It must also supply a utility function that describes the benefits from gains in the representation of blacks in the student body. These techniques do not remove the normative heart of this policy problem. But they do, I think, elevate the discussion of representation, inject facts into a value-laden discussion, and help us do better achieve objectives, whatever they may be.

The shape of the curves in figure 8.5 depends on several features of an institution's specific situation. Other things equal, the costs of increased representation will be greater (a) the better the prediction of academic performance; (b) the bigger the differences between groups in predicted academic performance; and (c) the greater the institution's utility for academic performance. Also, the more selective the institution is—the further out it is on the right tail of the distribution of academic performance—the greater the costs of representation will be.

As an example of this last point, consider figure 8.5. It is based on the results of the Graduate Record Examination Quantitative test of 1978–79, assuming that only the top 4 percent could be admitted to a very selective graduate school.[53] (This corresponds to the percentage of black and white students combined who scored over 750 on the GREQ.) The graph represents a sample further out on the extreme right tail and indicates that the academic costs of representation become steeper as an institution gets choosier.

The costs of affirmative action seem to be higher at the most selective universities. But this need not be so, especially if the very top schools practice vigorous affirmative action. This point, although tangential to the main line of argument, is worth a brief digression.

Suppose that the very top school admitted a student body on a race-blind basis and ended up with one percent blacks. Suppose this would allow the second top school to select on a race-blind basis 3 percent blacks, the third school 5 percent, and so forth. An average school might end up

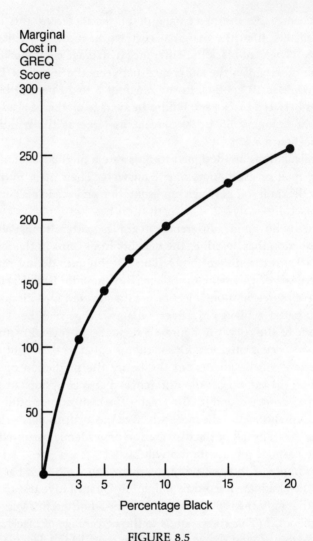

FIGURE 8.5

Marginal Cost of Minority Representation in Terms of GREQ Scores

NOTE: The graph shows the difference in GREQ scores between the last black admitted and the last white rejected for various percentages of black representation among those admitted, assuming that 3.5 percent of GREQ test takers were admitted.

with 8 percent blacks. For each school, black students would be about as academically qualified as white students.

But now suppose the top school wanted 7 percent of its students to be black. It would have to stretch academically, perhaps 120 to 150 points at the margin on each SAT aptitude test, to get that many blacks. This stretching, however, takes away precisely those blacks who would have been admissible without preferential treatment at schools two and three.

These schools therefore must stretch to get the same percentage of blacks as before, and then this stretching process might ripple back through the rest of the schools. Instead of the first situation where black students at each school were the academic equals of their white classmates, the result in the second case could be uniform discrepancies. Black students at each school might be a standard deviation below the white students and therefore might disproportionately occupy positions at the bottom of the class. Because of this ripple effect, if the very top schools give strong preferential treatment to blacks, other schools may also end up doing so. At each school this could entail high academic costs of the type we have been discussing.

Few empirical studies are available of how much universities are willing to give up to get more minority students. In a fascinating paper, economist Leonard S. Miller analyzed Stanford University's implicit utility function for test scores, racial representation, and financial aid, as expressed in undergraduate admissions and aid decisions. At the margin, being black meant as much to Stanford as having about a 310-point higher combined SAT verbal plus math score, or the equivalent of about $3,400 (in 1971 dollars).[54] Computer programs are available that analyze the average and total costs of various percentages of representation. These can be useful, but those I have seen assume a threshold utility function for later academic performance, which seems unrealistic at right-tail institutions.[55] Moreover, the decision about optimal representation should be based on marginal, not average, costs as described above.[56]

Summary

This chapter contains three major findings concerning the representation of groups.

1. At the right tail of academic qualifications, there are surprisingly large differences in the performance of various ethnic groups. This is particularly true of scores on standardized tests. For example, only 143 blacks who took the Graduate Record Examination quantitative test in 1978–79 scored 650 or above, compared to 27,470 whites who did. Only 39 blacks scored 600 or above on the Law School Admissions Test in the fall of 1976 and had a B+ or better college grade average, compared to 13,151 whites who did. In 1983, only about 570 blacks had combined SAT verbal plus math scores above 1,200, compared to 60,400 whites who did.[57] The pattern is the same on all the usual standardized tests. Of course more whites than blacks take these tests, but the percentages scoring at the right tail are disproportionately lower for blacks. Absolute numbers define the

available pool of potential applicants, and the unfortunate fact is that not many blacks have very high test scores and grades.

2. Differences in scores cannot be attributed to predictive bias in the tests. Indeed, predictions made using test scores and high-school grades actually overstate the later performance of blacks relative to whites. Compared to whites with the same test scores, blacks on average underperform in college, in graduate schools, and on some measures of job performance. The degree of this underperformance is from one-third to two-thirds of a standard deviation at typical right-tail institutions. Extensive study of the causes of this phenomenon is needed, which has been inhibited by understandable sensitivities surrounding discussions of racial differences in academic achievement.

Whatever its causes, overprediction means that for racially unbiased academic prediction at the right tail, blacks' scores should be adjusted downward by perhaps a standard deviation.

3. Techniques exist to help make the trade-off between the representational benefits and the academic costs of increased minority enrollments. Many universities value the representation of blacks and other minorities in their student bodies. The practical issue often becomes, "How much representation?" I provided a way for taking the first step toward an answer: Calculate the marginal costs in terms of later grades of admitting more members of certain minorities than a race-blind policy would select. Exhibit 8.1 contains a summary of the benefits and costs of representation. A conclusion emerges: Even across institutions with identical views about the marginal benefits of increased representation of blacks, there is no one "right" amount of affirmative action. The marginal costs of representation will differ across institutions, depending in part on how selective they are and how well they can predict the later academic performance of whites and blacks. In general, the more selective the institution and the better its prediction of later performance, the higher the costs of increased representation will be.

These analytical techniques are applicable to a broader range of policy choices. Using such tools could help move discussions of affirmative action, or of the preferential treatment of athletes or alumni children or other groups, from sterile absolutes to useful questions of degree.

This chapter concentrated on one aspect of the general problem of group representation, that of blacks at universities. Even with this restriction, it did not cover many pertinent questions. For example, what is the evidence about the relevant later-life contributions of blacks as opposed to whites, about the social value added of the education for different groups? What is known about the effectiveness of preparatory programs, tutoring services, and other policies that might enhance the academic performance of

EXHIBIT 8.1

Outline of the Calculation of the Benefits and Costs of Representation in Selecting Elites

I. Calculate the academic costs of additional representation of a particular group (ethnic, region, sex, and so forth).
   A. Obtain the distributions of predictors for each group.
   B. Calculate prediction equations for each group separately. (Notice that this adjusts for over- or underprediction by group.)
   C. Define what percentage of the combined applicant pool can be accepted.
   D. For various proportions of each group in the student body, use a, b, and c to calculate differences in the predicted criterion for the marginal admit in each group.
   E. Evaluate the predicted criterion in terms of the institution's utility function.
   F. Evaluate the marginal costs for various proportions of each group's representation in the student body.
   G. Consider qualitatively ecological costs—for example, costs arising from disproportionate numbers of the bottom of the class being from one or another group.

II. Consider the benefits of additional group representation.
   A. For different proportions of group representation, calculate how much better it is if one more group member is added. The benefits may be to students' educations, their later-life success, the contributions the institution thereby makes to a just or mobile or stable society, or the satisfaction of your constituencies. The result is the marginal benefit function.
   B. Alternatively, looking at the marginal cost curve, ask how much the institution is willing to give up in terms of that criterion for one additional group member.

III. Calculate optimal group representation for the institution by equating costs and benefits. Notice that the answer depends on what percentage of the applicant pool is selected, the group distributions of predictors, and the equations relating predictors to performance criteria. It also depends, of course, on the institution's utility function for the criteria and for group representation.

blacks? Are there harmful ecological effects to an institution's overall academic environment from the admission of less academically qualified students? What happens when other academic performance measures, such as achievement tests or indices of general intellectual skills, are used as measures of outcome?

I can only plead limitations of time, space, and capability in not attempting to answer these questions. There is no pretense here of a definitive assessment of the complex issue of group representation. Nor, as I have emphasized throughout, does my focus on issues of fact countermand the view that the issue is driven primarily by questions of ethics and politics. But here, as with other difficult issues, we need more facts and analyses, not fewer. Universities in particular should try to illuminate the debate over racial representation in choosing elites, not cloud things over with rhetoric and white lies. As elsewhere, we must hope that thinking harder is part of the solution.

9

Concluding Remarks

ONE OFTEN SIGHS in frustration after reading the annual book preview sections in magazines and newspapers. So many books seem valuable and fascinating, but there is so little time. Book buyers face a version of the problem of selection at the right tail. Among many attractive candidates, how should you decide which to choose?

Defining your objectives here is not that easy. You select books for several reasons. You care about how much reading a book will enhance your knowledge. You care about the book's practical applications. You want a "good read." You want a certain representation of different topics, authors, and so forth. Your choice depends on what you have already read, and perhaps on what other people are reading. Because all these factors vary in disparate groups of people, your objectives and mine may not agree.

After you have defined your objectives, you face further difficulties. You don't have perfect information. You must use various bits of unreliable data to predict which among many books are most likely to satisfy your objectives. You read book reviews, listen to friends' recommendations, consider the reputations of authors and publishers, take a look at advertisements, and perhaps flip through the pages to see how typical paragraphs read. After a while, you learn what sorts of information you can rely on. Many books look excellent, however, and you must make choices under uncertainty.

In this book, I have been analyzing a more complicated version of this problem of informed choice—that of selective universities choosing students. Yet many of the methods I have used apply to a range of other selection problems—such as deciding which patients should be eligible for a liver transplant, funding research proposals at the National Science Foundation, or choosing among applicants for entry-level jobs at Goldman Sachs. The problem of selection at the right tail comes to full flower when only a few among many candidates can be chosen, the objectives are multiple and vague, and information is imperfect about future performance or value.

When we talk about selecting at the right tail—about "choosing elites" —the mixed emotions we have about excellence and elitism, about the need for quality but our wish for equality, and about what makes a person worthy, are all brought into play. "A sudden sharp change has occurred in the meaning and impact of knowledge for society," wrote management expert Peter Drucker in 1959. "Because we now can organize men of high skill and knowledge for joint work through the exercise of responsible judgment, the highly educated man has become the central resource of today's society, the supply of such men the true measure of its economic, its military, even its political potential."[1] But we distrust the mechanisms used to select such men and women. Max Weber wrote:

> Democracy takes an ambivalent stand in the face of specialized examinations, as it does in the face of all the phenomena of bureaucracy—although democracy itself promotes these developments. Special examinations, on the one hand, mean or appear to mean a "selection" of those who qualify from all social strata rather than a rule by notables. On the other hand, democracy fears that a merit system and educational certificates will result in a privileged "caste."[2]

How we choose elites matters for social efficiency and social justice. It is hard to imagine a more central issue in society's allocation of opportunity than how a relatively few young people are selected for positions offering a distinctive advantage in education or influence. Most authors who have written about the selection of elites have focused on the ways elites perpetuate themselves. The aim is to explain why certain policies exist, often to show that what appears "meritocratic" is actually a disguised and nefarious way of winning at class warfare. These studies provide a useful reminder, but they may not provide much help with the prescriptive question: How should we go about choosing an elite?

As with the problem of deciding which books to read, the answer to the question begins first with the specification of the objectives sought. Second, we must confront the facts that in the real world these objectives are poorly measured and that predictions of the likely later performance of candidates are imperfect. Third, there may be a need to worry about the appropriate representation among those selected of certain social groups. What would be desirable to achieve in an ideal world of perfect information may be radically constrained by what is feasible in this imperfect society.

The Objectives of Selection

Universities have educational and social aims as well as narrower ones such as making enough money to stay in business. Choosing some students rather than others makes a difference in determining how close they come to achieving their goals. Chapter 3 analyzed the objectives of selection under the simplifying assumption of perfect information about the past and future attainments of all applicants. Several lessons emerged.

First, the objectives of selection can be usefully analyzed under the general rubric of maximizing the social value added of choosing one set of students rather than another. To determine this, several questions require answers for different sets of students:

1. What is the social value added of the education for students' later lives?
2. What is the value of the various contributions the students make to the university?
3. What are the social effects of the incentives that admissions policies may create?
4. Does the selection of some students have an intrinsic social value?

Each of these questions is complicated, even in an ideal world of perfect information. Chapter 3 provides no answers, but it does present a useful framework for the inevitably value-laden and controversial discussion of what ends admissions offices, and indeed the educational institution itself, should pursue.

Second, admissions policies should not be considered in isolation. They interact with other educational policies, such as the choice of curricula, social and cultural activities, financial aid policies, and others. They also interact with what other universities offer as competition. Ideally, students and educational policies should be chosen simultaneously, taking into account comparative advantage vis-à-vis other universities, the desires of potential students, and the needs of society. Consequently, there is no one correct admissions policy for selective universities. Rather, it depends on many specifics of the institution.

Third, in an ideal world of perfect information, students should not be chosen solely on the basis of "academic merit." If a university aspires to produce leaders in the real world, then it should also select students for the qualities that make leaders. Grades and scores on standardized tests are insufficient; using these alone substitutes precision for accuracy. The ancients added "virtue" to "wisdom" as criteria for rulers; today, we talk of character and commitment and personality in addition to academic achievement. Indeed, even the developers of aptitude tests have repeatedly said that tests should be only part of the answer in choosing elites. William Turnbull, former president of the Educational Testing Service, spoke often along these lines:

> The day when a single entrance measure or an array of traditional academic measures was an adequate yardstick for all candidates has vanished forever, if indeed that day ever existed. The academic dimension is relevant to only a fraction of the tasks to be performed.[3]

The eminent developer of intelligence and other tests Raymond Cattell admonished:

> We need to beware of the constant tendency to select, for privileged schools and universities, those who will *do best in those schools and universities.* The real criterion is surely that involved in selecting for such special education those who will contribute most to society *after* such education.[4]

The testers' repeated disclaimer that the tests are not everything is reassuring only during polemical enthusiasm. Critics of testing worry rightly that the disclaimers may be forgotten in practice, with a resulting "testing trap," or "tyranny of testing," or even "mismeasure of man."[5] Some critics identify tests as a conspiratorial device to keep the poor and minorities and women in their place—a particularly insidious device because tests offer the illusion of objectivity and allow a limited degree of mobility.[6]

But the animus of many of the critics of testing is itself polemical, and in the end this animus betrays them. It is a mistake to imagine that reducing tests to a mechanism of an elite's self-perpetuation proves the tests' intellectual inconsequence or social irrelevance. (This reductionism is common enough; why such sociological or psychological explanations appear to their authors—and some of their audience—as reductive in this way is itself a promising subject of sociological and psychological investigation.)[7] Often these criticisms are coupled with the reassurance that each individual is unique and equal, unmeasurable and worthy of our finest efforts. However, for the central problem—how to select in practice among many qualified applicants—such a declaration provides little operational guidance.

Academic achievement is only one of the factors that affect later social contributions, and it is imperfectly gauged by standardized test scores and grades. Let us etch these two facts in our minds. And then let us go beyond them. In selecting among promising young people, what can we use to supplement, or replace, imperfect academic indicators? How can we do better?

Prediction at the Right Tail

We must leave the ideal world of perfect information and enter the real world of imperfect measures and prediction to find better selection policies. Here the conventional wisdom may mislead.

The first step is to appreciate the special features of prediction at the right tail. Chapter 4 reviews many of the statistical pitfalls in such an endeavor—pitfalls in which I believe the current controversy over aptitude testing has been mired. The chapter provides a framework to judge the strength and usefulness of various brands of imperfect information in selecting an elite. The main lesson is this: the value of a piece of information does not depend solely on the size or significance of a statistical relationship, such as a correlation coefficient. It also depends on specific features of the situation, which vary from institution to institution:

- How completely and reliably objectives can be measured
- How the sample studied has been chosen
- The applicant pool and what proportion of applicants will be selected
- What other information is available.
- How much gains in objectives are valued—or the "utility function" for the outcome measures used.

Thus, a predictor may be highly useful for one institution and worthless for another—even when the statistical relationship between the predictor and a valued outcome is identical in both settings. As in the discussion of the objectives of selection, my primary aim is to provide a framework for policy analysis, rather than a brief for one or another particular choice of policies.

With the contingencies of this framework in mind, I reviewed in chapters 5 through 7 what is known about how well young people can be predicted to fulfill certain objectives. My strategy was to look at a variety of measures of success, each of them imperfect, and see what patterns of prediction emerged: grades, earnings, professional success, and others. Based on current knowledge, I would hazard these propositions:

1. In highly selective universities, test scores and previous grades are quite helpful in assembling a class that on the whole will perform well academically (see chapter 5 and appendix 1).

2. At the right tail, test scores and grades are much less powerful in forecasting various kinds of success in later life (see chapter 6 and appendix 2).

3. Other information now used in selection—such as essays, recommendations, interviews, and biographical information—do not add much of importance to the prediction of various kinds of later success (see chapter 7).

4. Using personality measures and other psychological information in selection at the right tail would probably not help—in part because there is no evidence that they predict later performance, and in part because an applicant can easily be coached to give the right answers. "Assessment centers" are a promising, but for now probably too expensive, alternative (see chapter 7).

Thus, the only objective of selection that we seem able to predict is academic performance.[8] A study of successful physicians provides a good example of the inability to predict which applicants will best achieve our institution's other objectives. Three researchers surveyed hundreds of physicians, administrators, educators, and citizens in an effort to identify the attributes of a good physician. The result was a list of 87 desirable attributes and 29 undesirable ones, which were summarized as five factors: dependability and commitment; problem solving, thought processes, and clinical skills; emotional stability, eliciting of trust, and frankness; fund of knowledge; and surgical skills.

The researchers applied these measures to a random sample of physicians practicing in Utah. The results were a wash—physicians' ratings showed no important relationship to the grades they got as medical students. Nor were there other predictors that might be useful to admissions committees. The conclusion was, "Only a very small amount of data can now emerge from premedical education . . . to enable admissions committees [to select] those who will become excellent physicians rather than . . . those who will become excellent medical students."[9]

No wonder a former director of admissions at an unnamed "major medical school" confessed to the *Chronicle of Higher Education:* "After four years of medical-school admissions I am sure of only one point, that is that I know very little about choosing good future physicians!"[10] And no wonder that Harvard President Derek Bok, after applauding the Harvard Medical

School's efforts to inculcate desirable personal as well as intellectual attributes, added:

> Some readers may believe that medical schools can best ensure proper attitudes by taking greater care in selecting students. In fact, most medical schools do interview applicants and try to give weight to traits of character such as those listed by the planning group. While these efforts are commendable, their impact is unclear. The interviewing process is sufficiently unreliable and the traits involved sufficiently intangible and easy to simulate that we have no reliable evidence that such procedures can have much effect on the characteristics of a medical school student body.[11]

The problem is not with our objectives but with what at present can be measured and predicted. I have cited Raymond Cattell's view that the ultimate object is not to select those who will do well in school. In theory, we should also look for those other attributes that go along with success after school. But how might we do that in practice? Not with the usual alternatives, wrote Cattell: "The weakness and bias of the interview, the essay, and countless other devices of the past have been exposed."[12] What about better and more varied tests? Not yet:

> Let us recognize, however, that we stand today only at the beginning of this new movement in mental testing . . . . We do not, at this moment, however, have more than a fraction of the necessary feedback of criterion information from the use of these new, structural tests whereby we might achieve the aims envisaged . . . . The motivation-analysis measures and the objective (performance) personality measures are still experimental . . . .[13]

Cattell and educator H.J. Butcher's review of how well such measures predict various kinds of later performance concludes agnostically:

> The brutal fact is, however, that we just do not know. . . . Without question, it can be concluded that there is little certainty as to just how adequate achievement prediction may be, and that the situation will continue until researchers begin to apply more sophisticated methods and concepts. [14]

David McClelland also concluded that grades and test scores don't help much in predicting later success at the right tail. He worried that "the testing movement is in grave danger of perpetuating a mythological meritocracy in which none of the measures of merit bears a significant demonstrable validity with respect to any measures outside the charmed circle" of academic performance.[15] I think he underestimated the predictive power of grades and tests, but that is not the point here: What would McClelland use instead? His own pioneering work on measures of motivation was mentioned in chapter 7, and he has formed a consulting firm that has applied motivational measures to promotion policies in the Department of State and elsewhere. Should such measures be used in university admissions? No, McClelland concluded, because those measures are too unreliable.

> Unreliability is a fatal defect if the goal of testing is to *select* people, let us say, with high *n* achievement. For rejected applicants could argue that they had been excluded improperly or that they might have high scores the next time they took the test, and the psychologist would have no good defense.[16]

Moreover, as with most other psychological tests, applicants could readily be coached to produce answers known to be those the admissions committee was seeking.

Or take Turnbull's point that "ability" is not adequately captured with a single score, but comes in many varieties. This venerable idea seems beyond debate.[17] The next question is what to do with it in practice. Howard Gardner's *Frames of Mind* presented a theory of multiple intelligences. "I hope that the point of view that I articulate here," he wrote, "may prove of genuine utility to those policy makers and practitioners charged with 'the development of other individuals.' "[18] But at the end of the book, Gardner said: "There does not yet exist a technology explicitly designed to test an individual's intellectual profile."[19] He noted that research so far has failed to document improvements as the result of matching specific aptitudes with appropriate teaching techniques:

> Educational scholars nonetheless cling to the vision of the optimal match between student and material. In my view, this tenacity is legitimate: after all, the science of educational psychology is still young; and in the wake of superior conceptualizations and finer measures, the practice of matching the individual learner's profile to the materials and modes of instruction may still be validated.[20]

"Carrying out relevant research," he continued, "is a task for the future." But it is research that is needed now, not yet the application of this theory to problems like choosing elites. "Even good ideas have been ruined by premature attempts at implementation, and we are not yet certain of the goodness of the idea of multiple intelligences."[21]

When it comes down to what to do, most psychologists call for more investigation. I agree. With more research, after a decade or two, who knows? We may have better studies of existing predictors, or new predictors, that enable us to do a better job of choosing which students will best serve the objectives of selection. The research needed is not "more of the same" but better.

Better measures of success. At the university, we need broader measures of educational progress. The pathbreaking work of Dean K. Whitla and his colleagues (see chapter 5) is an important step forward and deserves continued effort and encouragement. On a narrower educational front, grades could be improved as a measure of how much students learn, by adjusting grades to take account of the "quality" of students taking particular courses, as well as the reliability and relative standard of grading of different instructors. But of course the greatest need is for success measures after graduation, so that students can be chosen with an eye to their contributions to society and not just their earnings or professional status.

Better predictors of success. Perhaps research on multiple intelligences will bear practical fruit. Assessment centers look promising, focusing on specific competences, measured via performance on simulations of professional problems. The centers get away from interviews and recommendations, which are too subjective and unreliable. Although they are still too expensive for large-scale use in screening applicants to selective universities, something like assessment centers may someday be helpfully employed in the later stages of admissions.

Better studies. We need more studies done with samples at the right tail. In their statistical methodologies, studies must take account of the problems reviewed in chapter 4. The results must be placed in a decision-making context before it is said that a particular statistical relationship is "strong" or "weak," "useful" or "worthless."

This book provides guidelines and examples for improving and expanding predictive research. Without such research, choosing elites must be done in an atmosphere of great uncertainty. For now, we simply cannot predict well among applicant pools encountered by universities at the right tail. Indeed, the situation has not changed much from 1922, when the eminent jurist Learned Hand wrote a letter on admissions policy to the chairman of Harvard's Committee on the Faculties:

> If anyone could devise an honest test for character, perhaps it would serve well. I doubt its feasibility except to detect formal and obvious delinquencies. Short of it, it seems to me that students can only be chosen by tests of scholarship, unsatisfactory as those no doubt are . . . . A college may gather together men of a common tradition, or it may put its faith in learning. If so, it will I suppose take its chance that in learning lies the best hope, and that a company of scholars will prove better than any other company. Our tests do not indeed go far to produce such a company but they are all we have.[22]

The Representation of Groups

Learned Hand's verdict that tests of scholarship are all we have would not bother us so much were it not that our criteria of academic achievement disproportionately exclude certain groups whose welfare we wish to advance. Many of us are willing to give up something in academic excellence in order to include more people from these groups. The question I addressed in chapter 8 was how best to do so.

The problem of representation is by no means confined to the United States. Ethnic preferences in university admissions have been studied in China, Indonesia, India, Sri Lanka, Malaysia,[23] and even in the Soviet Union. "The Soviet elite universities have had special quotas for non-Russian students since the 1920s," reported political scientist Rasma Karklins. In his research among Soviet emigres "a majority of respondents pinpointed nationality as the one decisive factor" in answer to the question "who do you think is most easily admitted to higher educational institutions?" He cited evidence that "the experience of 'reverse discrimination' is resented and is highly divisive politically" :

> Further dilemmas arise from the fact that the ethnic quota system is covert and unpublicized and that in practice admissions apparently also include illegal aspects such as outright cheating on exam results . . . and various corrupt practices, thus increasing popular suspicions and resentments.[24]

The secrecy and sensitivity surrounding many American programs of preferential treatment may enhance "popular suspicions and resentments" here as well. A leading educator once remarked to me that there were two issues about which many university presidents deluded themselves or lied: preferential admissions for athletes and affirmative action. The facts presented in chapter 8 may be controversial simply because they are presented. Some people would like others, and perhaps themselves, to believe the facts were not so. One may wish top universities did not have to stretch so far to obtain their representation of blacks. Chapter 8 shows that at selective institutions being black frequently adds 40 to 50 percentage points to the probability of being admitted, other things equal. One may wish that standardized tests underestimated the later performance of blacks, but as we have seen, at the right tail black students typically do worse at the university and in some measures of job performance than whites do with the same test scores, perhaps one to two thirds of a standard deviation worse. The tests may be biased, but if so, they turn out to be less biased than commonly used criteria of later performance such as grades, scores on qualifying tests for the professions, and ratings of performance on the job.

The costs of affirmative action in terms of foregone academic performance are likely to be largest at highly selective universities. The benefits may also be the greatest at such universities—it is by no means an argument against affirmative action to note that affirmative action has academic costs. As elsewhere in this book, in chapter 8 I tried to provide a useful framework for assessing alternative policies, to help achieve whatever objectives an institution might have. Costs as well as benefits must be kept in mind.

If minorities are admitted with much lower test scores and prior grades, they tend to be overrepresented at the bottom of the class. This result can create new challenges. Dean of Harvard College John B. Fox, Jr., described one consequence:

> In the 1970's, when the College first found itself with a significant number of minority students, it began to seem that certain problems of self-confidence —shared to some degree by most students—afflicted minority students disproportionately. Minority students reported experiencing even more academic stress than their non-minority counterparts . . . . Dr. Jeffrey Howard has described it as ". . . in the first year . . . a rapid and unchecked erosion of their confidence in their capacity to compete."[25]

As with student-athletes who do not perform as well academically, it may be mistakenly inferred that group membership itself accounts for these results, rather than the major culprit, the fact that many of these students were admitted with lower test scores and grades than their peers.

But there are advantages of group representation beyond academics. These include the broader educational benefits of a diverse student body, the university's substantive and symbolic contributions to a more just and mobile society, and the satisfaction of constituents, among others. The educational benefits of diversity, however, are difficult to substantiate. Consequently, instead of justifying the preferential admission of people from particular regions, races, and social classes on the grounds of educational benefits from diversity, should one not forthrightly declare that helping these groups is a positive objective of the university, thereby warranting preferential treatment on their behalf? Why not face up to these values and announce them? There are counterarguments. It is difficult to agree on values.[26] It may be illegal to show preferential treatment in order to advance the welfare of an ethnic group. Some argue that the major business of a university is to transmit knowledge, and it should try to enhance academic, not social or moral, values.

But don't most universities already imply value judgments about a just society in what they do? For example, consider financial aid policies. Imagine we lived in a society with a perfectly just distribution of income and wealth and a perfectly efficient capital market. Presumably, we would then not think it necessary to offer scholarships on the basis of "need." Therefore, the fact that we now offer such scholarships implies that we *are* taking a substantive position that the current distributions of income and wealth, and the current capital market, are imperfect. Shouldn't we also stand up for our considered judgments about the distribution of social benefits across regions, races, and sexes? Isn't this what we would advise the Sri Lankans or the Malaysians or even the Soviets to do? And wouldn't we tell them to balance the gains from representation against the costs in terms of foregone performance? So why should we do differently?

The Process of Choosing Elites

About their policies of preferential admissions, and about other criteria used in selection, many top American universities have remained conspicuously vague. There is rhetoric about the attributes of ideal candidates and student bodies, but little to show exactly how various attributes contribute to a student's chance of being admitted or doing well.

In part this is because admissions officers would prefer to keep the discretion to themselves. Those of us who work in admissions may have abiding but unwarranted confidence in our "clinical judgment" of aspirants' merits. We tend to believe that an outstanding candidate will automatically cause our finely tuned antennae to quiver—this despite numerous studies that show quite imperfect agreement among raters or interviewers or, indeed, clinicians in a wide range of fields.[27] Some may believe that because choosing elites is so complicated and political, the best option is to leave the whole matter to us admissions officers and our experienced and dedicated judgments. The English educator W. D. Furneaux described a prevalent view at British universities:

> It is necessary to point out at this stage, however, that some of those who are concerned with university education are unwilling to admit that any selection problem really exists, except in so far as the procedures which they employ are time consuming and laborious. They believe that they are entitled to admit to their department those students who impress them as being in some way suitable material, and they refuse to accept academic achievement as providing a satisfactory criterion in terms of which their judgments can be evaluated. In their view, in fact, the criteria are so complex as to be almost beyond the possibility

of formal specification, and they thus seek to exclude all possibility of evaluation of any kind.[28]

But this position seems to many people simply to beg the important questions. Admissions committees distribute scarce resources, exercise considerable discretion, and display internal disagreement over the appropriate criteria for selection. Moreover, the fact that the objectives of selection are so difficult to specify, and predictions about applicants so dubious, makes the questions of who decides and how of prime importance.

There is, of course, a strong argument for not dissembling about what we do. But how open should we be about how we make admissions decisions? Some argue that legal and ethical issues of equal treatment and due process demand greater publicity:

> A primary consideration that ought to govern the admissions policies of colleges and universities is the development and application of the concept of "educational due process" to admissions. The lack of systematic, demonstrable, clearly documented guidelines for making judgments about applicants is a valid issue which may in some circumstances demand resolution by the courts.[29]

Several arguments can be given for more openness in admissions policies. Aspiring students would benefit from more information about their chances of being selected, the characteristics of their potential classmates, and their prospects for academic success at the university. Admissions policymaking might be improved by the internal and external debates such public revelation would entail. And, some ask, shouldn't a university stand for forthrightness in what it does and why it does so?

There are arguments for secrecy, too. Some of them are not compelling. Admissions offices and the selectivity of schools are sometimes judged by the surplus of applicants over admits, and the number of applicants is probably increased when applicants are unsure of their prospects. Politically, it is probably easier to satisfy diverse constituencies with policies generally phrased rather than specifically defined. Sub-groups may be embarrassed to learn about the true weights given to them in admissions.

More interesting is David Riesman's distinction between "democratic" and "aristocratic" variants of meritocracy:

> What Lowell sought both in recruiting students and in recruiting faculty might be defined as an aristocratic variant of Eliot's democratic and more impersonal meritocracy. It is this latter with which we are largely familiar in American life. It is egalitarian in the sense that placement depends on a contest judged in terms applicable to expanded candidate pools, with "merit" being assayed in publicly defensible forms . . . .
> In an unequivocally democratic meritocracy, any number can play—or rather,

work. What I have here termed the aristocratic variant would only appeal to those who felt confident in their fair-minded but sprightly ability to bet on able young people and to advance them, but who did not believe themselves required to consult widely and to justify their selections to a large and distant audience . . . . The aristocratic style of selection tends to disparage tests, and to put its faith instead in the unarticulated judgment of men who are satisfying each other and their own consciences.[30]

Riesman is describing an *organizational culture.* In deciding how an institution should choose an elite, one should worry about the process as well as the outcome. Let me describe how this aspect of selection at the right tail might enter into the choice of policies.

This book, and this was a surprise to me, has ended up supporting an admissions system giving more weight to "academic merit" at selective universities like Harvard. This tentative conclusion depends of course on many value judgments, but its primary source was factual: Given the current state-of-the-art of prediction at the right tail, selective universities will do better achieving their objectives by choosing the academically ablest students, with appropriate allowance for the representation of groups. We simply cannot predict much of interest with the other intuitively pleasing criteria now available.

To some, this might imply "admissions by the numbers." But that may not be the right conclusion. Not just because the numbers have a magical and misleading simplicity: That problem can be counteracted by making sure that admissions committees are presented with numbers that indicate expected academic performance (of various kinds) and the uncertainty associated with that prediction. Computers make it practical to create data like figure 9.1 on each candidate. Admissions officers should be trained in the interpretation of such data. As chapters 4 and 5 made clear, relying on untutored judgments about academic prediction simply invites problems.

But take the case of interviews. Chapter 7 showed that their predictive power is highly questionable, especially when the interviewers are untrained and the interviews are not carefully standardized. In addition, interviewing is expensive.

But interviews have other purposes in an institution's culture. As officials at the Harvard Medical School noted, those faculty members who serve on admissions committees enjoy interviewing candidates, and this may induce them to undertake the other burdens of serving. Alumni interviewers may gain a sense of participation in the life of the institution. As one admissions official said, "Interviews involve a wider group of people in the process. They tie people to the school. It's not just a means of fundraising but a way of building loyalty and maintaining the university's ties to the hinterlands. You can't buy that kind of public relations."

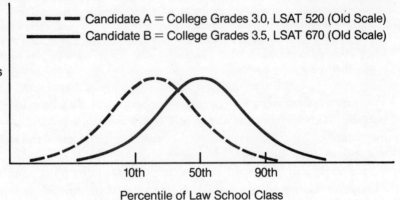

Probability of Finishing at Various Percentiles of the Law School Class

- - - Candidate A = College Grades 3.0, LSAT 520 (Old Scale)
——— Candidate B = College Grades 3.5, LSAT 670 (Old Scale)

10th 50th 90th

Percentile of Law School Class

	A 3.0, 520	B 3.5, 670
Predicted Percentile Rank in Class	15th	50th
50% Confidence Interval	6th–32nd	29th–71st
95% Confidence Interval	< 1st–73rd	5th–94th
Chance in Top 10% of Class	< 1%	6%
Chance in Bottom 10% of Class	38%	6%

FIGURE 9.1

Indicating the Uncertainty of Academic Prediction for Two Law School Applicants

NOTE: Based on my calculations from ten law schools with high LSAT average scores.

Interviews may also serve the purpose of persuading promising candidates to choose one institution over another.

Similarly, who decides in selection at the right tail matters to an institution's culture. Especially when objectives are vague, it is important that valued constituencies such as faculty, students, alumni, and others believe that their judgments are heard. Selections made by human beings, in lively disagreement, using their best if subjective judgments on a variety of subjective data, is qualitatively different in this cultural dimension from selection by a computer based on standardized test scores. The declaration of what is being sought—vague and idealistic as that may be—and the involvement of the culture's best representatives—its "aristocracy" in the good sense—help to create and reinforce an institution's mission. This is so even if someone comes along and shows that what is sought cannot be reliably measured or effectively predicted among young people at the right tail.

This is not a paean to ignorance nor the unqualified endorsement of an institutional myth. But it is a reminder that if we are in charge of choosing an elite, we have more than one responsibility. We do have the task of providing information about the implications of alternative decisions and policies, which has been the main aim of this book. But we also have to create legitimacy for decisions via a fair process of choice. We have to locate responsibility for decisions at the appropriate levels and positions of our institutions. We must create opportunities for later review of the decisions made—developing more information, checking on implementation, and so forth. All these dimensions should be included among an institution's criteria for a successful selection policy.

For these reasons it may be fitting that admissions committees struggle with subjective but also collective judgments, instead of routinizing those judgments into formal decision rules. Choosing elites may have some of the attractive qualities of a ritual, where students, faculty, administrators, and alumni contribute their views about the ideal student and the ideal class. Perhaps at universities like Harvard, the selection process should ultimately be one generation of the institution selecting the next, using as much discernment as the university has been capable of passing on.

Analytical models and empirical research can, I hope, improve this process. After all, what admissions committees debate are the objectives of selection, differing predictions about the prospects of one candidate versus another, and the right degree of preferential treatment and diversity. The framework provided in chapter 3 may help direct the discussion of objectives down constructive channels. As selection committees confront the many brands of patchy, imperfect information that are available on applicants, chapters 4 to 7 may be of assistance. Chapter 8 presents a framework for thinking about group preferences. Should selection committees make their decisions with or without such analyses? I have cited the judgment of the Harvard Medical School's Admissions Review Committee:

> We are aware of the absence of hard data bearing on the relative success or failure of our present process of selecting applicants . . . . Each procedure used in the selection of students has its strong advocates and detractors but the arguments advanced for or against a given procedure are based more on custom, emotion and "instinctive feelings" than on scientifically accepted facts.[31]

Is this by choice or necessity?

The complications of this topic—not just the uncertainties of current knowledge, but the philosophical and statistical complexities involved—create a certain psychological barrier to the use of analysis and empirical data. We may be reluctant to connect statistical distributions and predictions to the real candidates encountered, however sketchily, in selection files and interviews. We may even resist putting subjective judgments to the test—finding out whether pet theories and intuitive hunches serve better than the alternatives.

Such barriers are common in the human sciences, but they are even found in fields like physics. Steven Weinberg described the impact of a 1947 paper by physicist Willis Lamb as follows:

> Why was quantum field theory not taken more seriously? . . . I think that the deepest reason is a psychological difficulty, that may not have been sufficiently appreciated by historians of science. There is a huge apparent distance between the equations that theorists play with at their desks, and the practical reality of atomic spectra and collision processes. It takes a certain courage to bridge this gap, and to realize that the products of thought and mathematics may actually have something to do with the real world. Of course, when a branch of science is well under way, there is continual give and take between theory and experiment, and one gets used to the idea that the theory is about something real. Without the pressure of experimental data, the realization comes harder. The great thing accomplished by the discovery of the Lamb shift was not so much that it forced us to change our physical theories, as that it forced us to take them seriously.[32]

Perhaps this will be the path of progress on our topic as well—that new research will lead us to question productively our values and our theories about selection at the right tail, and eventually to improve policies for choosing elites.

Appendix 1

Evidence on Academic Prediction at the Right Tail

THIS APPENDIX shows several ways of predicting academic performance at an institution, and how to use and interpret the prior grades and test scores of its applicants. Evidence is summarized about selective undergraduate institutions, graduate schools, and professional schools.

Undergraduate Institutions

The meaning of various test scores and prior grades can be calibrated through comparisons:

Compare applicants to college-bound high-school seniors.   Figure A1.1 shows the approximate distributions of Scholastic Aptitude Test (SAT) verbal plus math scores for college-bound seniors. The average SAT V+M is 894, with a standard deviation of 207. If you took the average student and somehow could add 200 points to his or her SAT V+M score, the student would move from the 50th to about the 83rd percentile of college-bound seniors who took the SAT. You could make similar calculations in order to calibrate American College Testing Program (ACT) scores or high-school grade-point averages (HSGPA). In terms of where changes place a student in the distribution of college-bound seniors, 200 points on the SAT V+M is equivalent to about 5.6 points on the ACT and 0.58 points in HSGPA.

Compare applicants to students in your institution. In a highly selective college, students' test scores and high-school grades will be much higher than those of typical college-bound seniors. Distributions will also be tighter. For example, figure A1.1 superimposes the test scores of students at an institution at the right tail (with average SAT V+Ms over 1,200).[1] A 200-point difference in SAT V+M means relatively more, in terms of where it puts a student at one of these schools in relation to his or her classmates. At these colleges, a 200-point gain on the SAT V+M is about the same as 4.75 points on the ACT and 0.50 points in HSGPA.[2]

Compare applicants to students at other institutions. Colleges vary enormously in their academic standards and in the academic preparation of their students. With the cooperation of the College Board, the Educational Testing Service, and the American College Testing Program, I have assembled heretofore unavailable data on a spectrum of American colleges and universities.[3] Tables A1.1 and A1.2 provide data for institutions grouped by

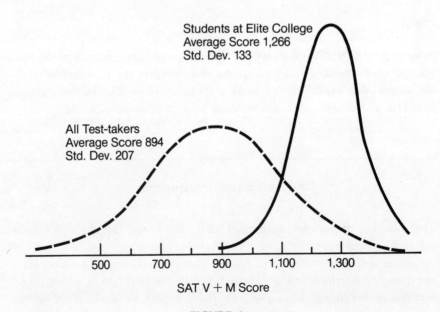

FIGURE A1.1

Distribution of SAT Verbal Plus Math Scores among College-Bound Seniors and Freshmen at a Highly Selective College

their students' average test scores. (None of the testing services identified particular institutions; it is their policy to keep such data confidential. I have listed "illustrative colleges" for the categories of SAT test scores based on other sources.)[4]

Among the 191 colleges in the SAT sample, the average SAT V+M was 900. But these colleges' average students differed by more than 600 points, more than three standard deviations. Average HSGPAs ranged from under 2.5 to over 3.7. A student with a 1,060 SAT V+M score would be at about the 10th percentile from the bottom at colleges with SAT averages over 1,200. The same student would be at the 97th or 98th percentile at a college with an SAT average of 700 to 800, and at about the 84th percentile in the modal college.

To put it another way, 200 points in SAT V+M, or roughly 0.4 points in HSGPA, are about the differences between the average student at Stanford/Rice/Duke/Northwestern/U.C. Santa Cruz and the average student at Texas/Michigan State/Pittsburgh/Marquette. These are also the approximate differences between the average student at the latter schools and the average student at Northeastern/Indiana State/Lamar/Morehouse.

Predict the grades of applicants. Tables A1.1 and A1.2 give regression results for various groups of universities. Look at the colleges with SAT averages over 1,200. There, a 200-point increase in SAT V+M raises the expected college GPA by about 0.28, or about four-tenths of a standard deviation —and this is after controlling for high-school GPA. This shift, equivalent to moving a student from the 32nd percentile of the college class to the 48th percentile. How does this compare to gains in high-school grades? A 200-point gain has the same expected effect on college grades as about an 0.85-unit gain in HSGPA, other things equal.[5] Based on the seven schools with SAT V+M averages between 1,100 and 1,200, a 200-point increase in SAT V+M is roughly equivalent to an 0.6-unit increase in HSGPA, both of which predict an 0.26-unit gain in first-year college grades, with the other variable held constant.

These results differ from the results for colleges around the middle of the distribution, as tables A1.1 and A1.2 show. At those schools, high-school grades are relatively stronger predictors, and test scores are weaker. In part, this is because the right tail schools have an extremely restricted range of high-school grades—relatively more restricted than their SAT V+M scores. Test scores are relatively stronger predictors at the right tail than at the average institution, compared to high-school grades. On the other hand, given both predictors, academic performance is less predictable at the right tail.[6]

Predict the grades applicants would obtain at other institutions. Colleges differ in their grading standards. Roughly, a 2.7 grade-point average at Stanford/

TABLE A1.1
Data on Colleges Grouped by Average SAT Scores

Number in Sample	Colleges' Average SAT V+M	Illustrative Colleges	SAT V+M Std. Dev.	HSGPA Avg.	HSGPA Std. Dev.	College GPA Avg.	College GPA Std. Dev.	Prediction Equation for College	Multiple Correlation (R)
2	1,200+	Stanford, Duke, Rice, Colgate, Northwestern, U.C. Santa Cruz	138	3.72	0.34	3.02	0.69	0.01 + 0.0014 SAT + 0.33 HSGPA	0.41
7	1,100–1,200	Georgia Tech, Michigan, Wake Forest, Notre Dame, U.C. Davis, Drexel	142	3.51	0.44	2.85	0.61	−0.24 + 0.0013 SAT + 0.45 HSGPA	0.50
25	1,000–1,100	Texas, Michigan St., North Carolina, Pittsburgh, Marquette	154	3.27	0.51	2.75	0.66	0.05 + 0.0011 SAT + 0.47 HSGPA	0.52
61	900–1000	Oregon St., Maryland, Texas Tech., North Carolina St., Florida St.	163	3.12	0.53	2.63	0.70	−0.02 + 0.0011 SAT + 0.52 HSGPA	0.55
64	800–900	Northeastern, Lamar, Indiana St., Morehouse, Nevada Las Vegas	155	2.92	0.52	2.46	0.73	−0.22 + 0.0012 SAT + 0.56 HSGPA	0.56
23	700–800	Prairie View, Texas El Paso, Delaware St., Bluefield St. (W. Va.)	151	2.79	0.54	2.36	0.81	−0.04 + 0.0013 SAT + 0.51 HSGPA	0.50
6	600–700	Bethune-Cookman, North Carolina A&T, Texas Southern,	133	2.64	0.53	2.16	0.76	−0.12 + 0.0020 SAT + 0.38 HSGPA	0.48
3	<600	Grambling St.	92	2.46	0.52	2.11	0.84	−0.53 + 0.0026 SAT + 0.49 HSGPA	0.48
191	Overall		155	3.03	0.52	2.55	0.72	−0.10 + 0.00123 SAT + 0.516 HSGPA	0.535

NOTE: Based on printouts from 1977–1981, provided by the College Board and the Educational Testing Service, 1983. The data include all validity studies for four-year colleges and universities that used HSGPA and SAT V+M in the prediction of freshman grade-point averages. The mean SAT V+M for these 191 schools was 900. The column headed "Prediction Equation for College" gives the best linear combination of SAT V+M and HSGPA for predicting freshman GPA for each cluster of colleges.

TABLE A1.2
Data on Colleges Grouped by Average ACT Scores

Number in Sample	Colleges' Average ACT	ACT Std. Dev.	HSGPA Avg.	HSGPA Std. Dev.	College GPA Avg.	College GPA Std. Dev.	Prediction Equation for College GPA	Multiple Correlation (R)
3	25+	3.28	3.62	0.40	2.90	0.64	$0.15 + 0.055$ ACT $+ 0.36$ HSGPA	0.38
11	23–25	4.21	3.34	0.52	2.71	0.73	$0.18 + 0.051$ ACT $+ 0.41$ HSGPA	0.42
9	21–23	4.73	3.17	0.60	2.66	0.76	$0.18 + 0.059$ ACT $+ 0.39$ HSGPA	0.50
14	19–21	4.94	3.00	0.61	2.40	0.86	$0.26 + 0.081$ ACT $+ 0.40$ HSGPA	0.41
9	17–19	5.20	3.00	0.64	2.38	0.94	$-0.15 + 0.060$ ACT $+ 0.48$ HSGPA	0.50
5	15–17	5.31	2.75	0.69	2.27	0.91	$0.38 + 0.052$ ACT $+ 0.38$ HSGPA	0.42
3	12–15	4.80	2.71	0.61	2.30	0.88	$0.67 + 0.052$ ACT $+ 0.32$ HSGPA	0.39
4	<12	3.67	2.55	0.60	2.43	0.72	$1.18 + 0.059$ ACT $+ 0.26$ HSGPA	0.39
58	19.8	4.66	3.05	0.59	2.51	0.82	$0.26 + 0.062$ ACT $+ 0.395$ HSGPA	0.44

NOTE: Figures shown are means for each variable with the group of schools. The data are from 58 colleges and universities that are members of the National Collegiate Athletic Association's Division I and refer to the 1982–1983 academic year.
SOURCE: American College Testing Program, summer 1983. ACT calculated regressions based on four ACT sub-scores and HSGPA; the regression coefficients on the sub-scores were added together to obtain the estimated coefficients given here for the ACT composite score.

Rice/Duke/Northeastern/U.C. Santa Cruz is about equivalent to a 2.9 average at Texas/Michigan State/Pittsburgh/Marquette and a 3.1 average at Northeastern/Indiana State/Lamar/Morehouse. There is no universal grading standard; some colleges are easier than others for equivalent students.[7]

But notice that the "easier" colleges—those having students with lower test scores and HSGPA—also give lower college grades. The average freshman grade in the Stanford/Rice/Duke/Northwestern/U.C. Santa Cruz group is about 3.0, but at Texas/Michigan State/Pittsburgh/Marquette it is roughly 2.75 and at Northwestern/Indiana State/Lamar/Morehouse it is about 2.5. Thus, the latter schools may look tougher, but students with equivalent academic preparation will actually find these will give higher grades. In effect, colleges' grading systems partially, but do not completely, adjust for differences in the prior preparation of their student bodies.

Using these data you could not only forecast where a candidate would be in a school's grade distribution, you could also assess the candidate's predicted position if he enrolled in other institutions. For example, a candidate with a 3.5 HSGPA and an 1,100 SAT V+M would be expected to attain a 2.7 grade average at Stanford/Duke and similar schools, or be at about the 32nd percentile of those institutions' grade distributions. The same student would be predicted to be at the 60th percentile in grades at Texas/Michigan State and similar schools (2.91) and the 79th percentile at Northeastern/Indiana State and so forth (3.06).

Evaluate the utility of using each predictor. Here I will need to make several simplifying assumptions, in the absence of more detailed data. I will assume that the reliability of college grade averages is 0.7, that a given applicant pool has standard deviations of test scores and of high-school grades that are both one-and-one-half times the standard deviations in the students actually admitted, and that 1 in 5 applicants will be selected. I will also assume linear, homoscedastic regressions and that grades are normally distributed.

Using the machinery of chapter 4, we can now calculate the increase in academic performance of the average admit, from using various pieces of information in admissions. (The expression "academic performance" is used because in calculating this gain I have adjusted college grades for their unreliability.) The calculations are based on the correlations shown in table A1.3.

With a selection ratio of 1 in 5 or 0.20, the corresponding ordinate of the standard normal distribution is 0.280. (In a standard normal distribution, 20 percent of the population have standard scores above 0.84; the ordinate corresponding to 0.84 is 0.280.) The formula for gain in college grades per selectee is:

Appendix 1: Evidence on Academic Prediction at the Right Tail

$$\Delta CGPA = \Delta r^{\phi}/\pi = \Delta r \cdot \frac{0.28}{0.20} = 1.40 \cdot \Delta r.$$

The calculation of Δr is made from table A1.3. I assume in these calculations that collecting and using the information is costless. Note that with perfect foresight, the average admit would perform 1.40 standard deviations higher than if we selected randomly (see table A1.4).

How much are such gains worth? A utility function must be used to assess this. In thinking about it, we might ask: "How much would it be worth to raise a student from the 16th percentile in academic performance up to the 50th percentile or median level of academic performance?" This would be a change of about one standard deviation. Using table A1.1, we might be tempted to think of this change as equivalent to replacing the average student at Oregon State/Maryland/Texas Tech/North Carolina State/Florida State by the average student at Stanford/Duke/Rice/Colgate/Northwestern/U.S. Santa Cruz, in terms of prior grades and test scores.[8] If this increase could be caused—say, with a better recruiting and admissions system—would it be worth $1,000 per student, or $10,000, or

TABLE A1.3

Correlations with Freshman GPA

Variable(s)	Uncorrected*	Corrected for:	
		Unreliability in College GPA	Restriction of Range
SAT V+M	0.372	0.445	0.598
HSGPA	0.273	0.326	0.459
SAT V+M & HSGPA	0.412	0.492	0.647

*Average correlations based on printouts from the two colleges in the ETS sample with average SAT V+M greater than 1,200.

TABLE A1.4

Gains in Per Student Academic Performance Using Different Selection Criteria

	Increase in Academic Performance (in Standard Deviations)
Perfect prediction vs. random selection	1.40
High-school grades vs. random selection	0.64
SAT scores vs. random selection	0.84
SAT scores and high-school grades	
vs. random selection	0.91
vs. high-school grades only	0.27
vs. SAT scores only	0.07

$100? This may seem a peculiar question, as most people are not accustomed to putting a price tag on academic achievement. Selection officers, however, often implicitly make such assessments, as when they decide whether a recruiting trip would be cost-effective, or whether additional predictors should be used in a selection system. As long as we take our answer as a tentative one—and see that the purpose of the exercise is in part to help us decide how much we should care—then we can proceed, perhaps using a range of possible answers.

After deciding how much one standard deviation in academic performance according to a given institution's current criteria is worth, then we multiply the chosen amount by the fractions of a standard deviation in table A1.4. This shows the gain *per student* from using various predictors. Finally, multiply that gain by the number of students.

For example, by selecting on the basis of SAT scores and HSGPA, instead of HSGPA alone, an average student's academic performance increases by 0.27 standard deviations. If one standard deviation (σ) is worth $1,000 and there are 10,000 students, then the gain is equivalent to $2,700,000 per year. If by some stroke of magic we could perfectly forecast academic performance, the gain compared to using just HSGPA to select students is $1.40\sigma - 0.64\sigma = 0.76\sigma$, or the equivalent of $7,600,000 per year. (Perfect forecasting would be worth $4,900,000 per year, compared to selection via test scores and HSGPA.)

These comparisons are precarious. For one thing, they assume that the prediction equation found within an already selected student body holds for a broader applicant pool, or indeed for the sorts of students who have such low test scores and grades that they do not apply to a highly selective college. My bet is that the equations would actually be changed if these lower-scoring students were admitted. I would guess that the correct extrapolations would lead to even lower performance for lower-scoring students. If so, the calculations in the text underestimate the gains in utility.

Another point is that I am assuming here that we only care about students' contributions to academic values at a particular institution. That is, I assume that we overlook what happens to academic values at other universities as the result of a particular choice of students. To take account of these larger effects would necessitate looking at *comparative advantage* in generating "academic values" from different sorts of students.

Indicate the uncertainty of grade predictions. There is another angle to think about when interpreting test scores and high-school grades. The predictions made for any individual student are highly uncertain. Chapter 5 provided examples of how the uncertainty of academic prediction for each student could be presented graphically to a selection committee (see page

113, figure 5.3) It is crucial in choosing the elite to emphasize this uncertainty in prediction.

Part of this uncertainty resides in college grades themselves. Recall the typical result that college GPAs in adjacent semesters correlate only 0.6 to 0.7. Looked at in this way, the 0.4 to 0.5 correlation between college grades and a combination of high-school grades and test scores seems stronger. Still, predicting any individual student's grades has a large margin of error.

I think two findings stand out at the undergraduate level. First, using test scores and prior grades as admissions criteria leads to important gains in the later academic performance of the student body as a whole. Second, the ability to predict the later academic performance of any *individual* student, however, is highly imperfect. Understanding that both these findings are true is the beginning of wisdom about academic prediction.

Let us now, in briefer fashion, review evidence on academic prediction after the undergraduate years.

Graduate Schools of Arts and Sciences

How well can academic prediction be carried out at graduate schools of arts and sciences? Figuring out how to measure academic performance is perhaps even more problematic here than elsewhere in the university. Grade averages are extremely tight, and as two authorities on the subject point out, grades and other proposed measures of graduate school achievement have serious shortcomings.[9] Moreover, small sample sizes hamper efforts to study academic prediction within a single graduate department.

In a recent study, educational researcher Kenneth Wilson pooled samples of the same departments across different universities. Table A1.5 presents the findings for graduate departments of bioscience, chemistry, psychology, English, and history.[10] The results were comparable to those at elite undergraduate institutions. Multiple correlation coefficients (R) were in the 0.4 area, and a standard deviation change in both test scores usually predicted a larger change in graduate school grades than did a standard deviation change in undergraduate grades. The weights for the verbal and quantitative test scores, however, varied greatly by field of study.

TABLE A1.5

Predicting First-Year Graduate School Grades with Pooled Data

Department	Number of Schools Pooled	Students Pooled	Standardized Regression Coefficients			Multiple Correlation (R)
			GREV	GREQ	College GPA	
Bioscience	13	390	0.18	0.24	0.21	0.39
Chemistry	6	203	0.01	0.29	0.33	0.44
Psychology	8	326	0.23	0.18	0.20	0.39
English	5	151	0.37	0.08	0.18	0.44
History	7	228	0.16	0.15	0.30	0.42

Law Schools

Law schools differ on the academic qualifications of their students. Educational researcher Donald E. Powers studied thirty-one law schools, whose average Law School Admission Test scores varied by over 150 points. I have analyzed the results for the ten law schools with the highest average LSAT scores. How well did test scores and college grades predict grades at these law schools at the right tail?

First-year grades in law schools have some attractive features as performance measures. Most students take the same core courses, which are deemed to convey the basic cognitive skills needed for the successful practice of law. Grading is usually done "blind," without the teacher knowing which student is being graded. On the other hand, as with other institutions, grades are incomplete and unreliable measures of academic performance.

Table A1.6 presents a revealing set of data on the ten highest-scoring law schools. Notice that Powers converted all grading scales to one with an average of 50 and a standard deviation of 10. Thus, a grade of 40 is one standard deviation below the school's average grade, or about the 16th percentile of the class. Powers' study reported prediction equations for different racial groups, not for the student body as a whole. The differences in these equations between the races was discussed in chapter 8; here, let us examine the results for white students, who were the vast majority at all ten schools.

The equations differ among schools, in part because of sampling error and other statistical artifacts.[11] The equation based on all ten schools shows that a 100-point increase in the LSAT score (on the old scale) corresponds to about a 0.46 standard deviation increase in first-year law school grades. The same increase in law school grades would be predicted

TABLE A1.6

Predicting First-Year Grades for Black and White Students at Ten Law Schools with High Average LSAT Scores

Percent Black*	LSAT Scores				College GPA				First-Year Law School Grades‡					Prediction Equations		Multiple Correlation (R)	Overprediction§
	Black		White		Black		White		Black		White						
	μ	σ	μ	σ	μ	σ	μ	σ	μ	σ	μ	σ					
7	477	51	647	47	3.0	0.4	3.4	0.4	33.6	8.9	51.3	8.8		B: 4.66 + 2.63 CGPA + 0.04 LSAT	W: −13.54 + 9.09 CGPA + 0.05 LSAT	0.24 / 0.34	−2.1
9	>550	44	>675	52	3.1	0.3	3.5	0.3	35.0	10.4	51.5	8.7		B: −19.65 + 7.19 CGPA − 0.06 LSAT	W: −4.17 + 5.25 CGPA + 0.06 LSAT	0.24 / 0.36	−3.8
11	526	76	>675	46	3.2	0.3	3.6	0.2	35.9	7.8	51.9	8.6		B: −42.79 + 8.96 CGPA + 0.06 LSAT	W: 10.17 + 3.97 CGPA + 0.04 LSAT	0.60 / 0.21	−2.0
3	514	61	659	44	2.9	0.4	3.2	0.3	36.5	10.0	50.4	9.7		B: −0.95 + 10.70 CGPA + 0.01 LAST	W: −16.01 + 8.03 CGPA + 0.06 LSAT	0.37 / 0.32	−2.2
9	>550	76	>675	46	3.1	0.3	3.5	0.2	34.7	8.2	51.9	8.4		B: −27.60 + 10.86 CGPA + 0.04 LSAT	W: −8.49 + 10.45 CGPA + 0.03 LSAT	0.54 / 0.30	−3.0
9	544	77	>675	59	3.0	0.4	3.5	0.3	37.9	8.8	52.7	8.5		B: 18.97 + 0.43 CGPA + 0.03 LSAT	W: 8.77 + 4.43 CGPA + 0.04 LSAT	0.28 / 0.29	−2.6
10	501	77	652	63	3.0	0.4	3.4	0.3	38.2	10.0	51.5	8.9		B: −2.18 + 4.62 CGPA + 0.05 LSAT	W: 0.38 + 6.55 CGPA + 0.04 LSAT	0.45 / 0.40	−2.2
6	542	57	669	43	2.9	0.4	3.5	0.2	35.8	9.9	51.0	9.2		B: −13.40 + 4.19 CGPA + 0.04 LSAT	W: 3.26 + 5.33 CGPA + 0.04 LSAT	0.32 / 0.20	−2.80
7	504	52	659	46	2.9	0.4	3.5	0.3	37.1	8.0	52.3	8.2		B: −0.08 + 9.86 CGPA + 0.05 LSAT	W: 1.41 + 6.69 CGPA + 0.04 LSAT	0.34 / 0.26	−1.9
2	486	79	647	55	3.0	0.4	3.4	0.3	35.1	7.7	51.0	9.4		B: 9.80 + 7.86 CGPA + 0.02 LSAT	W: −16.20 + 8.64 CGPA + 0.06 LSAT	0.31 / 0.38	−2.2
Means† 7	520	65	664	50	3.0	0.4	3.5	0.3	35.1	9.0	51.5	8.8		B: −7.34 + 6.73 CGPA + 0.004 LSAT	W: −3.44 + 6.84 CGPA + 0.046 LSAT	0.37 / 0.31	−2.5

*Number of blacks divided by number of blacks plus number of whites.
†Medians were used for LSAT μ's (averages)
‡Converted to have a mean of 50 and a standard deviation (σ) of 10.
§Difference between actual and predicted first-year grade-point average for black students based on a combined group of black and white students.
SOURCE: Donald E. Powers, "Comparing Predictions of Law School Performance for Black, Chicano, and White Law Students," Report LSAC-77-3 in *Reports of LSAC Sponsored Research: Volume III* (Princeton: Law School Admission Council, 1977) with additional information provided by Dr. Powers.

by an 0.65 increase in college grade-point average (CGPA). In other words, in terms of predicted grades in law school, 100 points on the LSAT is about the same as two-thirds of a college grade point—either would correspond to moving a student from the 50th percentile of the law school class to about the 68th percentile.

These relationships parallel those for the right-tail colleges we analyzed earlier. Multiple correlations are slightly lower. Law schools are usually even more selective than those colleges, though, so the utility analysis may have different results. Here is one example based on a number of reasonable but hypothetical assumptions:

	Increase in Academic Performance (in Standard Deviations)
Perfect prediction vs. random selection	2.18
College grades vs. random selection	0.78
LSAT scores vs. random selection	1.00
LSAT scores and college grades	
vs. random selection	1.35
vs. college grades only	0.57
vs. LSAT scores only	0.35

The uncorrected mean correlations with first-year law school grades are: CGPA alone, 0.16; LSAT alone, 0.21; CGPA and LSAT, 0.31. Assuming a reliability of 0.7 in grading, these become 0.19, 0.25, and 0.37, respectively. Assuming the ratio of standard deviations of law school grades is twice as high in the applicant pool as in the student body actually admitted, these correlations corrected for restriction of range become 0.36, 0.46, and 0.62, respectively. Assuming that one in eight applicants is admitted, $\phi/\pi = 0.272/0.125 = 2.18$; so perfect foresight would raise the average academic performance of those selected by 2.18σ compared to random selection of the one in eight. The other utilities follow from multiplying the corrected correlations by 2.18σ. As before, these calculations depend on a number of statistical assumptions about the linearity of the predictive relationships and the normality of the outcome measure.

How much using these predictors is worth again depends on the utility function. For example, suppose a one-standard-deviation gain in academic performance at a certain law school is worth $3,000. If there are 2,000 students, $3,420,000 would be gained by using LSAT scores along with college grades—as opposed to admitting students solely on the basis of college grades.

Medical Schools

Several researchers at the Rand Corporation looked at how well performance on the National Board of Medical Examiners (NBME) tests could be predicted. Many medical schools have their students take these certifying exams:

> Part I of the NBME exam measures a student's knowledge of material in the standard basic science courses of anatomy, behavioral science, biochemistry, microbiology, pathology, physiology, and pharmacology. The medical school course material for these subjects are usually a combination of lecture, small section, and laboratory sessions. Thus, the basic science course material and the teaching approach are both familiar to medical students from their undergraduate education, and this first part of medical school may reasonably be viewed as an extension of premedical training.
>
> The Part II NBME exam, unlike Part I, covers material that few students have been exposed to before medical school. The six exam sections deal with basic problems of diagnosis and patient treatment encountered in the different medical specialties: internal medicine, obstetrics and gynecology, pediatrics, psychiatry, public health, and surgery. In general, very little of the material on which Part II is based is presented to the student in the normal lecture or laboratory format. Most is either presented at the bedside, in small group discussion of diagnosis and treatment of patients in the clinical service, and at clinical conferences; or the student learns it through independent study of clinical journals and texts. Both the material and the learning process are so different from what the student has encountered before medical school that the Part II exam cannot be viewed merely as another in a series of tests measuring the absorptive capacity for knowledge presented by conventional educational means. Like the MCAT, the NBME examination results are reported in standardized scores. [On the old scale, MCATs had means of 500, standard deviations of 100; so did the NBME exams.][12]

The Rand researchers chose ten "representative" medical schools and studied how well scores on the two parts of the National Boards could be predicted by students' college grades, colleges' selectivity, scores on the four parts of the Medical College Admission Tests (MCAT), medical school attended, race, and several other variables. Among their findings:

• A 100-point increase (on the old MCAT scale) for each of the four parts of the MCAT corresponded to about a 60- to 70-point gain in both parts of the National Boards, other variables held constant. This in turn meant about two-thirds of a standard deviation on the National Boards. So, comparing the average medical student and an identical student with MCATs 100 points higher on the old scale (about 2.5 points higher on the new scale), the second student would be expected to be at the 75th percentile on the National Boards, compared to the 50th percentile for the first student.

· A one-point increase in college GPA corresponded to a gain of about 32 to 35 points on both parts of the National Boards, other things equal. The rough "exchange rate" between MCAT scores and college grades, in terms of predicting National Board scores, was 200 points on all the MCATs corresponding to about 2.0 grade points on a 4.0 scale, other things equal.

· With other variables held constant, medical schools differed in their apparent effects on their students' National Board scores. On Part I, the difference between the effects of the highest and lowest scoring medical schools was 84 points; on Part II, the difference was 57 points; the same two schools were highest and lowest. Remember, this is after statistically adjusting for the college grades, college selectivity, and MCAT scores of the students from these schools. Phrasing this result differently, the difference between the apparent value added of the "best" and "worst" medical schools was roughly the same as the effect of a 100-point increase in students' MCAT scores (or a 2.5-point increase on the new MCAT scale).

· With all the variables, the multiple correlation (R) reached about 0.5 for both National Boards.[13]

Business Schools

How does academic prediction at the right tail fare in graduate schools of business? Regression results are not publicly available, so we can only look at various correlation coefficients.

In 1979–80, thirty-eight business schools participated in the Graduate Management Admission Council's validity studies. These schools were a bit above average in the college grades and GMAT scores of their students. For example, the average GMAT quantitative score was about 30, compared to a national average among GMAT test takers of 27.

Six of the schools had both GMAT verbal and quantitative averages above 32 and reported first-year business school grades on a 4.0 scale. Their students' average test scores were about a half a standard deviation higher than the averages of all thirty-eight schools. The first-year business school grades at these schools, however, were about the same as at the other schools in the sample. So were the correlations between GMAT scores, college grades, and business school grades[14]:

Appendix 1: Evidence on Academic Prediction at the Right Tail

	Median Correlations between First-Year Grades and:		
	GMAT V+Q	College GPA	GMAT V+Q and College GPA
All 38 schools	0.36	0.25	0.44
The 6 above-average schools	0.39	0.26	0.47

These results correspond well with sixteen years of findings as summarized in a technical report on the GMAT test. The correlation between business school grades and college grades averaged 0.25, and the correlation between business school grades and GMAT verbal and quantitative scores combined with college grades averaged 0.43.[15]

In 1982, the results of eighty-five studies at seventy-four different business schools from 1978–79 to 1980–81 were published.[16] Three studies involved schools whose average student scores on both GMAT verbal and quantitative tests were above 35 and reported business school grades on a 4.0 scale. The average correlations with first-year business school grades at those schools were: GMAT V+Q, 0.35; college GPA, 0.24; and GMAT V+Q and college GPA, 0.44.

My conclusions from these analyses are summarized at the end of chapter 5. Table A1.7 provides a quick overview of some of the quantitative findings.

TABLE A1.7

Examples of Calibrating Academic Predictors

| Institutions | Admissions Tests | Holding the Other Variable Equal: | | In Predicting This Standard Dev. Increase in Later Grades | Which Corresponds to the Difference between a Student at the 50th Percentile and One at This Percentile |
		This Increase in Test Scores Is Equivalent to	This Increase in Prior Grade Avg.		
Colleges with SAT V+M 1,200+	Scholastic Aptitude Test verbal & math	100 in each	0.85	0.4	66th
Law Schools with LSAT 630+	Law School Admission Test	100 (old scale)	0.65	0.46	68th
Graduate Schools of Arts and Sciences	Graduate Record Examination verbal and quantitative	100 in each	1.65	0.40*	66th
Medical Schools	Medical College Admission Tests verbal, general information, quantitative, and science	100 in each (2.5 on new scale)	2	0.6–0.7†	73rd–76th

*Calculation based on averages from table A1.5, using a within-department standard deviation of 90 for GREV and GREQ and of 0.4 for college GPA.
†Increase in National Board scores, Parts I and II.

Appendix 2

Summary of Some Studies of the Relationship Between Academic Variables and Later-Life Success

THE STUDIES presented here by no means exhaust the literature, but neither are they intentionally selected to be a biased representation of the evidence. First, some of the broad studies of income and status are presented. Then we shall look at particular professions, examining earnings along with other success measures.

Income and Academic Predictors

Brown and Reynolds[1] report only simple correlations between earnings and IQ or education. Their sample consists of about 25,000 white and 4,000 black males who received scores on the Armed Forces Qualification Test during the Korean War. They find the correlations between IQ and general earnings to be between 0.24 and 0.35 for white males, the period from 1958 to 1964. The correlations between education and earnings of whites are almost identical, 0.26 to 0.34. The correlations for black males differ from those for whites, but again IQ and education are practically equivalent predictors of earnings. The correlation of IQ and earnings ranges from 0.08 to 0.13, and that of education and earnings from 0.09 to 0.15.

Weisbrod and Karpoff[2] related the earnings of 7,000 AT&T employees, all college graduates, to the selectivity of their college and to their class rank. Earnings were positively related to both. Even among graduates of the most selective colleges, class rank was important. Within the group, the ratio of earnings to earnings of all college graduates averaged 1.19 for those who graduated in the top tenth of their classes, 1.13 for those from the remainder of the top third, 1.04 for those from the middle third, and 0.97 for those from the bottom third. Moreover, the rate of salary increase was correlated with class rank for graduates of the most selective colleges. About a quarter of the difference between the higher incomes earned by college graduates as opposed to high-school graduates reflected their higher average ability and motivation.

Tyler[3] finds that income is positively related with having a college education, but ability is important as well. Among individuals with education beyond high school, those having IQs in the top 10 percent—that is, above 119—earned distinctly more. Solomon and Taubman[4] demonstrate that high income is related to college quality, as measured by average student SAT score and average family salary. They suggest that interactions with brighter students and better faculty serve to increase earnings potential. They also find the effect of college quality is greater for more able students.

Jencks[5] found that a graduate from a four-year college was associated with a 49 percent earnings advantage. Controlling for academic ability and family background reduced this advantage to 30 to 40 percent. A one-standard deviation difference in test scores was associated with a 9 to 30 percent earnings advantage in different samples. Controlling for family background reduced this effect by about one-quarter, which is consistent with the results of Weisbrod and Karpoff. They found that eight years after graduation from high school, ability and later schooling had no influence on earnings. But the influence of both variables increased over the next six years. Fourteen years after graduation, a clear association between ability and earnings had appeared. Men with IQs over 120 earned on average 20 percent more than men with IQs of 100, and 40 percent more than men with IQs under 80 (all were high-school, but not college graduates). The earnings differential associated with a year of college was constant across experience levels—about 10 percent if an A.B. was received, only 6 percent if not.

A variety of evidence indicates that income differences may be most significantly related to differences in ability or achievement in school at the extremes. Among a sample of male college graduates in 1947 and 1958, those who reported that they had received mostly A's in college earned significantly more than others, but between B, C, and D students the differences were negligible.[6] In a study of 309 members of the Dartmouth class of 1926, the median income of those with GPAs in five intervals between 1.7 and 3.1 ranged between $13,125 and $15,000. Of those with GPAs in excess of 3.3, however, the median income exceeded $20,000, and for those with GPAs between 1.5 and 1.7, median income was only $10,625. Those with more extracurricular achievements also had higher earnings.[7]

On the other hand, several studies have found no relation between income and ability, apart from the influence of educational achievement. Sharp[8] found that grades had little correlation with salary; one's "early career," age, and work experience mattered most. But he also found that college GPA was the best predictor of who would enter graduate school, regardless of the quality of the college.

Ashenfelter and Mooney[9] found that ability measures were not helpful in predicting earnings, but profession, degree level, and field of graduate study were. Their sample was of 1,322 Woodrow Wilson fellows between 1958 and 1960, a reasonably homogeneous group in terms of ability.

Griliches[10] also found that ability measures (IQ, knowledge of world of work, test scores, and family background) did not explain much of the dispersion of wage rates among a sample of 5,225 men aged seventeen to twenty-seven. Years of schooling, experience, and union membership were the best predictors. He also suggests that differences in schooling can make up for differences in ability—a one-standard deviation disadvantage on both background and IQ could be removed by an additional four years of schooling. A one standard deviation increase in IQ is associated with a one-fourth standard deviation increase in the logarithm of wages.

In contrast, Bowles and Nelson[11] find that childhood IQ and socioeconomic background are helpful predictors of income, but years of schooling add little to the accuracy of prediction. A one-standard deviation difference in IQ is associated with a 0.12- to 0.18-standard deviation difference in earnings, and a one-standard deviation difference in family background with a 0.24- to 0.41-standard deviation in earnings. Including years of schooling in the prediction equation has a negligible effect on the explanatory power of their regression.

Terman and Oden[12] reach a similar conclusion in their study of 1,500 individuals identified as gifted children forty years earlier. The average income for this group, all of whom had IQs in excess of 140, was well above that of the general population and of individuals with the same education and occupation. Moreover, the amount of formal education made little difference in earnings for this group. High-school graduates earned about as much as college graduates, and of the highest-paid six, only one had completed college.

According to Hartog, general academic ability commands a wage approximately three times that of general manual ability; a variable for "social ability" fell between these two in effect on wages. After controlling for a variety of variables including factors for both manual and social ability, a one-standard deviation increase in general academic ability is associated with an 0.57-standard deviation increase in earnings.[13]

In summary, the weight of evidence seems to show that both IQ and educational achievement correlate somewhat, perhaps as high as 0.3, with income. Graduation from college is associated with an earnings advantage of perhaps 40 to 50 percent, or 30 to 40 percent for persons of equal ability, as measured by IQ and family background. The difference in average income corresponding to a one-standard deviation difference in IQ is perhaps 10 to 30 percent, or 7 to 25 percent for those with equal schooling. Finally, it should be noted that although these income differences are significant, they seem to account for only a modest part of the existing inequality of income. In the United States, men in the highest paid fifth of the male population earn approximately five times as much as those in the lowest paid fifth, and the difference between the extremes is of course even greater. Most of the variation in income is not explainable with variables like academic ability, education, social background, or demographic variables.[14]

Occupational Status, Ability, and Education

The findings concerning the relationship between occupational status, academic ability, and educational achievement parallel those concerning income, except the correlations of the predictors with status are generally higher than those with income. Most of the studies report correlations and do not statistically resolve questions of independent causation, although they do provide useful clues.

The first problem obviously is how to measure such a slippery concept as "status." Usually it is assessed through ratings of the prestige of different occupations or, within professions, of different jobs. Tyler[15] produces evidence that occupational ratings are relatively stable over time. She reports that the correlation between the average ranking of twenty-five professions, by 450 high-school and college students in 1946 correlated highly ($R = 0.97$) with ratings of the same occupations by students in 1925. This correlation is between the average ranking of a large number of students; the correlations between rankings by individuals would be lower. Because of this consistency, scholars have been able to construct several standard scales of occupational status.

The general results found in the literature on the correlation of occupational status with academic ability and education are that ability and status correlate from 0.45 to 0.70. The correlation generally increases with the age of the person whose job is being rated. Among individuals with the same level of education, the correlation is about 0.15 or 0.20. The simple correlation between educational achievement and status is 0.6 to 0.7. For individuals with similar IQ it is nearly as high, 0.5 to 0.6.

For a sample of fathers and sons, Waller[16] analyzed IQ at age thirteen and later occupational status. He found the simple correlation between IQ and status to be 0.50. Controlling for education, the partial correlation was 0.21. Between fathers and sons, the correlation between IQ and status was 0.37. The correlations with education were somewhat higher: 0.72 between education and status, and 0.63 controlling for IQ.

In an extensive review of the literature, Jensen[17] finds IQ correlated with status about 0.5 to 0.6 for men aged eighteen to twenty-six, and about 0.7 for men over forty. He also cites results comparable to those of Waller cited above. In one major study, the simple correlation of IQ with status was 0.46, controlling for education, 0.15. The simple correlation between education and status was 0.63, controlling for IQ, 0.50.

Matarazzo's[18] review of the literature finds the correlation between IQ and level of occupational attainment to be around 0.50. In contrast, the correlation between IQ and actual success in one's job is only about 0.20.

Ball's[19] sample of 219 men measured occupational status for fourteen to nineteen years after taking the IQ test while in school. The simple correlations between status and IQ were 0.57 to 0.71. Those measured later in their careers had the higher correlations.

Several other studies support the general finding of a correlation between IQ and occupational status, but do not report correlation coefficients. Lewis[20] reports on 619 male liberal arts graduates of the University of Iowa from 1948–49, 1954–55, and 1959–60. Occupational level was classified into three levels. Among graduates with IQs in the top tenth of the sample, 24 percent held jobs in the highest status group, and 10 percent held jobs in the lowest status group. In contrast, among graduates with IQs below the median, only 9 percent held jobs in the highest status group, but 19 percent held the lowest status jobs.

Lewis's and several other studies are of particular interest because they concentrate on those toward the right tail of the distribution of academic ability. Thorndike and Hogen[21] studied a sample of 10,000 World War II Air Force cadets, all of whom were high-school graduates with IQs exceeding 105. Upon stratifying the group by postwar occupation at age thirty-three, Thorndike and Hogen found the average IQ of those in high status occupations—accountants, architects, engineers, lawyers, physicists, professors, scientists, treasurers, controllers, and writers—was 0.53 standard deviations above the mean of the group. The IQs of those in low-status occupations—bus and truck drivers, guards, miners, product assemblers, tractor and crane operators, railroad trainmen, and welders—averaged 0.54 standard deviation below the overall mean.

Coffman and Mahoney[22] studied the relationship between SAT scores and occupational status for 1,218 Phi Beta Kappa graduates of the Yale classes of 1931 through 1950. Their conclusion was that no important relationship existed. Terman and Oden[23] reported on a group of 1,500 adults who were identified as gifted children forty years earlier. All had IQs over 140; the average was 152. By the time they reached middle age, 85 percent were employed in high status occupations. The ten most popular occupations were lawyers, engineers, professors, managers of major businesses, financial executives, physicians, scientists, educational administrators, top business executives, and accountants, in that order. Only 3 percent were foremen or semiskilled or unskilled laborers.

Finally, several studies assess the relationship between college grades and occupational status. Spaeth[24] analyzed a large national survey of college graduates of the class of 1961. The graduates completed questionnaires every year from 1961 to 1964, and again in 1968. The best predictors of occupational status in 1968 (excluding career expectations reported in earlier years of the survey) were graduate school attendance, college grades, academic ability, and college quality in that order.

Munday and Davis[25] report the results of a study of self-reported "adult accomplishment" two years after college. They found no significant correlation between short-term accomplishment and college GPA.

Olsen[26] considered a sample of 1,072 leaders in business and education listed in *Who's Who.* High grades were not a prerequisite for eminence, but they were associated with higher probabilities of becoming eminent.

In an old 1917 study, Bevier[27] developed two lists, one of "eminent" and one of "highly successful," graduates of the Rutgers classes of 1862 through 1905. The classification was performed independently by four men with knowledge of the alumni, but not of their grades, on the basis of "reasonable judgment." Of the 1,326 male graduates, 54 were considered eminent and 480 highly successful. Analysis of college grades revealed that both lists were drawn disproportionately from the top of the classes. Of the eminent, 67 percent were graduated in the top third of their classes, 30 percent in the middle third, and 3 percent in the bottom third. Of the highly successful, 45 percent were graduated in the top third, 35 percent in the middle, and 20 percent in the bottom third.

To recapitulate, the literature generally shows status across occupations is substantially correlated with both academic ability and education. Simple correlations between education and status are generally slightly larger than between ability and status. The partial correlation of education and status, controlling for ability, is usually higher than the partial correlation of ability and status, controlling for education.

Income and Stature Within Professions

"Success," "performance," or "contribution within a profession" are obviously difficult to quantify. In this section I will first discuss some general results concerning professional performance, as opposed to status, then review specific results for law, business, engineering, medicine, and science.

A number of studies have examined the predictability of "success" in general, without reference to any particular profession. In an interesting study, Cox[28] examined a sample of 301 extremely eminent and creative people born between 1450 and 1850 (taken from Cattell's 1906 list of 1,000 famous men). People were removed from the sample if their eminence was not of their own making or available data on their childhoods were insufficient to estimate their IQs. The remaining 301 creative individuals included creative and scientific writers, statesmen and politicians, scientists, soldiers, religious leaders, philosophers, artists, and musicians. Using early childhood evidence, three psychologists estimated the IQ of each individual. Over half had IQs estimated to be greater than 140. They were generally found to be superior on all traits considered, but especially on persistence, depth of understanding, and originality.

MacKinnon and Hall[29] examined the relationship between creativity, as measured by peer ratings, and IQ for 185 architects, mathematicians, scientists, and engineers who were selected for being among those who had made the most creative contributions to their fields. Within this sample, rated creativity and IQ correlated by $R = 0.11$, but the sample included only individuals with high IQs. The mean was 131, the 98th percentile for the standard population.

Torrance[30] reported results of a study of fifty-one students identified as mathematically precocious, from a group of 185. Twelve years later, about half held university teaching or research positions, although only four were in mathematics or the physical sciences. In general, members of this select group had held more jobs, received more honors, and were rated as more inventive, creative, and original than their peers.

Chauncey and Hilton[31] cited seventeen studies that showed a relationship between either IQ or one or more ETS aptitude tests and various measures of performance, including grades, completion of degree program, faculty or supervisor ratings, or professional recognition and appearance in *Who's Who*. In a later article, however, Wallach[32] cites five studies showing no relation between GRE scores and peer ratings.

Ghiselli[33] reviewed the then-existing literature on the correlation between intelligence tests and job performance. He found the reported correlations to differ systematically with the type of job—presumably, he argued, with the "general intelligence" demands of the job. For managers, professionals, and electrical workers, most correlations ranged between 0.35 and 0.47; for supervisors, clerks, and assemblers, from 0.20 to 0.34; and for sales and service occupations, machinery workers, packers and wrappers, and repairmen, 0 to 0.19. In another work, Ghiselli[34] concluded that trainability is more readily predicted from intelligence tests than is actual job performance.

LAW

Carlson and Werts used scores on the Multistate Bar Exam as their measure of performance for 6,779 graduates of seventy-seven law schools. Bar exam scores correlated 0.31 to 0.33 with undergraduate grade point average, 0.51 with LSAT scores, and 0.55 with GPAs and LSATs combined. Law school GPA correlated about 0.6 with bar scores. After adjusting the data for unreliability of measurement:

The "true" correlation between MBE scores and the combination of LSAT, first-year law grades, and second-year law grades is .79. The addition of third-year law grades or undergraduate grades does not increase this correlation.[35]

Using the California State Bar Exam as the criterion, Watkins[36] found a slightly higher correlation between law school GPA and scores. The median correlation for graduates of five law schools was 0.67. Lind and Yarbrough[37] examined the proportion of University of Toledo Law School graduates passing the Ohio Bar Exam as a function of their law school grade point averages. Law school grades were a useful predictor of performance on the bar exam—about 94 percent of those with GPAs of 3.0 or better passed, while only 68 percent of those with GPAs between 2.0 and 2.2 passed.

Other studies have looked beyond the bar exam to assess performance. Baird[38] sampled 1,600 graduates of six law schools, from the classes of 1955, 1965, and 1970. Those who claimed to have been graduated in the top third of their classes more frequently worked for the bigger and more prestigious firms, had become partners or associates, and practiced corporate law. These graduates were less frequently solo practitioners or government employees, except as legislators or judges.

In a 1964 study, Smigel[39] examined twenty large New York firms, each with fifty or more partners. He found 71 percent of the partners were graduates of Harvard, Yale, or Columbia Law Schools. Members of these firms were disproportionately from the top of their respective classes; the top students in a class went disproportionately to New York firms, often after a short period as clerk to a judge. (Perhaps even more than the other studies, this result, of course, does not assess causation.)

At the Harvard Law School, Guttentag and Dewhirst studied the predictors of job placement among a stratified sample of graduates from 1971 to 1974.[40] After controlling for type of employment and geographical location, starting salary showed no statistically significant relationship to law school grades, race, marital status, or presence of financial aid. Both law school grades and membership in the Law Review predicted employment as a judicial clerk. Among students employed in law firms, those with higher grades received more job offers, other things equal. As one Harvard Law School official said, "Over 20,000 job interviews for just 540 graduates a year leaves a lot of room for all GPA-level students." None of the available measures except sex predicted who would take legal aid jobs.

Studies of performance as a lawyer have found that law school grades, LSAT scores, and, to a lesser extent, undergraduate grades are related to performance on the bar exam, and that those who do well in law school more often join and become partners in the large corporate firms.

BUSINESS

Two studies by Wise exhibit particularly strong methodology. For each he used a stratified sample of 976 white male college graduates employed by Ford Motor Company. Wise[41] examined salaries and the rate of salary increase. He found the best single predictor of salary to be years employed, which accounted for nearly half of the variance in salaries within his sample. Academic variables (college GPA, college selectivity, and whether the employee received a master's degree) and nonacademic variables (socioeconomic status, and indices of leadership, ability, need for job security, initial job and supervisor experience) were approximately equally useful for explaining the remaining variance. Academic variables alone accounted for an additional 19.6 percent of the variance in salaries, for 12.1 percent if nonacademic variables were used as well. Nonacademic variables alone explained 21.9 percent and 14.5 percent when academic variables are controlled for.

Differences in average rates of salary increased for employees with different academic attributes were significant in Wise's study. The average annual rate of salary increase for the sample was 4.5 percent. A one-point difference in GPA was associated with a difference in rate of increase of between 0.84 and 1.6 percent per year, depending on the selectivity of the employee's college. A difference in college selectivity from the lowest to the highest of Wise's six groups was associated with a 1 percent difference in annual rate of increase. Nearly all of this difference was concentrated at the high end of his selectivity index; the difference in average rates between the most selective and the second most selective categories was 0.8 percent.

Wise[42] also examined the frequency of promotion for the same sample of employees. He found a clear association between college GPA and probability of promotion. For graduates of the most selective colleges, the annual probabilities of promotion associated with GPAs of 3.5 to 4.0, 3.0 to 3.5, 2.5 to 3.0, and less than 2.5 were 0.526, 0.458, 0.420, and 0.383. College selectivity had a similar association. The average promotion probability for a graduate of one of the least selective colleges, with a GPA greater than 3.5, was only 0.329, lower than that for a low-GPA graduate of a highly selective college. These differences can be quite important over a period of years. For example, the probability of receiving six or more promotions in ten years is 0.45 for an employee with promotion rate 0.53; but only 0.11 for an employee whose rate is 0.36.

In a study of 352 MBAs from the University of Michigan and Cornell, Crooks and Campbell[43] found significant correlations between grades and scores on the Admission Test for Graduate Students in Business (ATGSB, now the GMAT), and graduates' salaries. Starting salaries, including bonuses and stock options, correlated 0.22 with business school GPA and 0.16 with the verbal part of the ATGSB. No correlation between beginning salary and the quantitative part of the ATGSB was found.

In a later monograph, Crooks and her colleagues were able to go further and analyze career success six years after graduating from business school. Fortunately, regression coefficients (standardized) are available in this pre-publication monograph. The regression results are summarized in table A2.1. For example, a one-standard-deviation increase in business school grades was associated with no gain in salary for staff people and a 0.11 standard deviation increase in salary for line managers, after controlling for test scores and college selectivity.[44]

Harrell[45] used a sample of 266 white male Stanford MBAs to develop a model to predict earnings five and ten years after business school. Pre-

TABLE A2.1

Regression Results on "Success" Six Years after Business School

	Salary and Salary Progress			
	Staff N = 266 R = .12 Standardized Regression Coefficients	Line Mgr N = 138 R = .21 Standardized Regression Coefficients	Specialist N = 72 R = .44 Standardized Regression Coefficients	Combination N = 198 R = .19 Standardized Regression Coefficients
ATGSB-V	.11	−.10	.40	.16
ATGSB-Q	.04	−.19	−.30	−.08
UGPA	.00	.11	.08	.05
CES index	−.05	.09	.41	.11
	Level and Type of Responsibility			
	Staff N = 266 R = .29 Standardized Regression Coefficients	Line Mgr N = 138 R = .31 Standardized Regression Coefficients	Specialist N = 72 R = .31 Standardized Regression Coefficients	Combination N = 198 R = .13 Standardized Regression Coefficients
ATGSB-V	.19	−.17	−.32	−.05
ATGSB-Q	−.27	.09	.09	.00
UGPA	−.10	.07	.03	.02
CES index	−.02	−.24	−.19	.14

NOTE: The ATGSB has been renamed the GMAT; V = Verbal, Q = Quantitative. UGPA is undergraduate grade-point average. CES refers to an index of the "excellence" of the person's undergraduate college. Combination refers to people who had jobs in more than one of the other categories. Regression weights greater than 0.08 "may be considered statistically significant."
SOURCE: Lois Crook, Joel T. Campbell, and Donald A. Rock, *Predicting Career Progress of Graduate Students in Management* (Princeton: Educational Testing Service, February 1979) p. 78.

dicted earnings, using personality tests, age, and ATGSB scores, correlated 0.38 with actual earnings. Using business school GPA as well raised the correlation to 0.45. Harrell's summary measure of personality characteristics was the best single predictor, but controlling for this measure GPA had a significant positive correlation with earnings. In a later article based on the same sample, the Harrells and their co-authors found that second-year GPA correlated 0.44 with earnings five years after graduation and 0.32 with earnings ten years after graduation.[46]

In contrast, Pfeffer[47] considered a sample of 215 MBAs and 156 bachelor's degree graduates in business from a large state school. He found that neither GPAs nor ATGSB scores were useful predictors of current or starting salary. Working more years, occupying a line rather than staff position, and higher socioeconomic status were all associated with higher salaries, although the effect of socioeconomic status was less important for the MBAs than for those with only bachelor's degrees.

Bisconti[48] studied the subset of a group first surveyed when they entered college in 1961 who eventually became business executives. She found that a high salary was associated with having a college-educated father, high-school GPA, and college selectivity, but not with field of college study.

Weinstein and Srinivasen[49] studied 136 graduates of the Carnegie-Mellon University Graduate School of Industrial Administration. GPA was significantly related to salary, adjusted for years of experience, and it was a more useful predictor for line managers ($R = 0.49$) than for staff ($R = 0.24$).

One of the earlier studies of executive salaries was by Bridgman.[50] His sample was of 1,310 American Telephone and Telegraph employees who had graduated from college in or prior to 1926, and who had spent at least half their careers with AT&T. Bridgman found that those employees who graduated in the top tenth of their classes earned 60 percent above the median of those with similar length of service with AT&T, while graduates from the lowest third of their classes earned 20 percent below the median. In a complementary study, Walters and Bray[51] sampled 10,000 AT&T employees who had graduated prior to 1950 and were employed by the company within five years of graduation. After controlling for length of service, geographic region, and company department, 45 percent of those who graduated in the top third of their classes earned salaries in the top third of the sample. In contrast, only 25 percent of graduates from the bottom third of their classes earned salaries in the top third.

Calhoon and Reddy[52] surveyed fifteen studies of GPA and business success. They reported four showing definite correlations, four showing weak correlations, and seven with no correlations at all. Of eight studies of extracurricular activities and business success, five show weak correlations and three show no correlation.

In business, then, the results are mixed. Most studies find a modest relationship between grades or test scores and salaries, but some find no such relationships. O'Leary's recent review estimates that in many studies the average correlation between business school grades and various criteria of success is 0.23.[53] The more sophisticated studies, however, such as those by Wise, show significant and practically important relationships.

ENGINEERING

Fewer studies of success in engineering are available than for law or business. A pair of reports by Muchinsky and Hoyt,[54] who analyzed the results of questionnaires completed by 127 graduates of the College of Engineering at Kansas State University who had at least five years of postgraduate employment, and by the engineers' supervisors, found that graduates who had received outstanding senior grades were more likely to be recognized as creative and to receive higher supervisor ratings, but they did not earn more, produce more or better work, or score better on other measures of success. Muchinsky and Hoyt found supervisor ratings were significantly related to scores on several psychological tests.

The Perruccis[55] also found no correlation between engineers' grades and salaries. But they did discover that both salaries and amount of responsibility were correlated with college selectivity, at least for the high-GPA students. A high level of education and high grades were associated with participation in many professional activities.

Among the older studies, Pierson[56] found that faculty ratings of occupational success correlated 0.43 with engineering GPA for a sample of 463 graduates and 337 dropouts from the University of Utah. Rice[57] found correlations of 0.16 to 0.46 between salary four to six years after graduation and GPA for three classes of mechanical and electrical engineering graduates of Pratt Institute. Of the six correlation coefficients, only two were statistically significant at conventional levels. The weighted average correlation was 0.27.

Walters[58] used professional eminence—defined as holding office in a professional society—as his measure of success. Of 392 eminent engineers, 189 (48 percent) were graduates of one of five schools (Columbia, Cornell, MIT, Lehigh, and Stevens Institute of Technology). These engineers were disproportionately from the top, but not the very top, of their classes—29 percent graduated in the top fifth, 36 percent in the second, 26 percent in the third, and only 9 percent in the bottom two-fifths. The eminent engineers who graduated from other schools were skewed toward the top of their classes: 66 percent from the top fifth, 17 percent from the second, 9 percent from the third, and 8 percent from the bottom two-fifths.

Studies of success in engineering show little relation of salaries to grades, but a number have found significant relationships between other measures of success and grades and college selectivity.

MEDICINE

The performance of physicians is as difficult to measure as that of any other profession considered here. The criteria which have been used are scores on professional qualifying exams and subjective ratings. In a methodologically superb study, Rolph, Williams, and Laniear[59] use scores on the National Board Exams as their criterion. They developed separate multiple regression equations to predict Board scores for 268 minority and 1,899 majority medical students at nine medical schools. They found minority students' scores could be predicted slightly more accurately than majority students' scores by using a different combination of predictor variables. MCAT scores and undergraduate GPAs are statistically significant. For majority students, the Science MCAT score and undergraduate GPA are by far most important. With many other variables held constant, a one-standard deviation difference in Science MCAT is associated with a 0.436 standard deviation difference on the Board exam, and a one-point difference in GPA (for example, 2.5 to 3.5) corresponds to a 0.354 standard deviation difference on the Board exam. College selectivity, although statistically significant, is less important—the predicted difference in Board score is only 0.288 standard deviations between the least and most selective colleges.

Bell considered the prediction of scores on a specialty certification exam, that of the American Board of Internal Medicine (ABIM).[60] In his sample of 438 graduates of nine medical schools, he found medical school class rank to be a significant predictor of ABIM scores. The correlation was 0.52. A one-standard deviation difference in class rank was associated with a 0.466 standard deviation difference in ABIM score, after controlling for school and MCAT scores. After controlling for class rank, only Science MCAT and undergraduate GPA were statistically significant predictors. MCATs and GPA alone correlated 0.38 with ABIM scores. Bell was particularly interested in differences in medical schools as related to ABIM scores. He found that, controlling for class rank, the average ABIM scores for graduates of the nine schools varied by as much as 0.55 standard deviations. After controlling for other measures of student ability (MCATs and GPA), however, these differences approached zero.

Richards, Taylor, and Price[61] used two measures of physicians' performance—subjectively quantified evaluations by hospital administrators and an objective measure of the quality of the hospital where employed. For their sample of 139 interns (all graduates of the University of Utah Medical School), they found undergraduate GPA correlated only 0.06 and 0.03 with the two criteria. But the correlations with third-year medical school GPA were 0.33 and 0.45, and grades for the first and second years correlated around 0.20 to 0.25 with the criteria.

Peterson[62] attempted to assess the performance of eighty-eight North Carolina general practitioners, aged twenty-eight to thirty-five, as it related to class rank in medical school. The performance measure was a subjective rating assigned by an intern after three days observing the physician. He found that those doctors who graduated in the top third of their classes received significantly higher ratings, but that there was no difference between those who graduated in the middle or bottom thirds.

Price, Richards, Taylor, and Jacobsen[63] studied physician performance using a number of criteria. Their sample included 102 full-time medical school faculty, 190 board-qualified specialists, 110 urban, and 105 rural general practitioners. They found no significant relationships between any of their performance measures and either undergraduate or medical school GPA. The authors[64] cite a number of studies showing that college grades have only a modest correlation with physician performance. Similarly, Wingard and Williamson[65] conclude that there is little or no correlation between physicians' academic and professional performance.

In medicine, there are reasonably strong correlations between grades and test scores and qualifying examination scores. The evidence on correlations between academic and actual professional performance, however, is mixed, but the majority of the literature finds at most weak correlations.

SCIENCE

The literature on predicting success in science is extensive. In *Fair Science: Women in the Scientific Community,* Cole concluded that IQ is mildly related to some forms of occupational success in science, even though much earlier research has shown scientists usually are at the right tail of academic ability. The IQ correlates with the quality of a graduate department and with later jobs. He found stronger correlations for women than for men. The correlations between IQ and job after eight and thirteen years were 0.19 and 0.11 for men, 0.30 and 0.31 for women. Cole also concludes that in his sample, "for men there seems to be some positive, albeit not very strong, relationship between native ability and scientific output."[66] The correlations between citation counts and IQ were about 0.20 for men and 0.10 for women. After controlling for measures of research performance and the quality of the university where the Ph.D. was received, a one-standard deviation increase in IQ within this sample was associated with about one-sixth of a standard deviation increase in "prestige of academic job."

A number of studies have attempted to measure contribution to scientific knowledge by number of publications or by counts of the number of times an author's publications are cited. Citation counts are assumed to reflect not only the quantity of an author's work, but its quality and importance as well. As Price writes in his classic *Little Science, Big Science,* "On the whole there is, whether we like it or not, a reasonably good correlation between the eminence of a scientist and his productivity of papers."[67] Cole and Cole found no significant relation between IQ and either number of papers or of citations ($R = 0.05$ and 0.06, respectively) for a sample of 499 physical, biological, and social scientists.[68] They did, however, find a significant correlation, 0.27, between IQ and prestige of the scientist's academic department.

Craeger[69] studied the relation of Graduate Record Exam scores to citation counts for seventy-three psychologists. He calculated correlations of -0.03, 0.23, and 0.33 for the Verbal, Quantitative and Advanced scores on the GRE.

Schrader examined the relationships between SAT and GRE scores and both citation and publication counts for a sample of 215 psychologists who received Ph.Ds in 1963–64. He found GRE scores correlated with citation counts ($r = 0.27$ with GRE-V, 0.31 with GRE-Q, and 0.41 with GRE-Achievement) and somewhat less with publication counts ($r = 0.18, 0.29$, and 0.32, respectively). Scores for SATs correlated less with his criterion measures. The group above 700 on the GRE quantitative and advanced tests were four times as cited and twice as published as the 500 to 690 group.[70]

Bayer and Folger[71] measured citation counts for 224 biochemists for whom they had IQ scores, but the correlation was insignificant ($R = -0.05$).

Harmon[72] studied a group of 355 mathematicians, physicists, chemists, engineers, and biologists who applied for Atomic Energy Commission fellowships. His criterion was based on both scientific and technical contributions and supervisor ratings. For the 219 who were awarded fellowships, GRE-Q and GRE-Advanced scores were statistically significant predictors of the criterion ($r = 0.21$ and 0.28). GRE-V was insignificant. For the 136 applicants who were not awarded fellowships, no significant correlations with GRE scores were found.

Taylor[73] reported the results of a number of studies. For a sample of sixty-six research physicists, he found significant correlations between undergraduate grades and supervisors' ratings of quantity of work (0.31), initiative (0.31), attitude (0.28), quality of work (0.26), and creativity

(0.29), for 103 physicists and electrical engineers. He also compared creativity ratings to scores on three psychological tests and found significant correlations of 0.29 for the Owens-Bennett Mechanical Comprehension Test, 0.24 for the Psychological Corporation Test of Productive Thinking, and 0.36 for the AIR Test for Selecting Research Personnel. None of these tests, however, correlated significantly with productivity ratings.

In a classic study of psychologists who received their Ph.D.s between 1940 and 1944, Clark[74] found that although 37 percent of all psychologists graduated in the top 5 percent of their college classes, 65 percent of those who made significant contributions graduated in the top 5 percent.

Taylor and Ellison[75] developed a predictor of scientific performance and creativity based on scientists' responses to questions about their backgrounds, experiences, opinions, attitudes, and self-images. Correlations between this predictor and several measures of performance and creativity were quite high, ranging between 0.4 and 0.7. High-school and college grades were useful predictors of creativity, although the best single predictors were measures of self-image and self-confidence.

Despite severe attenuation due to restriction of range, the majority of studies of success in science have found significant, modest relations between performance and tests and grades.

Notes

1. How Should Elites Be Chosen?

1. Russell A. Simpson, "Admissions at Harvard Law School," *Harvard Law School Alumni Bulletin* (Spring 1979): 23.

2. Alan M. Dershowitz and Laura Hanft, "Affirmative Action and the Harvard College Diversity-Discretion Model: Paradigm or Pretext?" *Cardozo Law Review* 1, no. 2 (Fall 1979): 384n.

3. Simpson, "Admissions at Harvard Law School."

4. Nathan Glazer, "The Schools of the Minor Professions," *Minerva* 12 (1974).

5. Calvin N. Mosley, "The Impact of the Merger of the Office of Admissions at Harvard and Radcliffe Colleges" (Ed.D. diss., Harvard Graduate School of Education, 1981) chap. 2.

6. "Report of the Admissions and Financial Aid Policy Subcommittee, December 6, 1976," mimeographed (Boston: Harvard Business School) p. 6.

7. Thomas F. Donlan and Gary J. Echternact, "A Feasibility Study of the SAT Performance of High-Ability Students from 1960 to 1974" (Valedictorian Study) (Prepared for the Advisory Panel on the SAT Score Decline, College Board and E.T.S., February 1977).

8. Rodney Hartnett and Robert Feldmesser, "College Admissions Testing and the Myth of Selectivity: Unresolved Questions and Needed Research," *AAHE Bulletin* 34 (March 1981).

9. A fascinating history is given in Lee J. Cronbach, "Five Decades of Public Controversy over Mental Testing," *American Psychologist* 30, no. 1 (1975).

10. Allan Nairn et al., *The Reign of ETS: The Corporation that Makes Up Minds* (Washington, D.C.: Ralph Nader, 1980); Warner V. Slack and Douglas Porter, "The Scholastic Aptitude Test: A Critical Appraisal," *Harvard Educational Review* 50, no. 2 (May 1980).

11. Gertrude Murray, "Marginal Notes to the 'Report of the Ad Hoc Committee on Admissions Policies and Procedures,'" *Harvard Medical Alumni Bulletin* (February 1980): 22.

2. How Admissions Works

1. "Report of the Admissions Review Committee," mimeographed (Cambridge: Harvard Medical School, 1975) p. 25.

2. Christopher Jencks and David Riesman, *The Academic Revolution* (Garden City, N.Y.: Doubleday, 1977) p. 254.

3. William Fitzsimmons, Memorandum from Harvard College for University-wide meeting on admissions, 10 June 1980, mimeographed, Harvard University, Cambridge, Mass.

4. Derek C. Bok, "On the Purpose of Undergraduate Education," *Daedalus* 103, no. 4 (Fall 1974).

5. Fred L. Glimp and Dean K. Whitla, "Admissions and Performance in the College: An Examination of Current Policy," *Harvard Alumni Bulletin* (11 January 1964): 306.

6. Dean K. Whitla, "A Study of College Admissions," in *Handbook of Measurement and Assessment in Behavioral Sciences,* ed. Dean K. Whitla (Reading, Mass.: Addison-Wesley, 1968) p. 472.

7. Chase N. Peterson *Harvard Alumni Bulletin* (7 April 1969): 20.

8. Wilbur Bender, *Final Report . . . 1952–1960* (Cambridge: Admissions and Scholarship Committee, Harvard College, 1960) pp. 22–23.

9. David Riesman, "Educational Reform at Harvard College: Meritocracy and Its Adversaries," in Seymour Martin Lipset and D. Riesman, *Education and Politics at Harvard* (New York: McGraw-Hill, 1975) pp. 306, 317n.

10. Bender, *Final Report,* pp. 26–34; Chase N. Peterson, *Report of Admissions and Scholarship Committee, 1967–68* (Cambridge: Harvard College) p. 14.

11. Bender, ibid., p. 38. See also Peterson, ibid., p. 15.

12. See, for example, Dean K. Whitla, "Candidate Overlap Studies and Other Admissions Research," in *College Admissions Policies for the 1970's,* Dean K. Whitla, ed. (New York: College Entrance Examination Board, 1968) pp. 161–62.

13. Penny Hollander Feldman, "Recruiting an Elite: Admission to Harvard College," (Ph.D. diss., Department of Government, Harvard University, 1975).

14. Bender, *Final Report,* pp. 31–32.

15. Chase N. Peterson, *Harvard Alumni Bulletin* (7 April 1969): 25–26.

16. Whitla, "A Study of College Admission."

17. Feldman, "Recruiting An Elite," p. 111.

18. Ibid. *See also* Appendix 1.

19. See the conclusions of Harold S. Wechsler, *The Qualified Student: A History of Selective College Admission in America* (New York: Wiley-Interscienes, 1977) pp. 298–99.

20. John K. Fairbank et al., "Report of the Task Force on the Composition of the Student Body", (March 1977), Harvard College, Cambridge, Mass.

21. Feldman, "Recruiting An Elite," pp. 82 83.

22. Memorandum from the Graduate School of Arts and Sciences for the University-wide meeting on admissions, 10 June 1980, p. 1.

23. Sidney Verba, Memorandum from the Department of Government for the University-wide meeting on admissions, 10 June 1980, p. 1.

24. R. Duncan Luce, Memorandum from the Department of Psychology and Social Relations for the University-wide meeting on admissions, 10 June 1980, p. 3.

25. Gwynne B. Evans, Memorandum from the Department of English to the University-wide meeting on admissions, 10 June 1980, p. 2, Harvard University, Cambridge, Mass. Professor Evans estimates the departmental cost of interviewing about 60 candidates as $6,500, including travel to various parts of the country.

26. Evans to Klitgaard, 1980.

27. Graduate School of Arts and Sciences, "(Preliminary) Admissions Report for Fall 1980," (Cambridge: Harvard University, n.d.) p. 1.

28. Memorandum from Graduate School of Arts and Sciences, p. 2.

29. *Harvard Law School, Official Register of Harvard University,* 8th ed. (Cambridge, 1979) p. 5.

30. Russell A. Simpson, "Admissions at Harvard Law School," *Harvard Law School Bulletin* (Spring 1979).

31. Ibid., p. 18.

32. Ibid., p. 27.

33. Ibid., p. 17.

34. "A variety of procedures could be used to select a diverse entering class. At one end of the scale an admissions committee might establish a fixed list of factors and decide for each factor how many students to enroll who demonstrate a sufficient measure of that factor. The Harvard Law School admissions process has been more like the other end of the scale where an overall goal of diversity is assumed and an *ad hoc* series of judgments are made based in part upon the available diversity within the population and partly upon some sense of the relative importance of the various diversity factors." Ibid., p. 23.

35. Ibid., p. 22.

36. Ibid., p. 19.

37. Ibid., pp. 19–20.

38. Simpson, "Admissions at Harvard Law School," is source of table 2.3.

39. Harvard Medical School, 1980 admissions brochure, (Cambridge, 1980) p. 1.

40. "Report of the Admissions Review Committee," mimeographed, (Cambridge: Harvard Medical School, 1975) p. 5. In a similar vein, a 1979 report observes, "We were unable to evaluate the relative weighting of the criteria used and perhaps these should be more explicitly stated." "Report of the Ad Hoc Committee on Admissions Policies and Procedures," *Harvard Medical Alumni Bulletin* (February 1980): 24.

41. Harvard Medical School, 1980 admissions brochure, p. 1.

42. "Report of the Ad Hoc Committee," p. 24.

43. From guidelines given in the late 1970s to interviewers for the Harvard Medical School.
44. This aim appears to be justified in part in terms of future careers and contributions: "If possible, this goal should be surpassed in recognition of the fact that these minority groups *in toto* represent a greater proportion of the U.S. population under twenty-five years of age as compared to the population at large. This lends additional obligation to increase the output of minority group physicians as rapidly as possible." Ibid., p. 8.
45. "Report of the Admissions Review Committee, 1975," pp. 6–7.
46. Ibid., pp. 9–10.
47. "Report of the Ad Hoc Committee," pp. 22–23. Reprinted by permission of the *Harvard Medical Alumni Bulletin*.
48. "Report of the Admissions and Financial Aid Policy Subcommittee, 6 December 1976," mimeographed (Cambridge: Harvard Graduate School of Business Administration) p. 6.
49. Ibid., p. 1.
50. Ibid., p. 12.
51. Ibid., pp. 6–7.
52. Ibid., Appendix 2, p. 14.
53. Ibid., p. 15. Recommendation adopted by the faculty in March 1970.
54. Minutes of the MBA Faculty Meeting, 9 December 1976, Harvard University, Cambridge, Mass., p. 3.
55. "Report of the Admissions and Financial Aid Policy Subcommittee," p. 2.
56. Ibid., pp. 8–9.
57. One black student told a 1976 faculty meeting that the second-tier process "placed a burden on a black person during the interview process by industry thinking there were two degrees—one black and one white." She asked that "this burden to becoming effective managers be relieved by this procedure being discontinued." Minutes of the M.B.A. Faculty Meeting, 9 December, 1976, p. 3.
58. "If the failure rate remains high for several years many faculty may begin to make individual adjustments in their evaluation of individual students. Such a grading practice would over time result in an inferior graduate of the School—in other words, a 'white' degree and a 'black' degree. The price of a two-degree system is particularly high to minority students, who would successfully complete the regular MBA curriculum." From a 1974 report cited in "Report of the Admissions and Financial Aid Policy Subcommittee," p. 8.
59. American Association of Collegiate Registrars and Admissions Offices and the College Board, *Undergraduate Admissions: The Realities of Institutional Policies, Practices, and Procedures* (New York: College Entrance Examination Board, 1980).
60. Table 2.4 is based on Warren W. Willingham and Hunter M. Breland, *Personal Qualities and College Admissions* (New York: College Entrance Examination Board, 1982).
61. R. L. Burns, *Graduate Admissions and Fellowship Selection Policies and Procedures, Parts I and II* (Princeton: Graduate Record Examination Board and Educational Testing Service, 1970).
62. Albert R. Turnbull, William S. McKee, and L. Thomas Galloway, "Law School Admissions: A Descriptive Study," in *Reports of LSAC Sponsored Research: Volume II, 1970–74* (Princeton: Law School Admissions Council, 1976) p. 319.
63. Walter F. Char et al., "Interviewing, Motivation, and Clinical Judgment," *Journal of Medical Education* 50, no. 2 (February 1975).
64. Warren W. Willingham et al., "The Status of Selective Admissions," in *Selective Admissions in Higher Education*, Carnegie Council on Policy Studies in Higher Education (San Francisco: Jossey-Bass, 1977), p. 120.
65. Gertrude Murray, "Marginal Notes to the 'Report of the Ad Hoc Committee on Admissions Policies and Procedures,'" *Harvard Medical Alumni Bulletin* (February 1980): 22.
66. H. J. Eysenck, *Psychology Is About People*, (Middlesex, England: Penguin, 1977) p. 172.

3. The Objectives of Selection

1. McGeorge Bundy, "An Overview: The Federal Government and the Major Research University, Indispensable Partnership for Excellence," in *Research Universities and the National Interest: A Report from Fifteen University Presidents* (New York: Ford Foundation, February 1978) pp. 16–17.

2. Kingman Brewster, "Admission to Yale: Objectives and Myths," *Yale Alumni Magazine* (October 1966): 31–2. Emphasis added.

3. Credentialing can be efficient, if it helps the labor market sort and allocate talent. It can also be inefficient, either by creating false and nonproductive barriers to powerful social positions or, in elaborate economic models, when students pursue an education in part to signal their underlying capabilities. Useful references are Randall Collins, *The Credential Society* (New York: Academic Press, 1979); and A. Michael Spence, *Market Signaling* (Cambridge: Harvard University Press, 1974). Some of these issues are examined in chapter 6.

4. David Riesman, "Educational Reform at Harvard College: Meritocracy and its Adversaries," in Seymour Martin Lipset and D. Reisman, *Education and Politics at Harvard* (New York: McGraw-Hill, 1975) pp. 281–84.

5. Faculty of Arts and Sciences, *Admission to Harvard College: A Report by the Special Committee on College Admission Policy* (Cambridge: Harvard University, February 1960) pp. 7–8.

6. Max Weber, "Wirtschaft und Gesellschaft" (1921), in *From Max Weber: Essays in Sociology,* Hans. H. Gerth and C. Wright Mills, eds. (New York: Oxford University Press, 1958) p. 243.

7. President Eliot also said, "As a people we have but a halting faith in special training for high professional employments . . . . The vulgar conceit that a Yankee can turn his hand to anything we insensibly carry into high places, where it is preposterous and criminal. We are accustomed to seeing men leap from farm or shop to court-room or pulpit, and we half believe that common men can safely use the seven-league boots of genius. What amount of knowledge and experience do we habitually demand of our lawgivers? What special training do we ordinarily think necessary for our diplomatists?" Quoted in Burton J. Bledstein, *The Culture of Professionalism: The Middle Class and the Development of Higher Education in America* (New York: W. W. Norton, 1976) p. 323.

8. Imagine there are two universities, H and Y, and two students, A and B. Both A and B will learn more at Y than at H, because Y is academically superior, but B will learn much more than A. At University H, B will learn a little more than A will. Call the amount learned ΔL:

$$\Delta L \text{ for } B \text{ at } Y = 10$$
$$\Delta L \text{ for } A \text{ at } Y = 7$$
$$\Delta L \text{ for } B \text{ at } H = 6$$
$$\Delta L \text{ for } A \text{ at } H = 5$$

Now suppose that because of outstanding nonacademic attributes, A will make more of each unit of L he adds than will B; the social utility of a one-unit change in L for student A is 3 and for student B, 2. How should we think about admissions?

If Y myopically acted as if H did not exist, Y would calculate as follows. "The social utility I add for A is 7 units of L times 3 equals 21. For B, it is 10 units of L times 2 equals 20. I should admit student A." But if H does exist and Y wants to maximize the social value added of its education, Y should take B. The utility added for A is now $(7-5) \times 3 = 6$. For B, the calculation is $(10-6) \times 2 = 8$. Admitting student B to Y has the higher social value added.

9. Seymour Martin Lipset, "Political Controversies at Harvard, 1936 to 1974," in S. M. Lipset and David Riesman, *Education and Politics at Harvard* (New York: McGraw-Hill, 1975) p. 150.

10. Karl A. Wittfogel, "Public Office in the Liao Dynasty and the Chinese Examination System," *Harvard Journal of Asiatic Studies* 10, no. 1 (June 1947): 28.

11. Most of the data came from Jonathan R. Cole, *Fair Science: Women in the Scientific Community* (New York: Free Press, 1979) chapters 3 and 4.

12. Winton F. Manning, unpublished memorandum, (Educational Testing Service, Princeton, May 1980).

13. E. Walster, T. A. Cleary, and M. M. Clifford, "The Effect of Race and Sex on College Admission," *Sociology of Education* 44, no. 2, (1971): 237–44.

14. John K. Folger, Helen S. Astin, and A. E. Buyer, *Human Resources and Higher Education* (New York: Russell Sage, 1970). See also J. Bernard, *The Academic Woman* (University Park, Pa.: Pennsylvania State University Press, 1964). Bernard writes: "However convincing individual cases of prejudiced discrimination are, it is difficult to prove its existence on a large or mass scale. The most talented women may be and, indeed, are victimized by it, but apparently not academic women *en masse*. At least the evidence from awards and from the

number of academic women in proportion to the qualified pool available is far from convincing." Quoted in Cole, *Fair Science,* p. 80.

15. The men and women in the sample were matched on the basis of year of doctorate, university where the Ph.D. was earned, field (biology, chemistry, psychology, and sociology), and specialty. It is interesting that Cole found no difference in publication rates during the first two years after gaining the Ph.D. Cole, *Fair Science,* chap. 3.

16. Ibid. There is one exception: other things equal, sex explains about 10 percent of the variance in academic rank.

17. These points are discussed at length in Jonathan R. and Stephen Cole, *Social Stratification in Science* (Chicago: University of Chicago Press, 1973).

18. Cole, *Fair Science,* p. 68.

19. David McClelland documents the finding that "scientists avoid interpersonal contact" and "scientists avoid and are disturbed by complex human emotions, perhaps particularly interpersonal aggression." Gerald Holton approvingly summarizes the work of Anne Roe that, as youths, natural and biological scientists "disliked social occasions" and avoided them "as much as possible," many had "quite specific and fairly strong feelings of personal isolation," and "were slow to develop socially and to go out with girls." The lack of early and continued attention to societal concerns is part of that general pattern, both of life history, of work, and of personality structure." Gerald Holton, *The Scientific Imagination: Case Studies* (Cambridge: Cambridge University Press, 1978) pp. 238, 241–43.

20. Lin Yutang, ed. and trans., *The Wisdom of Confucius* (New York: Modern Library, 1938) p. 204.

21. John Rawls, *A Theory of Justice* (Cambridge: Harvard University Press, Belknap Press 1971) p. 312.

22. Alan H. Goldman, *Justice and Reverse Discrimination* (Princeton: Princeton University Press, 1979) p. 171.

23. Ibid., pp. 165, 164.

24. Ibid., p. 35–48.

25. American Association of Collegiate Registrars and Admissions Officers and the College Board, *Undergraduate Admissions: The Realities of Institutional Policies, Practices, and Procedures* (New York: College Entrance Examination Board, 1980) Table 30.

26. For a fascinating general analysis of such externalities, see Thomas C. Schelling, "Hockey Helmets, Concealed Weapons, and Daylight Savings: A Study of Binary Choices with Externalities," *Journal of Conflict Resolution* 17, no. 3 (September 1973). A shorter, less technical version appears in Schelling's *Micromotives and Macrobehavior* (New York, W. W. Norton, 1978) chap. 7.

27. Harold S. Wechsler, *The Qualified Student: A History of Selective College Admission in America* (New York: Wiley-Intersciences, 1977) p. 148.

28. Cronbach to Klitgaard, 9 September 1980.

29. Riesman, "Educational Reform," p. 307n.

30. See, for example, Wechsler, *The Qualified Student;* and Alan M. Dershowitz and Laura Hanft, "Affirmative Action and the Harvard College Diversity-Discretion Model: Paradigm or Pretext?" *Cardozo Law Review* 1, no. 2 (Fall 1979).

31. Amanda Cross, *Death in a Tenured Position* (New York: Ballantine, 1982) p. 58.

32. Howard J. Savage et al., *American College Athletics,* Bulletin No. 23 (New York: Carnegie Foundation for the Advancement of Teaching, 1929) p. 254.

33. For a useful review with references, see Lee J. Cronbach, Elanna Yalow, and Gary Schaeffer, "Setting Cut Scores in Selection: A Mathematical Structure for Examining Policies," Project Report 79-A7, (Stanford University: Institute for Research on Educational Finance and Governance, School of Education, October 1979); and John E. Hunter and Frank L. Schmidt, "Fitting People to Jobs: Implication of Personnel Selection for National Productivity," in *Human Performance and Productivity,* E. A. Fleshman, ed., (Hillsdale, N.J.: L. Erlbaum Associates, 1982).

34. Riesman treats some of them, if anecdotally, in "Educational Reform," Dean Wilbur Bender includes some of the incentives on students, feeder schools, and alumni in his 1960 *Final Report . . . , 1952–1960* (Cambridge: Admissions and Scholarship Committee: Harvard College, 1960).

35. For example, India, Mexico, and Ecuador are widely believed to demonstrate this effect, where open admissions were followed by the deterioration of quality in secondary

schools. See, for example, Osvaldo Hurtado, *Political Power in Ecuador,* Nick D. Mills, Jr., trans. (Albuquerque: University of New Mexico Press, 1980) pp. 252–54.

36. A mostly positive account of the incentives created by Japan's system of admissions by competitive examinations is provided by Ezra F. Vogel, *Japan as Number One: Lessons for America* (Cambridge: Harvard University Press, 1979) pp. 163–67, 179.

37. Rebecca Der Simonian and Nan Laird, "Evaluating the Effectiveness of Coaching for SAT Exams: A Meta-Analysis," *Harvard Educational Review* 15 (1983) pp. 1–15.

38. In a recent study of Irish elementary schools, students' achievement test scores were apparently more susceptible than aptitude test scores to another "incentive effect," where because of scores students define themselves as "smart" or "dumb." Joseph J. Locascio, "Secondary Analysis of Major Societal Experiment: The Effects of Standardized Testing on Elementary Schools," *Evaluation Review* 8, no. 2 (April 1984).

39. This phenomenon depends on a binary reward (such as admit/reject) and a positive but imperfect correlation between student investment and the reward. The point is less important in educational systems like ours in the United States, where many levels of institutions exist and scholarships are sometimes a function of student investment; the reward structure facing a given student is no longer binary. There is a corollary to the phenomenon: If an admissions office is thought to be doing a good job when more candidates apply, the office may wish to have a mysterious admissions policy.

40. Wechsler, *The Qualified Student,* and Bledstein, *The Culture of Professionalism.*

41. Arthur Levine, quoted in "Scholastic Aptitude Test: Hints of Vulnerability," by Nina McCain, *The Boston Globe,* 12 December 1983.

42. See Robert Klitgaard, *Making Merit Work: Selection for Higher Education in Developing Countries,* chap. 6, in press.

43. Youssef M. Ibrahaim, "Iran's Holy City Teachers, Exports Revolution," *Wall Street Journal,* 12 April 1984.

44. Jan-Ingvar Löfstedt, *Chinese Educational Policy,* Atlantic Highlands, N.J.: Humanities Press, 1980) p. 126. The changing use of test scores and political criteria in China is examined in Klitgaard, *Making Merit Work,* chap. 2.

45. Jorge I. Dominguez, *Cuba: Order and Revolution* (Cambridge: Harvard University Press, Belknap Press, 1978) p. 396.

46. Joel Seligman with Lynne Bernabei, *The High Citadel: The Influence of Harvard Law School* (Boston: Houghton Mifflin, 1978) pp. 119–20.

47. "Report of the Ad Hoc Committee on Admissions Policies and Procedures," *Harvard Medical Alumni Bulletin* (February 1980).

48. Quoted from a Polish report, in Neil P. Eurich, *Systems of Higher Education in Twelve Countries: A Comparative View* (New York: Praeger, 1981) p. 83. Eurich also describes the elaborate socioeconomic and regional quotas used in admissions in Sweden and Germany.

49. Harvard President Derek Bok makes such arguments on behalf of preferential admissions for minorities, but rejects affirmative action for faculty members. Derek C. Bok, *Beyond the Ivory Tower* (Cambridge: Harvard University Press, 1982) chap. 4.

50. Klitgaard, *Making Merit Work,* chaps. 5 and 7.

51. Susan Rose-Ackerman, *Corruption: A Study in Political Economy,* (New York: Academic Press, 1978) p. 1.

4. Prediction and Selection

1. The former president of the Educational Testing Service, William Turnbull, made a similar point on numerous occasions. "In these circumstances," he wrote in 1968, "the day when a single entrance measure or an array of traditional academic measures was an adequate yardstick for all candidates has vanished forever, if indeed that day ever existed. The academic dimension is relevant to only a fraction of the tasks to be performed." William W. Turnbull, "Relevance in Testing," *Science* 160 (June 1968): 1426. See also his "On Educational Standards, Testing and the Aspirations of Minorities," (Paper delivered at Columbia University, 8 December 1974).

2. These remarks assume that data are normally distributed, which is approximately true for test scores, grades, logarithms of earnings, and several other measures. It may be a risky

assumption, however, within highly selected samples. The standard deviation is the square root of the variance, which is the average squared deviation from the mean:

$$\text{var} = \sigma^2 = \frac{(x_i - \mu)^2}{n}.$$

Some calculations use $n-1$ in the denominator, for technical purposes.

Figure 4.1 based on data in Leonard Ramist and Solomon Arbeiter, *Profiles, College-Bound Seniors* (New York: College Entrance Examination Board, 1984) p. 102.

3. Hunter M. Breland and Philip A. Griswold, *Group Comparisons for Basic Skills Measures,* College Board Report No. 81–6, (New York, College Entrance Examination Board) Table 5.

4. E. E. Ghiselli, *The Validity of Occupational Aptitude Tests* (New York: John Wiley, 1966) p. 125.

5. Christopher Jencks et al., *Who Gets Ahead? The Determinants of Economic Success in America* (New York: Basic Books, 1979) Table 4.1.

6. Lee J. Cronbach, *Essentials of Psychological Testing,* 2nd ed., (New York: Harper & Row, 1960) p. 349.

7. W. E. Coffman, "On the Validity of Essay Tests of Achievement," *Journal of Educational Measurement* 3, no. 2, (Summer 1966).

8. Judith A. Hall et al., "Profile of Nonverbal Sensitivity," in *Advances in Psychological Assessment,* vol. 4, Paul McReynolds, ed. (San Francisco: Jossey-Bass, 1978) p. 214.

9. Robert Klitgaard, "Beating the Spread," *Boston Observer* 2, no. 7 (September 1983). The correlation cited is for the 1978 season.

10. Jencks et al., *Who Gets Ahead?,* pp. 316–27.

11. Ibid., p. 57.

12. Ibid., Tables A2.13 and A2.14.

13. Robert L. Ebel, *Essentials of Educational Measurement,* (Englewood Cliffs, N.J.: Prentice-Hall, 1972).

14. Loren Spencer Barritt, "Note: The Consistency of First-Semester College Gradepoint Average," *Journal of Educational Measurement* 3, no. 2 (Fall 1966): 1262.

15. Roy D. Goldman and R. E. Slaughter, "Why College Grade Point Average Is Difficult to Predict," *Journal of Educational Psychology* 68 (1976): 14. David Riesman, in personal correspondence (Reisman to Klitgaard, May 1984), notes how Phi Beta Kappa students at Harvard College, in judging the merits of aspiring members, carefully "adjust" the grades earned depending on the difficulty of individual courses and of a candidate's overall courseload.

16. J. E. Singer, "The Use of Manipulative Strategies, Machiavellianism and Attractiveness," *Sociometry* 7 (1964); E. Caldwell and Rodney T. Hartnett, "Sex Bias in College Grading," *Journal of Education Measurement* 4, no. 3 (Fall 1967). David Riesman comments on "affirmative grading" and other sources of grade bias in chapter 3 of *On Higher Education* (San Francisco: Jossey-Bass, 1980).

17. Rodney T. Hartnett and Warren W. Willingham, *The Criterion Problem: What Measures of Success in Graduate Education?* GRE Board Research Monograph No. 77–4R (Princeton: Educational Testing Service, March 1979).

18. Table 4.1 is based on a survey of 650 colleges (448 responding) in Ohmer Milton and John W. Edgerly, *The Testing and Grading of Students* (New Rochelle, N.Y.: Change, 1976) p. 47.

19. Henry Chauncey and Thomas L. Hilton, "Are Aptitude Tests Valid for the Highly Able?" *Science* 148 (4 June 1967): 1299. Marshall K. Kirk has provided a table of rough equivalences among aptitude tests and intelligence tests:

Equipercentile Equation Table for Several Aptitude and Intelligence Tests, 140–190 IQ

Percent of U.S. Population Who Would Score Higher*	Childhood Stanford-Binet IQ Test	Deviation IQ Tests	SAT V+M	GREV	GREQ
0.0099	190	164	1563	830†	—
0.0042	180	159	1524	809†	—

(Continued)

Percent of U.S. Population Who Would Score Higher*	Childhood Stanford-Binet IQ Test	Deviation IQ Tests	SAT V+M	GREV	GREQ
0.021	170	153	1476	787	830†
0.086	160	147	1416	760	800
0.38	150	140	1343	672	718
1.17	140	134	1265	580	624

*Based on deviation IQ scores with average-100, std. dev. = 15.
†Based on extrapolation of raw scores.
SOURCE: Marshall Kirk, "Generic End-Testing of the Intellectually Brilliant at Early Maturity," A.B. thesis, Harvard College, 1980, pp. 43–44.

20. See Arthur R. Jensen, *Bias in Mental Testing* (New York: Free Press, 1980) p. 469.

21. Consider an example from sports. An incomplete measure of baseball hitting performance is the batting average. We may develop an excellent predictor of batting averages, and owners and managers of baseball teams might find our predictions useful. But they would certainly recognize that batting averages aren't everything, even in the domain of hitting, and until we had a more complete measure of "baseball hitting performance," we would be unable to tell how well our predictor of batting averages would perform.

22. For a discussion of adjustments for these effects, see Frederic M. Lord and Melvin R. Novick, *Statistical Theories of Mental Test Scores* (Reading, Mass.: Addison-Wesley, 1968) chap. 6.

23. It is inappropriate in this context to perform a similar correction on the unreliable predictor itself. We might be able with such a correction to appreciate the predictive power of some "underlying" trait or achievement that the predictor unreliably measures, and this may be of theoretical interest. But if the predictor cannot be made more reliable and is what we have to use, we want to assess its actual predictive power, with its unreliability included.

24. Dick Steinberg, Player Personnel Director of the New England Patriots, said "the acceptable level of speed" for a wide receiver is 4.5 or faster in the forty-yard dash on artificial turf. "We send our five scouts to every school in the country with a draftable player. If he's small or light, we still go if he has the speed. But if he can't run, we don't even look at him." Quoted in *Boston Globe,* 29 April 1984.

25. For example, if our highly selected sample has a standard deviation of the predictor that is half the size of the standard deviation in the broader sample we wish to consider, the correlation within our sample might have to be multiplied by more than one-and-one-half to estimate the correlation in the broader sample. Under restrictive assumptions, the adjustment formula is:

$$r = \frac{r^* \, (\sigma/\sigma^*)}{\sqrt{1 - r^{*2} + r^{*2}(\sigma^2/\sigma^2)}}$$

where r = the correlation in the larger sample, r^* = the correlation in the selected sample, σ = the standard deviation of the predictor in the larger sample, and σ^* = the standard deviation of the predictor in the selected sample. Thus if $\sigma/\sigma^* = 2$ and $r^* = 0.4, r = 0.66$.

More complicated ways of estimating the effects of restriction of range are actively under research. One involves pooling the results across universities, which differ in the academic qualifications of their students. For example, Donald B. Rubin, "Using Empirical Bayes Techniques in the Law School Validity Studies," *Journal of the American Statistical Association 75,* no. 372 (December 1980).

26. For a review, see Lord and Novick, *Statistical Theories,* pp. 140–48. They note the problems with the usual adjustment formulas for restriction of range when the selectivity is extreme: "The present writers feel that a more cautious attitude toward these formulas is called for in any applications in which the ratio of standard deviations in the unselected sample group to standard deviations in the selected group is more than 1.40. This condition corresponds to a selection of approximately the upper 70% from a standard normal popula-

tion. Unfortunately, in many applications the percentage selected is much lower than this and hence these applications of the theory should be questioned (pp. 147–48)."

27. If the "other variables" are ascertained judgmentally and not included in a prediction equation, multivariate predictive relationships would also suffer from omitted variable bias. I believe this is a common phenomenon in studies of selective universities, but not a particularly important one.

28. Another way of adjusting for selection bias is demonstrated in Charles F. Manski and David A. Wise, *College Choice in America* (Cambridge: Harvard University Press, 1983).

29. This is a biserial correlation, slightly different than the correlation coefficient used previously in this chapter.

30. These results and those in the paragraph following are derived from tables provided in H. C. Taylor and J. T. Russell, "The Relationship of Validity Coefficients to the Practical Effectiveness of Tests in Selection: Discussion and Tables" *Journal of Applied Psychology* 23 (1939).

31. These results are based on a table provided in C. W. Brown and E. E. Ghiselli, "Per Cent Increase in Proficiency Resulting from the Use of Selective Devices," *Journal of Applied Psychology* 37 (1953).

32. This leaves out the cost of the predictors. For many admissions variables, such as test scores, the information costs the university nothing. For a generalization, see Lee J. Cronbach and G. C. Gleser, *Psychological Tests and Personnel Decisions,* 2nd ed. (Urbana, Ill.: University of Illinois Press, 1965).

33. The report has been denounced by the testing establishment, but despite its too pessimistic interpretation of the predictive usefulness of tests, it is brilliantly written, replete with valuable references, and full of good questions about the proper role of tests and the Educational Testing Service. Allan Nairn et al., *The Reign of ETS: The Corporation that Makes up Minds* (Washington, D.C.: Ralph Nader, 1980).

34. As in the earlier example, I assumed that the correlations are calculated for the entire applicant pool. In practice, of course, the correlations are calculated within the sample of those already admitted. Thus to apply them to the broader population of the applicant pool, we should adjust the correlations for restriction of range, as outlined earlier. Suppose the standard deviations of college grades and test scores within the applicant pool are larger than the standard deviations among the admits, and after appropriate calculations, we obtained adjusted correlations. Suppose college grades now correlated 0.4 with passing at the law school and 0.5 with superb performance, and that using test scores raised these correlations to 0.65 and 0.75, respectively. Then the relevant table would become:

	Percentage Failing	Percentage Performing Superbly
Random selection	20	5
Admissions with college grades only	5	19
Admissions with college grades and test scores	1	32

35. A full treatment of regression analysis and the related techniques used in the next chapters exceeds the scope of this chapter. More details regrading the meaning of regression coefficients can be found in Frederick Mosteller and John W. Tukey, *Data Analysis and Regression* (Reading, Mass.: Addison-Wesley, 1977) among other texts. For an educational example stressing both the construction and interpretation of regression models, see Robert Klitgaard, Sadequa Dadabhoy, and Simin Litkouhi, "Regression Without a Model," *Policy Sciences* 13, no. 1 (1981).

36. T. Anne Cleary, "Test Bias: Prediction of Grades of Negro and White Students in Integrated Colleges," *Journal of Educational Measurement* 5, no. 2 (Summer 1968). Cleary's College 1 is omitted because high school grades were not available.

37. The standard deviation of black grades in College X is 0.69 and $0.48/0.69 = 0.70$.

38. Table 4.4 based on Cleary, "Test Bias."

39. Mancur Olson, "A Less Ideological Way of Deciding How Much Should Be Given to the Poor," *Daedalus* 112, no. 4 (Fall 1983).

40. James G. March *American Public School Administration: A Short Analysis,* Stanford University, mimeographed, 1977, p. 32.

41. John E. Hunter and Frank L. Schmidt, "Fitting People to Jobs: Implication of Personnel Selection for National Productivity, in *Human Performance and Productivity,* E.A. Fleshman, ed. (Hillsdale, N.J.: L. Erbaum Associates, 1982).

42. Robert Klitgaard, *Data Analysis for Development* (London and Karachi: Oxford University Press, 1985) chap. 7; and Klitgaard, *Making Merit Work: Selection for Higher Education in Developing Countries,* chaps. 4 and 7, in press.

43. On the construction of complicated utility functions, and usable proxies for those functions, see Robert Klitgaard, *Achievement Scores and Educational Objectives,* R–1217–NIE (Santa Monica, Calif.: Rand Corporation, 1974); and Robert Klitgaard, "Going Beyond the Mean in Educational Evaluation," *Public Policy* 23, no. 1 (1975).

44. Cronbach and Gleser, *Psychological Tests and Personnel Decisions;* and Edwin E. Chiselli, John P. Campbell, and Sheldon Zedeck, *Measurement Theory for the Behavioral Sciences* (San Francisco: W. H. Freeman, 1981) pp. 306–19. If information is free, the increase in utility per selectee ΔU from using a predictor X to forecast an outcome Y can be shown to be $\Delta U = r\,\sigma_y\,\phi/\pi$, where r is the adjusted correlation between X and Y, σ_y is the utility for a standard deviation increase in Y, and ϕ is the ordinate of the standard normal curve at the point on the X axis corresponding to the selection ratio π. This formula makes a number of restrictive assumptions.

5. Predicting Academic Performance

1. David G. Winter, David C. McClelland, and Abigail J. Stewart, *A New Case for the Liberal Arts* (San Francisco: Jossey-Bass, 1981) pp. 192–93, citing S. M. Huff, G. O. Klemp, Jr., and D. G. Winter, "The Definition and Measurement of Competence in Higher Education," in *The Assessment of Occupational Competence,* G. O. Klemp, Jr., ed. (Boston: McBer, 1980).

2. See Dean K. Whitla et al.; *"Value-Added: Measuring the Impact of Undergraduate Education,"* mimeographed (Cambridge: Office of Instructional Research and Evaluation, Harvard University, n.d.) especially chaps. I–IV and IX.

3. Winter, McClelland, and Stewart, *A New Case,* p. 206.

4. Frederic M. Lord and Melvin R. Novick, *Statistical Theories of Mental Test Scores* (Reading, Mass.: Addison-Wesley, 1968); Ronald K. Hambleton et al., "Developments in Latent Trait Theory: Models, Technical Issues, and Applications," *Review of Educational Research* 48, no. 4 (Fall 1978); Vernon W. Urry, "Tailored Testing: A Spectacular Success for Latent Trait Theory," Technical Study 77–2 (Washington, D.C.: United States Civil Service Commission, August 1977).

5. Frederic M. Lord, "An Analysis of the Verbal Scholastic Aptitude Test Using Birnbaum's Three-Parameter Logistic Model," *Educational and Psychological Measurement* 28, no. 4 (Winter 1968).

6. Marshall Kirk, "Generic End-Testing of the Intellectually Brilliant at Early Maturity," A. B thesis, Harvard College, 1980. reviews very difficult intelligence tests.

7. For reasons that go beyond the scope of this book, the right tail of academic aptitude may be even broader or longer than the tail of a normal distribution. The top 1 and 2 percent would therefore contain even more variation in ability. Greater variation in the predictor is, other things equal, associated with larger correlations with the criterion. See Kirk, "Generic End-Testing," and Arthur Jensen, "Genetic and Behavioral Effects of Nonrandom Mating," in *Human Variation: The Biopsychology of Age, Race, and Sex,* R. Travis Osborne, Clyde E. Noble, and Nathaniel Weyl, eds. (New York: Academic Press, 1978).

8. Hunter M. Breland, *Assessing Student Characteristics in Admissions to Higher Education: A Review of Procedures,* Research Monograph No. 9 (New York: The College Board, 1981) p. 34.

9. Robyn Dawes, "A Case Study of Graduate Admissions: Application of Three Principles of Human Decision Making," in *Statistics and Public Policy,* William B. Fairley and Frederick Mosteller, eds. (Reading, Mass.: Addison-Wesley, 1977); and Robyn Dawes and B. Corrigan, "Linear Models in Decision Making," *Psychological Bulletin* 81, no. 2 (Spring 1974).

10. Warren W. Willingham and Hunter M. Breland, *Personal Qualities and College Admissions* (New York: College Entrance Board Examination 1982) p. 161.

11. Both Willingham and Whitla are at work on research concerning the prediction of several sorts of longer-term academic outcomes. In personal communications, they have said that they believe biodata and certain other information may turn out to improve the prediction of several of those outcomes. At present, however, the evidence is not yet complete.

12. Certain demographic information is also helpful in predicting college grades. More on this in chapter 8.

13. Elisabeth Allison, "Educational Production Function for an Introductory Economics Course," Discussion Paper No. 545 (Cambridge: Harvard Institute of Economic Research, April 1977).

14. It is, of course, improper to extrapolate these results outside the actual range of the data observed in Allison's study. For example, presumably a student with zero hours of study per week would learn much less than an extrapolation would indicate.

15. For nine colleges with SAT V+M averages above 1,100, the average prediction equation is:

$$\text{Freshman GPA} = -0.17 + 0.0014 \text{ SAT V+M} + 0.41 \text{ HSGPA}$$

The R is 0.47 and the standard error of the estimate is 0.55. This equation is roughly equivalent to $-0.17 + 0.0014$ (PRED 300), where PRED 300 = SAT V+M + 300 (HSGPA). For students at these colleges, the average freshman GPA is 2.90 (std.dev. = 0.63), the average SAT V+M is 1,166, and the average HSGPA is 3.57.

16. See, for example, Frank L. Schmidt and John E. Hunter, "Development of a General Solution to the Problem of Validity Generalization," *Journal of Applied Psychology* 62 (1977): 529–40.

17. Derek de Solla Price, *Little Science, Big Science* (New York: Columbia University Press, 1963) pp. 59–61.

6. *Academic Performance and Later-Life Contributions*

1. Plato, *Republic*, Benjamin Jowett, trans. (New York: Random House, 1955) 503 b-d.

2. Friedrich Nietzsche, *Beyond Good and Evil*, Walter Kaufmann, trans. (New York: Vintage, 1966) §269.

3. Zvi Griliches, "Estimating the Returns to Schooling: Some Econometric Problems," *Econometrica* 45, no. 1 (January 1977): 1.

4. Douglas M. Windham, "The Benefits and Financing of American Higher Education: Theory, Research and Policy," No. 80–A19 (Stanford, Calif.: Institute for Research on Educational Finance and Governance, Stanford University, November 1980) pp. 5–6.

5. A. Michael Spence, *Market Signaling* (Cambridge: Harvard University Press, 1974), showed theoretically how non-optimal signaling equilibria can exist.

6. For subtler variants of this argument, see Samuel Bowles and Herbert Gintis, *Schooling in Capitalist America* (New York: Basic Books, 1976) especially chaps. 3–5; Randall Collins, *The Credential Society* (New York: Academic Press, 1979) chap. 2; Allan Nairn et al., *The Reign of ETS: The Corporation that Makes Up Minds* (Washington, D.C.: Ralph Nader, 1980) chap 3.

7. Spence to Klitgaard, June 1982.

8. Riley to Klitgaard, May 1982; see also John G. Riley, "Testing the Educational Screening Hypothesis," *Journal of Political Economy* 87, no. 5, (October 1979): S227–S252.

9. Joseph E. Stiglitz, "The Theory of 'Screening,' Education, and the Distribution of Income," *American Economic Review* 65, no. 3, (June 1975): 298. On the social productivity of educational screening, see especially pp. 287–90. "On the other hand, it should be emphasized, that whether there is 'too much' or 'too little' screening in a competitive economy depends on a number of assumptions concerning the screening technology, how well-informed individuals are concerning their own abilities, the nature of the production process, and whether screening is primarily hierarchical or 'job matching' " (p. 299). See also Kenneth Wolpin, "Education and Screening," *American Economic Review* 67, no. 5 (December 1977): 952–3.

10. Jencks to Klitgaard, June 1982.

11. Christopher Jencks et al, *Who Gets Ahead? The Determinants of Success in America* (New York: Basic Books, 1979) pp. 299–300. The more affluent of the two brothers is expected to earn

about twice as much as the less affluent. Christopher Jencks et al., *Inequality,* (New York: Basic Books, 1972) reaches the same qualitative conclusion.

12. Economists, though, often rely on such a measure. "Market transactions and competition among employers and employees will establish relative prices proportional to the different marginal productivities of different types of labor. . . . There are shortcomings to this view. But it is the only interpretation that makes a modicum of sense." Griliches, "Estimating the Returns," p. 2.

13. Jencks, *Who Gets Ahead?,* p. 297.

14. "Family background might explain anywhere from 15 to 35 percent of the variance in twenty-five- to sixty-four-year-old men's earnings. This means that 15 to 35 percent of a mature man's advantage or disadvantage in earnings typically derives from characteristics he shares with his brothers." Ibid., p. 217.

15. Ibid., p. 218.

16. Table 6.1 is based on Brian S. O'Leary, "College Grade Point Average as an Indicator of Occupational Success: An Update," PRR–80–23 (Washington, D.C.: GPO, Office of Personnel Management, August 1980).

17. David A. Wise, "Academic Achievement and Job Performance," *American Economic Review* 65, no. 3 (June 1975); and "Personal Attributes, Job Performance, and Probability of Promotion," *Econometrica* 43, nos. 5–6 (September-November 1975).

18. George W. Pierson, *The Education of American Leaders: Comparative Contributions of U.S. Colleges and Universities* (New York: Praeger, 1969) p. 244.

19. Ibid., p. xxiii.

20. Ibid., p. 251.

21. Ibid., p. 252.

22. Louis Bevier, "College Grades and Success in Life," *Education Review* 54 (1917): 33.

23. R. W. Husband, "What Do College Grades Predict?" *Fortune* (June 1957) pp. 157–58. Husband cited a study by John R. Tunis, which followed the Harvard College class of 1911 and discovered that those with higher scholastic ability had the highest earnings, athletes the lowest earnings.

24. Orley Ashenfelter and J. Mooney, "Graduate Education, Ability and Earnings," *Review of Economics and Statistics* 50, no. 1 (February 1968).

25. For example, L. M. Sharp, *Education and Employment: The Early Years of College Graduates* (Baltimore: Johns Hopkins Press, 1970).

26. See, for example, Robert Hauser and Thomas Daymont, "Schooling, Ability, and Earnings: Cross-Sectional Findings 8 to 14 Years After High School Graduation," *Sociology of Education* 50, no. 2, (July 1977). They found that effects of test scores on earnings were small after 8 years but rose rapidly in the next 6 years.

27. "The Relationship Between Scores on the Scholastic Aptitude Test and Certain Post-College Activities of Phi Beta Kappa Members of the Yale Classes of 1931–1950," Research Memorandum RM-67-18, (Princeton: College Entrance Examination Board, July 1967) p. 7.

28. Evrard Nicholson, "Success and Admission Criteria for Potentially Successful Risks," Brown University report, 1970, Educational Research Information Clearinghouse, #ED-041-534-1970.

29. Nicholson to Klitgaard, 1981.

30. R. M. Knapp, "The Man Who Led His Class in College and Others," *Harvard Graduate Magazine* 24, (1916): 597–600.

31. Dean K. Whitla et al., *Value-Added: Measuring the Impact of Undergraduate Education,* mimeographed (Cambridge: Office of Instructional Research and Evaluation, Harvard University, n.d.) p. VI–1. See especially chapters V–VII.

32. "The reader should be cautioned that these scales represent our best guesses about the conventional values of three professions: they do *not* purport to measure the 'true expertise' of the social contribution of respondents." Ibid., p. VI-18, emphasis in original.

33. Ibid., p. VI–22.

34. Ibid., p. VI–22 and 23.

35. Ibid., p. VI–26.

36. Ibid., p VI–37.

37. Ibid., p. VI–45.

38. Table 6.2 based on Ibid., p. VI–41.

39. Donald P. Hoyt, *The Relationship Between College Grades and Adult Achievement: A Review of the Literature,* (Iowa City: American College Testing Program, 1965) p. 1.

40. David C. McClelland, "Testing for Competence Rather Than for 'Intelligence,'" *American Psychologist* 28, no. 1, (January 1973).

41. McClelland to Klitgaard, 1980. Perhaps not coincidentally, the rough minimum for admission to the doctoral program in Professor McClelland's department is a combined GRE verbal plus quantitative score of 1,300; see chapter 2.

42. E. E. Ghiselli, *The Validity of Occupational Aptitude Tests* (New York: John Wiley, 1966).

7. Nonacademic Predictors of Later-Life Contributions

1. See, for example, A. R. Barro, "Survey and Evaluation of Approaches to Physician Performance Measurement," *Journal of Medical Education* 48, no. 11 (1973); Ramon J. Powell and Alfred B. Carlson, *Defining Competence in Legal Practice: Report of a National Survey of Solo and Small Firm Practitioners,* RB–78–3 (Princeton: Educational Testing Service, February 1978); Leonard L. Baird et al., "Defining Competence in Legal Practice: The Evaluation of Lawyers in Large Firms and Organizations," (draft of report for Educational Testing Service, Princeton, N.J., n.d.); Harry Levenson, "Criteria for Choosing Chief Executives," *Harvard Business Review* (July-August 1980).

2. On the nonacademic predictors of academic performance and extracurricular success in the university, see, for example, Robert C. Nichols, "Non-intellective Predictors of Achievement in College," *Educational and Psychological Measurement* 26, no. 4, (1966); Anne Anastasi et al., *The Validation of a Biographical Inventory as a Predictor of College Success* (New York: College Entrance Examination Board, 1960); Samuel Messick, "Personality Measurement and College Performance," *Proceedings of Invitational Conference on Testing Problems* (Princeton: Educational Testing Service, 1963); L. G. Rurer, "A Circuitous Route to Bootstrapping," in *Personality Measurement in Medical Education,* H. B. Haley et al., eds. (Washington D. C.: Association of American Medical Colleges, 1971). Warren Willingham of the Educational Testing Service and Dean K. Whitla of Harvard have very promising research underway on the prediction of various kinds of success in college.

3. Christopher Jencks et al., *Who Gets Ahead? The Determinants of Success in America,* (New York: Basic Books, 1979) chap. 5. Of course, personality measures may affect grades and cognitive tests scores; here we are assessing the extra predictive power gained when we add these personality varibles to the usual academic variables.

4. Ibid., p. 222. A slightly lower figure holds for earnings.

5. Ibid., p. 157. The authors discovered no interactions among personality variables, cognitive test scores, and family background.

6. Ibid., p. 216.

7. Joop Hartog, "Earnings and Capability Requirements," *Review of Economics and Statistics* 62, no. 2 (May 1980): 237.

8. For a recent review of the predictive power of biodata for academic and nonacademic success in the university, see Hunter M. Breland, *Assessing Student Characteristics in Admissions to Higher Education: A Review of Procedures,* Research Monograph No. 9 (New York: College Board, 1981) pp. 5–12.

9. Ibid., p. 54.

10. Professors Donald H. Brush and Lyle F. Schoenfeldt, Rensselaer Polytechnic Institute, School of Management, to Klitgaard, 1981.

11. Lyle F. Schoenfeldt, "Biodata for Management Selection," EIMT Research Report 6–80 (Paper presented at the conference "Biodata: An Alternative Selection Tool," Personnel Testing Council of Southern California, Los Angeles, May 28, 1980) p. 1.

12. Paul van Rijn, "Biographical Questionnaires and Scored Application Blanks in Personnel Selection," Personnel Research Report 80–31 (Washington, D.C.: U.S. Office of Personnel Management, GPO, December 1980) p. 12.

13. Paul van Rijn, "Self-Assessment for Personnel Examining: An Overview," Personnel Research Report 80–14 (Washington, D.C.: U.S Office of Personnel Management, GPO, June 1980).

14. See, for example, the reviews by E. C. Mayfield, "The Selection Interview: A Reevaluation of Published Research," *Personnel Psychology* 17, no. 2, (1964); Lynn Ulrich and Don Trumbo, "The Selection Interview Since 1949," *Psychological Bulletin* 63, no. 2, (February 1965); O. R. Wright, Jr., "Summary of Research on the Selection Interview Since 1964," *Personnel Psychology* 22, no. 4, (1969); Ronald Karren, "The Selection Interview: A Review of the

Literature," Personnel Research Report 80–14, (Washington, D.C.: U.S. Office of Personnel Management, GPO, August 1980); and Breland, *Assessing Student Characteristics,* pp. 18–23, 113–18.

15. Edgar Antsey, "A 30-Year Followup of the CSSB Procedure, with Lessons for the Future," *Journal of Occupational Psychology* 50, no. 2 (1977): 153.

16. This is a common phenomenon in the literature on interviews; for example, "No evidence was located in this review for the incremental value of interviews." Breland, *Assessing Student Characteristics,* p. 23.

17. Antsey continues: "This particular group of 'borderliners' at interviews must of course have obtained high marks in the written examination, or they would not have been successful in the Competition as a whole." "A 30-Year Followup," p. 155.

18. For a review, see Marvin D. Dunnette and Walter C. Borman, "Personnel Selection and Classification," reprint of a chapter in *Annual Review of Psychology,* vol. 30 (Palo Alto, Calif.: Annual Reviews, 1979) pp. 25–29.

19. Marvin D. Dunnette, "Personnel Management," *Annual Review of Psychology,* vol. 13, (Palo Alto, Calif.: Annual Reviews, 1962) pp. 291–92.

20. "Perhaps Kelly, after deploring the lack of reliability and validity evidence for the interview, best explained the reason for the interview's acceptability in noting 'all evidence suggests that it gives a great deal of satisfaction to the persons who use it'." Breland, *Assessing Student Characteristics,* p. 23.

21. David Riesman describes some circumstances in which he finds interviews to be helpful:

> I insist on getting transcripts and look at the pattern of courses taken, watching especially for non-required courses in difficult quantitative areas, and cumulative courses, i.e, not taking simply introductory courses. . . . I can look at transcripts from a fair number of colleges with some understanding of what they mean, partly because I know the test scores and general academic level of the institutions in question. I look very closely at essays, watching for overstatement and grandiosity, yet being generous at times out of realization these are young people without experience—in the case of post baccalaureate applications—of how long it takes to accomplish things. If I have done this kind of background work, then I find an interview helpful; I decide ahead of time how to use the essay to raise questions in the interview, to see the degree of openness to learning versus dogmatism, ideological fanticism . . . , flexibility as distinguished from desire to please the interviewer, presence and effectiveness in oral exchange, general breadth of ideas and curiosity, etc."

He points out that "so much work is involved" in such a careful process that one "could not process many cases this way." Riesman to Klitgaard, 16 March, 1982.

22. J. A. Thomas, cited in Breland, *Assessing Student Characteristics,* pp. 13–14.

23. R. C. Browning, "Validity of Reference Ratings from Previous Employers," *Personnel Psychology* 21, no. 3, (1968).

24. J. M. Cuca et al., *The Medical School Admissions Process: A Review of the Literature, 1955–1976* (Washington, D.C.: Association of American Medical Colleges, 1976).

25. "Sounding Board: Fantasy Land," a series of letters to the editors of *New England Journal of Medicine* 308, no. 11 (17 March, 1983): 651–53; and responses in vol. 309, no. 12 (22 September 1983) 735–37.

26. Nicholson to Klitgaard, 1981.

27. Richard A. Lilienthal, "The Use of Reference Checks in Selection," Personnel Research Report 80–12 (Washington, D.C.: U.S. Office of Personnel Management, GPO, May 1980) p. 4. Lilienthal concludes that references therefore have "poor validity."

28. Breland, *Assessing Student Characteristics,* p. 17.

29. P. Wells, cited in Ibid., p. 13.

30. E. A. Kracke, Jr., *Civil Service in Early Sung China, 940–1067, with Particular Emphasis on the Development of Controlled Sponsorship to Foster Administrative Responsibility* (Cambridge: Harvard University Press, 1953) p. 195.

31. Robert Henley Woody, ed., *Encyclopedia of Clinical Assessment,* 2 vols. (San Francisco: Jossey-Bass, 1980).

32. James C. Crumbaugh, "Graphoanalytic Clues," in *Encyclopedia of Clinical Assessment,* vol. 2, p. 922. The author goes on to discuss uses of handwriting analysis in predicting which students will have difficulty in school.

33. Ibid., pp. 922–23.

34. David Rapaport, Merton W. Gill, and Roy Schafer, *Diagnostic Psychological Testing,* rev. ed., Robert R. Holt, ed., (New York: International Universities Press, 1968); Paul McReynolds, ed., *Advances in Psychological Measurement,* vol. 4, (San Francisco: Jossey-Bass, 1978).

35. Herman A. Witkin et al., *A Longitudinal Study of the Role of Cognitive Styles in Academic Evolution During the College Years,* GRE Board Research Report BREB No. 76–10R, (Princeton: Educational Testing Service, February 1977) p. 4.

36. Ibid., p. 5.

37. James L. McKinney and Peter G. W. Keen, "How Managers' Minds Work," *Harvard Business Review* (May–June 1974).

38. Kenneth M. Goldstein and Sheldon Blackman, "Assessment of Cognitive Style," in McReynolds, in *Psychological Measurement,* p. 498.

39. See, for example, Norman Fredericksen and William C. Ward, *Development of Measures for the Study of Creativity,* GREB and Professional Report GREB No. 72–2P (Princeton: Educational Testing Service, June 1975); and Lloyd D. Noppe, "Creative Training," in Woody, *Encyclopedia,* chap. 58.

40. William C. Ward and Norman Fredericksen, *A Study of the Predictive Validity of the Tests of Scientific Thinking* (Princeton: Educational Testing Service, 1977).

41. Howard Gardner, *Frames of Mind: The Theory of Multiple Intelligences* (New York: Basic Books, 1983) p. 385.

42. Ibid., pp. 389–90.

43. Ibid., p. 392

44. David McClelland, "Testing for Competence Rather than for 'Intelligence,' " *American Psychologist 28,* no. 1 (January 1973): 12. Emphasis in original.

45. Crooks to Klitgaard, June 1981.

46. Robert Rosenthal to Klitgaard, May 1982.

47. Moreover, "there is considerable evidence to suggest that prior experience in taking the PONS serves to improve subsequent performance. For eight samples that were tested twice, the average increase in performance from first to second testing was very large (1.79σ)." Robert Rosenthal et al., "The PONS Test: Measuring Sensitivity to Nonverbal Cues," in *Nonverbal Communication: Readings with Commentary,* 2nd ed., Shirley Weitz, ed. (New York: Oxford University Press, 1979) p. 367.

48. We should probably worry less about coaching if it takes either a very little or a great deal of it, to raise scores. If it takes only a little coaching, one could imagine circumstances where all those taking the test would be given this small amount and, as a result, the test's reliability and validity might not suffer. If it takes a great deal of coaching—say, three months of intensive study—then the coaching starts to look like training or educating, and it may actually improve the skill we value. But if, say, a couple of weeks of coaching can artificially inflate or distort a score when not everyone has access to the coaching, then the test will present severe problems as a criteria for selection.

My review of the literature on the coachability of SAT and related cognitive tests leads me to believe that coaching of the two-week variety may have an average effect of 10 to 30 points on verbal or math scores, or perhaps one-fourth of a standard deviation. See especially Rebecca Der Simonian and Nan M. Laird, "Evaluating the Effect of Coaching on SAT Scores: A Meta-analysis," *Harvard Educational Review* 15 (1983): 1–15.

49. Donald P. Campbell, *Handbook for the Strong Vocational Interest Blank,* (Stanford, Calif.: Stanford University Press, 1971). Campbell was one of the designers of the revised SVIB.

50. Ibid., p. 14.

51. Ibid., p. 23.

52. Nancy Badore, interview with author, 20 June 1981.

53. The particular contexts of the problems tackled in these simulations are related to the future job. This is primarily for motivational purposes; there is no firm evidence that such contexts affect what is learned about the candidate. For example, Foreign Service candidates deal with simulated problems in the context of consular affairs. The assessment center for the Presidential Management Intern Program has candidates design a new agency and deal with personnel problems. At Sears, potential managers had to deal with the problems of a store in trouble; for Anheuser-Busch line supervisors and area foremen, a scheduling exercise was used. (This information comes from interviews with personnel within these organizations.)

54. Stephen A. Williamson and Mary Lou Schaalman, *The Assessment of Occupational Compe-*

tence. 2. Assessment Centers: Theory, Practice, and Implications for Education (Boston: McBer, 1980) Table 12.

55. Berkeley Rice, "From the OSS with Love: The Rise of a Testing Method," *Psychology Today* (December 1978).

56. Lois A. Crooks, "The Selection and Development of Performance Measures for Assessment Center Programs," in *Applying the Assessment Center Method,* Joseph L. Moses and William C. Byham, eds. (Elmhurst, New York: Pergamon Press, 1977) chapter 5. Reprinted with permission from Pergamon Press.

57. Author's interviews with Sheppeck, 16 July 1981; Pitlari, 17 July 1981; and Tokar 15 July 1981. See also Dale R. Baker and Charles G. Martin, "Evaluation of the Federal Executive Department Program Assessment Center," Technical Memorandum 74–4, (Washington, D.C.: U.S. Civil Service Commission, GPO, September 1974) p. 22: "In general, [candidates] were impressed with the entire assessment center process. They considered the assessment center process to be the most objective executive/management evaluation that they personally had experienced in the Federal government."

58. In addition to the studies cited later in this paragraph, see Marvin D. Dunnette's useful "The Assessment of Managerial Talent," in *Advances in Psychological Assessment: II,* P. McReynolds, ed. (Palo Alto, Calif.: Science Behavior Books, 1971) pp. 79–100.

59. Anthony J. Mento, "A Review of Assessment Center Research," Personnel Research Report 80–10 (Washington, D.C.: Office of Personnel Management, GPO, May 1980). Emphasis in original.

60. Barry M. Cohen, Joseph L. Moses, and William C. Byham, *The Validity of Assessment Centers: A Literature Review,* Monograph II (Pittsburgh: Development Dimensions, rev. 1977) p. 20.

61. "Research on reliability demonstrates a fair degree of reliability in measurement from the assessment center process, though in many cases there is a considerable variation among dimensions (suggesting the need for redesign)." Williamson and Schaalman, *Occupational Competence,* pp. 2.220–2.221.

62. J. R. Hinrichs and S. Haanpera, "Reliability of Measurement in Situational Exercises: An Assessment of the Assessment Center Method," *Personnel Psychology* 29, no. 1, (1976).

63. Douglas W. Bray et al., *Formative Years in Business: A Long-Term AT&T Study of Managerial Lives* (New York: John Wiley & Sons, 1974).

64. Notice that this is not the restriction of range problem discussed in chapter 4. There we considered the use of a predictor in selection where lower scorers were disproportionately not admitted and where performance ratings such as grades were not contaminated by the predictor (teachers do not generally know about their students' test scores, for example). Here the low scorers are not fired, so there is no restriction of range. But the later success measures may be affected by decisions based on the predictor and not just observed on performance.

65. Richard J. Klimoski and William J. Strickland, "Assessing Assessment Centers: A Comparative Approach," Ohio State University, unpublished paper, 1979.

66. Table 7.2 based on ibid., p. 23

67. Mento, "A Review of Assessment Center Research," p. 8.

68. Alverno College, Nova University, Colorado State University, Kalamazoo College, Mission College, and Pace University.

69. Alverno College and Brigham Young University's Graduate School of Management.

70. Colorado State University, Kalamazoo College, and Mission College.

71. Nova University and the University of Phoenix.

72. Kalamazoo College.

73. Badore, interview with author, 20 June 1981.

74. "This problem was highlighted when a divisional vice-president unfamiliar with his company's assessment center outlined in detail one of the exercises and the appropriate action to be taken to the assessment center director. In such a situation, uncontrollable bias in introduced into the performance of candidates and, indeed, the credibility of the entire process is jeopardized." Donald H. Brush and Lyle F. Schoenfeldt, "Identifying Managerial Potential: An Alternative to Assessment Centers," *Personnel* 57, no. 3 (May–June 1980): 71.

75. Reuben Fine, *The World's Great Chess Games* (New York: Crown, 1951) p. 287.

76. Eugene S. Wilson, Quoted in Edward B. Wall, *How We Do It: Student Selection at the Nation's Most Prestigious Colleges* (Alexandria, Va.: Octameron Associates, 1981) p. 4.

8. The Representation of Groups

1. American Association of Collegiate Registrars and Admission Offices and the College Board, *Undergraduate Admissions: The Realities of Institutional Policies* (New York: College Entrance Examination Board).

2. Penny Hollander Feldman, "Recruiting an Elite: Admission to Harvard College," (Ph. D. diss., Department of Government, Harvard University, 1975) pp. 126, 176.

3. Albert P. Williams, Wendy D. Cooper, and Carolyn L. Lee, *Factors Affecting Medical School Admissions Decisions for Minority and Majority Applicants: A Comparative Study of Ten Schools*, R–2030–HEW (Santa Monica: Rand Corporation, December 1979) p. x.

4. Ibid.

Average MCAT Scores (1975–76)

	Verbal	Quantitative	General	Science
Blacks				
accepted	479	515	466	500
rejected	411	429	419	391
Chicanos				
accepted	508	554	493	542
rejected	458	482	467	455
Whites				
accepted	584	629	559	627
rejected	533	573	523	552

MCAT scores have been rescaled. Instead of the old scale with avg. = 500, std. dev. = 100, the MCAT Science scores now have avg. = 8.0, std. dev. = 2.52 (based on April 1977 national data). Roughly, the following equivalences hold:

Old MCAT Science Score	New MCAT Science Score
400	5.5
500	8.0
600	10.5
700	13.0

5. The conclusion is not that only 18 percent of blacks would have attended law school with race-blind admissions. Without reverse discrimination, many of them would have been accepted at less selective law schools than those they ended up attending. See Franklin R. Evans, "Applications and Admissions to ABA Accredited Law Schools: An Analysis of National Data for the Class Entering in the Fall of 1976," in *Reports of LSCA Sponsored Research: Volume III, 1975–1977* (Princeton: Law School Admissions Council, 1977) p. 632.

6. Robert Klitgaard, *Making Merit Work: Selection for Higher Education in Developing Countries*, chap. 7, in press.

7. Ibid., chap. 5.

8. Allan Nairn et al., *The Reign of ETS: The Corporation that Makes Up Minds* (Washington, D.C.: Ralph Nader, 1980) p. 120.

9. David M. White, "Culturally Biased Testing and Predictive Invalidity: Putting Them on the Record," *Harvard Civil Right-Civil Liberties Law Review* 14 (1979): 127.

10. Ibid., p. 130.

11. Ibid., pp. 123, 131. Emphasis in original.

12. Evans, "Applications and Admissions," p. 604.

13. Ibid., p. 603.

14. Hilda Wong, "Profiles of Cognitive Abilities of Different Racial/Ethnic and Sex Groups on a Multiple Abilities Test Battery," *Journal of Applied Psychology* 5, no. 3 (1980): 289–98; M. E. Backman, "Patterns of Mental Abilities: Ethnic, Socioeconomic, and Sex Differences," *American Educational Research Journal* 9 (1972): 1–12; Arthur R. Jensen, "The Nature of the Black-White Difference on Various Psychometric Tests: Spearman's Hypothesis, in *The Behavioral and Brain Sciences,* forthcoming.

15. In 1978–79, 52 of 3,721 black candidates scored at or above the 600 LSAT with 3.25 college GPA threshold, compared to 13,518 of 42,709 white candidates. Franklin R. Evans, "Replication of Bakke Statistics," (13 March 1980), memorandum, Law School Admissions Council, p. 16.

16. Leonard Ramist and Solomon Arbeiter, *Profiles, College-Bound Seniors* (New York: College Entrance Examination Board, 1984). The standard deviations were: women's SATV = 110, SATM = 109; men's SATV = 110, SATM = 119.

17. Ibid. Despite a number of studies that show black women outscoring black men on aptitude tests, black men do better on the SATs. Their averages were SATV = 341 and SATM = 381, compared to the women's SATV = 327 and SATM = 350.

18. White, "Culturally Biased Testing," p. 122.

19. Arthur R. Jensen, *Bias in Mental Testing* (New York: Free Press, 1980); Lewis W. Pike, *Short-term Instruction, Testwiseness, and the Scholastic Aptitude Test: A Literature Review with Research Recommendations* (New York: College Entrance Examination Board, 1979); L. T. Sinott, *Differences in Item Performance Across Groups,* Research Report #80-19 (Princeton: Educational Testing Service, 1980); Rebecca der Simonian and Nan Laird, "Evaluating the Effects of Coaching on SAT scores: A Meta-Analysis," *Harvard Educational Review* 53 (1983): 1–15.

20. For example, using the mean equations, the expected law school grades for a student with a 650/3.5 are 44.82 for a black and 50.40 for a white, a difference of 5.58 or about 0.56σ.

21. For the black, $(3.0 \times 6.73) + (520 \times 0.044) = 43.97$; for the white, $(3.5 \times 6.84) + (664 \times 0.046) = 54.48$. The difference is 11.41, or about 1.1 standard deviations. Using common slopes (of 6.78 and 0.045), the difference would be $53.61 = 43.74 = 9.87$, or about 0.99 standard deviations.

22. Figure 8.2 is based on my reanalysis of data in Donald E. Powers, "Comparing Predictions of Law School Performance for Black, Chicano, and White Law Students," Report LSAC–77–3 in *Reports of LSAC Sponsored Research Volume III* (Princeton: Law School Admission Council, 1977).

I computed mean prediction equations for blacks and whites at the ten law schools. A one hundred-point increase in LSAT (on the old scale) corresponded to about an 0.45-standard-deviation increase in first-year law school grades, after holding college grade-point average constant—whether a student was black or white.

The equations were as follows:

Blacks: First-year grades = 7.34 + 6.73 CGPA + 0.044 LSAT; R = 0.37
Whites: First-year grades = 3.44 + 6.84 CGPA + 0.046 LSAT; R = 0.31

The regressions coefficients were not significantly different across groups, but the intercepts were.

This finding holds throughout research on prediction equations. In Powers' 29 law schools, for example, there were statistically significant differences in intercepts in 21 cases, in slopes zero times, and in standard errors of estimate 10 times (with blacks having the larger standard error 4 times). More generally, see Robert Linn, "Ability Testing: Individual Differences, Prediction and Differential Prediction," in *Ability Testing: Uses, Consequences, and Controversies,* vol. 2 (Washington, D.C.: National Academy Press, 1982).

Powers transformed law school grades so they had a mean of 50 and a standard deviation (σ) of 10. So, a 100-point LSAT increase corresponds to about a $0.045 \times 100 = 4.5$ increase in first-year law school grades, which is 0.45σ.

23. The difference was $51.5 - 35.9 = 15.6$, or 1.56σ using the overall σ of 10. But the standard deviation among blacks was 9; this was also the standard deviation among whites. Thus, the difference was $15.6/9 = 1.73$ within-group standard deviations.

24. These calculations are based on the regression equations reported above.

25. *Medical College Admissions Tests*
(Old Scale)

	Verbal		General Informa- tion		Quanti- tative		Science		College GPA		National Board Scores			
											Part I		Part II	
	μ	σ	μ	σ	μ	σ	μ	σ	μ	σ	μ	σ	μ	σ
Whites	580	79	571	72	634	70	586	67	3.39	0.34	509	87	498	91
Minorities	523	97	501	87	586	106	533	88	3.14	0.48	434	101	424	96

NOTE: Average = μ; standard deviation = σ. Based on 1,568 students from the class of 1975–76 at nine medical schools who took Part II of the National Boards. John Rolph, Albert Williams, and A. Lee Lanier, *Predicting Minority and Majority Medical Student Performance on the National Board Exams,* Report No. R–2039–HEW (Santa Monica, Calif.: Rand Corporation, November 1978).

26. This calculation is based on the combined standard deviation of about 100. Within-group standard deviations were usually smaller, averaging 94; based on those figures, the differences would be larger.

27. The minority group regression coefficients for the four MCAT subtests were:

	Verbal	General Information	Quantitative	Science
National Boards, Part I	0.110	0.062	0.202	0.269
National Boards, Part II	0.261	0.085	0.111	0.194

If you subtracted 50 points from each subtest score—about 1¼ points on the new MCAT scale—the predicted performance on both parts of the National Boards would drop by about 32 points, and this is about the extent of the overprediction of minorities compared to the majority group.

28. Studies usually show that, for blacks, test scores are better than high-school grades as a predictor of college grades. In particular, "High school GPA is a consistently poor predictor for black males." Albert S. Farver, William E. Sedlacek, and Glenwood C. Brooks, Jr., "Longitudinal Predictions of University Grades for Blacks and Whites," *Measurement and Evaluation in Guidance* 7, no. 4 (January 1975): 246.

29. See Robert Linn, "Ability Testing."

30. The calculation is based on equations in appendix 1. Kenneth Wilson, and William Sedlacek and his colleagues have shown that the overprediction remains, though at a slightly reduced level, when one looks at cumulative rather than first-year grade-point averages. The slight reduction may be an artifact of the greater self-selection into easier courses and majors, as described in R. D. Goldman and R. E. Slaughter, "Why College Gradepoint Average Is Difficult to Predict," *Journal of Educational Psychology* 68 (1976) and references therein. See also Kenneth M. Wilson, *Predicting the Long-term Performance in College of Minority and Nonminority Students: A Comparative Analysis in Two Collegiate Settings,* Research Bulletin #RB–78–6 (Princeton: Educational Testing Service, April 1978); Farver, Sedlacek, and Brooks, "Longitudinal Predictions," and references cited therein.

31. J. T. Campbell, L. A. Crooks, M. H. Mahoney, and D. A. Rock, *An Investigation of Sources of Bias in the Prediction of Job Performance—a Six-Year Study,* Report PR–73–37 (Princeton: Educational Testing Service, 1973). See also Frank L. Schmidt, *Differential and Single Group Validity, Test Fairness, and Test Utility,* 75–4 (Washington, D.C.: United States Civil Service Commission, May 1975) pp. 17–20.

32. For example, S. Gael and D. L. Grant, "Employment Test Validation for Minority and Non-minority Telephone Company Service Representatives," *Journal of Applied Psychology* 56 (1972).

33. Linn, "Ability Testing," pp. 381–82.

34. Ibid., summary, pp. 383–84.

35. Suppose a test has a reliability of 0.90 for whites and 0.85 for blacks. We compare a black and a white student with an identical, high score of 650 on the test. For the black, let's say this score is three standard deviations above the black mean. Suppose the same score is only 1.5 standard deviations above the white mean. (This is approximately the situation on the SAT math test.) The estimated true score ($\hat{T}$) is:

$$\hat{T} = r_{xx} (Z_x \cdot \sigma_x) + \bar{X}$$

where r_{xx} is the reliability of the measure, Z_x is the individual's score in standardized form, σ_x is the standard deviation of scores in the group, and $\bar{X}$ is the average score in the group. If one uses a different r_{xx}, Z_x, and $\bar{X}$ for each ethnic group, then the true score of the black with a 650 on the test is actually 608, and of the white the true score is 638, a thirty-point difference. If the result of regression toward the mean involved a similar sized effect for SAT verbal test and a weaker one for HSGPA, the total effect might amount to about a third of the overprediction observed in colleges at the right tail, which is about half a standard deviation. Notice that overprediction averages about a quarter of a standard deviation for blacks at the mean of the overall SAT distribution, a reduction of about 50 percent compared to the overprediction for blacks one standard deviation above the mean. However, overprediction occurs even at open admissions colleges, where the regression toward the mean effect might be expected to favor blacks. See, for example, Bernie I. Silverman, Florence Barton, and Mark Lyon, "Minority Group Status and Bias in College Admissions Criteria," *Educational and Psychological Measurement* 36(1976) (Incidentally, the authors find underprediction for Jewish students, who tend to have higher mean test scores than other whites.) See also the comprehensive review in Hunter M. Breland with Shula Minsky, *Population Validity and College Entrance Measures,* Research Bulletin RB–78–19 (Princeton: Educational Testing Service, November 1978) especially pp. 19–36; and J. Richard Harrison and James G. March, "Decision Making and Postdecision Surprises," *Administrative Science Quarterly* 29, no. 1(March 1984).

36. The variables used in these prediction equations do not include all the variables that were used in admissions decisions. If affirmative action is practiced, leaving out these other variables may lead to the overprediction of blacks. For example, suppose at a hypothetical college that among applicants with a test score of 600 and a high-school GPA of 3.5, one of every two blacks is chosen but only one of every ten whites. We would expect the white to do better in college than the black, because on all the other variables used by the admissions committee he is the best of ten while the black is the best of two. If performance were predicted using only the test score and the high school grades—without the other, perhaps nonquantified measures used by the admissions committee—overpredicting the black's college performance compared to the white's would be expected.

How much of observed overprediction might this phenomenon explain? In many contexts, such as job performance, it is hard to say. Based on studies of colleges and graduate schools, however, one can surmise that the effect there would be modest. In one careful analysis, adding a battery of twenty-three other variables only raised the multiple R by 0.04, compared to the prediction of college grades by test scores and high school grades alone. Omitting these twenty-three variables, then, would not lead to much overprediction by ethnic group. Warren W. Willingham and Hunter H. Breland, *Personal Qualities and College Admissions*(New York: College Entrance Examination Board, 1982) p. 159. See also Robert L. Linn, "Predictive Bias as an Artifact of Selection Procedures," in *Principals* [sic] *of Modern Psychological Measurement,* Howard Wainer and Samuel Messick, eds. (Hillsdale, N.J.: Lawrence Erlbaum Associates, 1983).

37. Most studies use linear regressions to predict grades. If reality is nonlinear, low-scoring, or for that matter other subsets of students may be over- or under-predicted.

For example, if floor effects exist—where failing grades are almost never given, no matter how badly one does—then a linear equation will underpredict the later performance of a lower-scoring group. If ceiling effects exist—many A's are given, and no matter how much better one does, that is the ceiling—then the lower-scoring group may be overpredicted. I have found few studies of the magnitude of these possible phenomena. See Robert L. Linn and Barbara Pitcher, "Predictor Score Regions with Significant Differences in Predicted Law School Grades from Subgroup Regression Equations," in *Reports of LSAC Sponsored Research: Volume II, 1970–1974* (Princeton: Law School Admission Council, 1977.)

Anecdotal evidence suggests both floor and ceiling effects at selective universities. Pending further research, my feeling is that these phenomena explain very little of the overprediction of blacks' performance.

38. Wilson found evidence of affirmative grading in the two colleges he studied in depth (*Predicting the Long-term Performance,* p. 75–76). David Riesman refers to the phenomenon in *On Higher Education: The Academic Enterprise in an Era of Rising Student Consumerism* (San Francisco: Jossey-Bass, 1980) chap. 3. See also Goldman and Slaughter, "Why College Gradepoint Average is Difficult to Predict."

39. Alan H. Goldman, *Justice and Reverse Discrimination* (Princeton: Princeton University Press, 1979) and the references therein.

40. See the massive review on this and related questions in Lee J. Cronbach and Richard E. Snow, *Aptitudes and Instructional Methods: A Handbook for Research on Interactions* (New York: Irvington, 1977).

41. For example, Alexander W. Astin reports these findings of a broad cross-sectional study:

> Attending a predominantly black college appears to reduce the black student's chance of persisting to the baccalaureate, an effect which was observed in both two-year and four-year institutions. Attending a predominantly black institution also shows a negative effect on undergraduate satisfaction, but the effects on undergraduate grades are positive and substantial in magnitude. Thus, it would appear that black undergraduates will tend to get higher grades at a black college than at other colleges, but they will also be less satisfied and less likely to persist to the completion of a baccalaureate.

In personal communication with Professor Astin, I tried to obtain the numerical results underlying these conclusions, in order to get an idea of the size of the effects. Unfortunately, Professor Astin said the numbers were not available. *Minorities in American Higher Education* (San Francisco: Jossey-Bass, 1982) p. 101.

42. Powers, "Comparing Predictions."

43. The original Coleman Report did find a "diversity effect" within high schools. But later analysis showed this finding was erroneous. "Thus the Report's finding that 'a pupil's achievement is strongly related to the educational backgrounds and aspirations of the other students in the school' is due in part to a mechanical error made by the Report's authors . . . . *Based on these data I find no evidence that characteristics of the student body have a strong independent influence on the verbal achievement of individual students.*" Marshall S. Smith, "Equality of Educational Opportunity: The Basic Findings Reconsidered," in *On Equality of Educational Opportunity,* Frederick Mosteller and Daniel P. Moynihan, eds. (New York: Vintage Books, 1972) pp. 272, 280, emphasis in original.

44. A. Anastasi, M. J. Meade, and A. A. Schneider, *The Validation of a Biographical Inventory as a Predictor of College Success* (New York: College Entrance Examination Board, 1960). Studies were done at Amherst, Cal Tech, Cornell (College of Engineering), Dartmouth, M.I.T., Rensselaer Polytechnic Institute, Rutgers, and Stanford.

45. T. D. Taber and J. D. Hackman, "Dimensions of Undergraduate College Performance," *Journal of Applied Psychology* 61, no. 5 (1976).

46. Robert Klitgaard and Ruth Katz, "Overcoming Ethnic Inequalities: Lessons from Malaysia," *Journal of Policy Analysis and Management* (Spring 1983).

47. Luisa M. Fernandes and Robert Klitgaard, "Ethnic Inequalities in Brazil," Kennedy School of Government teaching case (Cambridge: Kennedy School of Government, 1983).

48. Klitgaard, *Making Merit Work,* chap. 7.

49. This assertion is based on nine colleges (in the ETS sample of 191 colleges, described in appendix 1) whose students averaged over 1,100 on the combined SAT V+M.

50. The summary statistics on the black and white students in the sample of 100,000 SAT test takers in 1983 were as follows:

Summary Statistics from Random Sample of College-Bound Seniors Taking the SAT in 1983

	N	Mean	Std. Dev.
Both Groups			
SAT V+M	83,464	907	205
HSGPA	82,814	2.79	0.44
PRED 200	82,491	1,466	248

	N	Mean	Std. Dev.
PRED 300	82,491	1,746	277
Blacks			
SAT V+M	7,756	706	171
HSGPA	7,625	2.64	0.51
PRED 200	7,600	1,296	224
PRED 300	7,600	1,501	261
Whites			
SAT V+M	75,708	927	197
HSGPA	75,189	2.81	0.42
PRED 200	74,891	1,490	238
PRED 300	74,891	1,771	267

NOTE: "PRED 200" refers to SAT V+M + 200 (HSGPA), which is probably the best equation for colleges with SAT V+M over 1,200 or under 700.
"PRED 300" is SAT V+M + 300 (HSGPA). I use PRED 300 in chapter 8
because it seems the best equation for colleges with SAT V+M over 1,100
and has the attractive property of approximately equalizing the means of
SAT V+M and HSGPA.

51. Figure 8.4 is based on this table:

	Combined Predictor				College Grades	
Percent Black	Cut Score Black	Cut Score White	Δ Cut Score	Δ σ	Δσ	Δσ with Overprediction
1.4	2,100	2,100	0	0	0	0.33
3	2,010	2,103	93	0.34	0.20	0.53
5	1,933	2,106	173	0.62	0.36	0.69
7	1,885	2,110	225	0.81	0.47	0.80
10	1,829	2,114	285	1.03	0.60	0.93
15	1,757	2,122	365	1.32	0.77	1.10
20	1,699	2,131	432	1.56	0.91	1.24

Several assumptions were made in these calculations. Among the nine colleges in the ETS
sample of 191 (described in appendix 1) with SAT V+M > 1,100, the mean multiple R between the combined predictor and first-year grades was 0.487. I corrected this correlation for
unreliability by assuming an unreliability of 0.7, yielding a correlation of 0.582. I did not
correct for restriction of range since the correction would have to change for different percentages of blacks admitted; thus, the results slightly understate the academic costs of admitting
more blacks.

52. The calculations are based on the distributions of SAT V+M + (300) HSGPA for
blacks and whites in the sample of 100,000 college-bound seniors who took the SAT in 1983.
The figures were:

	Cut Scores		Average Scores		Differences in	
Percent Black	Black	White	Black	White	Cut Scores	Average Scores
1.4	2,100	2,100	2,200	2,212	0	12
3	2,010	2,103	2,120	2,212	93	92
5	1,933	2,106	2,058	2,216	173	158
7	1,885	2,110	2,016	2,219	225	203
10	1,829	2,114	1,968	2,222	285	254
15	1,757	2,122	1,909	2,228	365	319
20	1,699	2,131	1,862	2,235	432	373

Notice that, with the same cut score (zero marginal cost), the average black is lower than the average white.

53. Using linear interpolations within the frequency distributions provided by Cheryl L. Wild in *A Summary of Data Collected from Graduate Record Examinations Test-Takers During 1978–79,* Data Summary Report 4 (Princeton: Educational Testing Service, 1980), I calculated the following:

Percent Black	Difference between Marginal Black and Marginal White (GREQ)
0.2	0
3	112
5	144
7	166
10	193
15	226
20	253

The means and standard deviations were:

	Black		White	
	Avg.	Std. Dev.	Avg.	Std. Dev.
GREQ	358	107	525	122
GREV	363	99	511	111

54. Leonard S. Miller, "College Admissions and Financial Aid Policies as Revealed by Institutional Practices," *Economic Inquiry* 19 (January 1981): 129–31.

55. A considerable literature on the utility analysis of selection policies grew up in the 1970s. Most models, however, made the unreasonable assumption that outcomes were binary —a student either "succeeded" or did not. That is not the way most educators at right tail institutions think about academic performance. That literature did have the virtue, however, of reminding us that there may be thresholds or nonlinearities in our utility functions for academic outcomes. For helpful distillations, see Jensen, *Bias in Mental Testing,* pp. 391–420; Frank L. Schmidt and John E. Hunter, "Development of a General Solution to the Problem of Validity Generalization," *Journal of Applied Psychology* 62 (1977); and Lee J. Cronbach, "Equity in Selection—Where Psychometrics and Political Philosophy Meet," *Journal of Educational Measurement* 13, no. 1 (Spring 1976): 31–41.

56. For a description of the work behind existing programs, see Lee J. Cronbach, Elanna Yalow, and Gary Schaeffer, "Setting Cut Scores in Selection: A Mathematical Structure for Examining Policies," Project Report 79-A7, (Stanford University: Institute for Research on Educational Finance and Governance, School of Education, October 1979); and David T. Chuang, James J. Chen, and Melvin R. Novick, *Theory and Practice for the Use of Cut Scores for Personnel Decisions,* Technical Report 79–B (Iowa City: University of Iowa, September 1979).

57. These figures are based on extrapolations from my analysis of a sample of 100,000 college-bound seniors who took the SAT in 1983.

9. Concluding Remarks

1. Peter F. Drucker, *Landmarks of Tomorrow,* (New York: Harper and Brothers, 1959) p. 125.
2. Max Weber "Wirtschaft und Gesellschaft" in *From Max Weber: Essays in Sociology,* Hans H. Gerth and C. Wright Mills, eds. (New York: Oxford University Press, 1958) p. 240.
3. William W. Turnbull, "Relevance in Testing," *Science,* 160 (June 1968): 1426.

4. Raymond B. Cattell and J. J. Butcher, *The Prediction of Achievement and Creativity* (Indianapolis: Bobbs-Merrill, 1968) p. 320. Emphasis in original.

5. Andrew J. Strenio, *The Testing Trap* (New York: Rawson, Wade, 1981); Banesh Hoffmann, *The Tyranny of Testing* (New York: Collier, 1962); Stephen J. Gould, *The Mismeasure of Man* (New York: W. W. Norton, 1981).

6. Charles Elliott, assisted by Françoise de Morsier, *Patterns of Poverty in the Third World: A Study of Social and Economic Stratification* (New York: Praeger, 1975) chap. 9.

7. Stanley Cavell, "Austin at Criticism," in *Must We Mean What We Say?* (Cambridge: Cambridge University Press, 1976) p. 113.

8. Even here, I have noted important limitations. There is a lot of unexplained variation, part of which is in the grading system and the way grades are compared across dissimilar courses and majors. Some students with relatively low test scores and prior grades may do well at a selective university, although if an entire class were admitted with such characteristics the result would almost certainly be a lowering of overall academic performance.

9. Research by Philip B. Price, Calvin W. Taylor, and David E. Nelson, cited in "Attributes of Excellence," *Scientific American* (May 1982) p. 98. See also appendix 2.

10. Dr. Gerald C. Crary, *Chronicle of Higher Education* (14 October 1981) p. 25.

11. Derek C. Bok, "President's Annual Report" (March 1984), Harvard University, Cambridge, Mass.

12. Cattell and Butcher, *The Prediction of Achievement and Creativity,* p. 308.

13. Ibid., p. 324.

14. Ibid., p. 251.

15. David C. McClelland, "Testing for Competence Rather than Intelligence," *American Psychologist* 28, no. 1 (January 1973) p. 2.

16. Ibid., p. 12. Emphasis in original.

17. The selections in Stephen Wiseman's *Intelligence and Ability* 2nd ed. (Middlesex, England: Penguin, 1973) convey the long pedigree of this notion: see especially those by Vernon, Burt, and Guilford.

18. Howard Gardner, *Frames of Mind* (New York: Basic Books, 1983) p. 10.

19. Ibid., p. 385.

20. Ibid., p. 390.

21. Ibid., p. 392.

22. Learned Hand, *The Spirit of Liberty: Papers and Addresses of Learned Hand,* 3rd ed. Irving Dilliard, ed. (New York: Knopf, 1960) pp. 22–23.

23. See Robert Klitgaard, *Making Merit Work: Selection for Higher Education in Developing Countries,* in press, references therein.

24. Rasma Karklins, "Ethnic Politics and Access to Higher Education: The Soviet Case," *Comparative Politics* 16, no. 3 (April 1984): 288–90.

25. John B. Fox, Jr., *Annual Report of the Dean of Harvard College* (April 1984) Harvard University, Cambridge, Mass.

26. For example, David Riesman has written: "The older convictions about what Harvard should be doing have unevenly lost their assurance; we live within the secular cathedrals of the higher learning in the absence of the convictions which built the cathedrals." "Educational Reform at Harvard College: Meritocracy and Its Adversaries," in S. M. Lipset and D. Riesman, *Education and Politics at Harvard* (New York: McGraw-Hill, 1975) p. 392.

27. P. E. Meehl, *Clinical Versus Statistical Prediction: A Theoretical Analysis and Review of the Literature* (Minneapolis: University of Minnesota Press, 1954); Robyn M. Dawes, "A Case Study of Graduate Admissions: Applications of Three Principles of Human Decision Making," in *Statistics and Public Policy,* William B. Fairley and Frederick Mosteller, eds., (Reading, Mass.: Addison-Wesley, 1977); and Hunter M. Breland, *Assessing Student Characteristics in Admissions to Higher Education: A Review of Procedures,* Research Monograph No. 9 (New York: College Board, 1981).

28. W. D. Furneaux, *The Chosen Few: An Examination of Some Aspects of University Selection in Britain* (London:Oxford University Press, 1961) p. 103.

29. Winton Manning, "The Pursuit of Fairness in Admissions to Higher Education," in *Selective Admissions in Higher Education,* Carnegie Council on Policies Studies in Higher Education (San Francisco: Jossey-Bass, 1977) p. 41.

30. Riesman, "Educational Reform," pp. 288–89.

31. "Report of the Admissions Review Committee," mimeographed (Cambridge: Harvard Medical School, 1975) p. 25.

32. Steven Weinberg, "The Search for Unity: Notes for a History of Quantum Field Theory," *Daedalus* 106, no. 4 (Fall 1977): 30.

Appendix 1

1. The Educational Testing Service provided the percentile distributions of SAT V+M for seven unnamed institutions with SAT V+M averages above 1,200. I chose one from the middle of that group, with an SAT V+M of 1,266 and a standard deviation of 133. The distribution was fairly well approximated by a normal distribution. The actual percentile scores compared to those expected from a normal distribution with $\mu = 1,266$, $\sigma = 133$ were:

Percentile	Actual SAT V+M	Normal Distribution
90th	1,430	1,436
75th	1,359	1,356
50th	1,278	1,266
25th	1,182	1,176
10th	1,104	1,095

2. In SAT V+M, 200 points is 1.45 standard deviations within schools having average SAT V+M over 1,200. For the ACT distribution, I used the data in table A1.2 for the three schools with averages above 25. And 1.45 standard deviations in terms of ACT is (1.45) (3.28) = 4.75; in terms of HSGPA, (1.45) (0.34) = 0.50.

3. The Educational Testing Service provided "validity studies" conducted through the College Board Validity Study Service that had the following characteristics: the study was on an entering class from 1977–1981; the criterion was freshman GPA on a scale of 0–4; the predictors were SAT Verbal, SAT Math, and high-school GPA on a scale of 0–4; and all students with SAT scores were analyzed in one regression equation. If a college had more than one such study, the most recent was used.

4. Computer printouts of institutionally self-reported data were provided by Peterson's Guides, Princeton, N.J., in the summer of 1983. I also used unpublished data used by the U.S. Air Force in the construction of its "Patton College Quality Index." The data are based on the late 1970s and early 1980s; college averages may now be different.

5. These calculations are based on the regression equation for the two schools with SAT V+M averages above 1,200. On SAT V+M, 200 points corresponds to a (200) (0.0014) = 0.28 unit gain in first-year college grades, or 0.28/0.69 = 0.41σ. With the coefficient of 0.33 for high-school grades, it would take an increase of 0.28/0.33 = 0.85 in HSGPA to yield the same 0.28 unit gain in college grades as a 200-point gain in SAT V+M.

6. This result is confirmed by other data:

Correlations Are Lower at Right-Tail Institutions

Number in Sample	Average SAT V+M	SAT V+M	H.S. Record	SAT V+M and H.S. Record
22	>1,200	0.31	0.31	0.40
46	1,100–1,200	0.38	0.44	0.52
80	1,000–1,100	0.44	0.50	0.57
260	900–1,000	0.44	0.51	0.58
150	800–900	0.44	0.48	0.56
31	700–800	0.42	0.43	0.55
16	600–600	0.35	0.42	0.50
15	<600	0.39	0.47	0.54

Correlations between College Grades and (columns 3–5).

SOURCE: Based on an unpublished summary of 620 validity studies carried out by the Educational Testing Service from 1961 to 1977. "H.S. record" can either be HSGPA or rank in high-school class.

7. Here is another way of seeing this result:

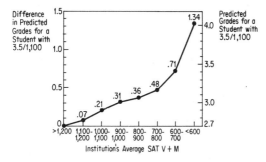

Institution's Average SAT V + M

8. The average student at the group of colleges with SAT means between 900–1,000 has an SAT of about 950 and an HSGPA of 3.12. At a school with SAT means over 1,200, this predicts college grades of 2.37, which is almost one standard deviation below the median (the 17th percentile).

9. Rodney T. Hartnett and Warren W. Willingham, *The Criterion Problem: What Measures of Success in Graduate Education?* GRE Board Research Monograph No. 77–4R (Princeton: Educational Testing Service, March 1979).

10. Kenneth M. Wilson, *The Validation of GRE Scores as Predictors of First-Year Performance in Graduate Study: Report of the GRE Cooperative Validity Studies Project*, GREB No. 75–8R (Princeton: Educational Testing Service, June 1979).

11. For the law schools with LSAT averages under 550, the mean equation for whites was GPA = 4.00 + 6.84 CGPA + 0.04 LSAT, with *R* = 0.40.

12. John E. Rolph, Albert P. Williams, and A. Lee Laniear, *Predicting Minority and Majority Medical Student Performance on the National Board Exams*, Report No. R-2039-HEW (Santa Monica, Calif.: Rand Corporation, November 1978).

13. Ibid., p. 48. The variables were: medical school attended, date took exam, four MCAT scores, college GPA, year 1975, repeat test taker, college selectivity, and sex. The authors ran separate regressions for blacks and whites; in racially grouped regressions, summary statistics were not reported, but I obtained them from Dr. Rolph.

14. My calculations, based on Tables 1 and 2 in Donald E. Powers and Pamela A. Moss, *A Summary of the Results of the Graduate Management Admission Council (GMAC) Validity Study Service for 1979–1980*, GMAC Research Report 80–3 (Princeton: Educational Testing Service, December 1980).

15. My calculations, based on Table 2 in William B. Schrader, *The Graduate Management Admission Test: Technical Report on Test Development and Score Interpretation for GMAT Users* (Princeton: Educational Testing Service, 1979).

16. My calculations, based on Tables 1 and 2 in Lawrence W. Hecht and Donald E. Powers, *The Predictive Validity of Preadmission Measures in Graduate Management Education: Three Years of the GMAC Validity Study Service*, GMAC Research Report 82–1 (Princeton: Educational Testing Service, April 1982). Regression results were not available.

Appendix 2

1. W. W. Brown and M. O. Reynolds "A Model of IQ, Occupation and Earnings," *American Economic Review* 65 (1975): 1002–7.

2. Burton A. Weisbrod and Peter Karpoff, "Monetary Returns to College Education, Student Ability and College Quality," *Review of Economics and Statistics* 50, no. 4 (November 1968): 491–97.

3. Leona E. Tyler, *Individual Differences: Abilities and Motivational Differences* (Englewood Cliffs, N.J.: Prentice-Hall, 1974).

4. L. C. Solomon and P. J. Taubman, eds., *Does College Matter? Some Evidence on the Impacts of Higher Education* (New York: Academic Press, 1973).

5. Christopher Jencks et al., *Who Gets Ahead: The Determinants of Economic Success* (New York: Basic Books, 1979).

Notes to pages 213 to 219

6. E. Haverman and P. S. West, *They Went to College* (New York: Harcourt, 1952).
7. R. W. Husband, "What Do College Grades Predict?", *Fortune* (June 1957).
8. L. M. Sharp, *Education and Employment: The Early Careers of College Graduates* (Baltimore: Johns Hopkins Press, 1970).
9. O. Ashenfelter and J. Mooney, "Graduate Education, Ability and Earnings," *Review of Economics and Statistics* 50 (February 1968): 78–86.
10. Zvi Griliches, "Wages of Very Young Men," *Journal of Political Economy* 84, no. 4 (1976): 569–86.
11. S. Bowles and V. Nelson, "The Inheritance of IQ and the Intergenerational Transmission of Inequality," *Review of Economics and Statistics* 56, no. 1 (February 1974): 39–51.
12. L. M. Terman and M. Odin, *The Gifted Group at Mid-Life* (Stanford, Calif.: Stanford University Press 1959).
13. Joop Hartog, "Earnings and Capability Requirements," *Review of Economics and Statistics* (May 1980): 230–40.
14. Christopher Jencks et al., *Inequality* (New York: Basic Books, 1972); Jencks et al., *Who Gets Ahead?*
15. L. E. Tyler, *The Psychology of Human Differences*, 3rd ed. (New York: Appleton-Century, Crofts, 1965).
16. J. H. Waller, "Achievement and Social Mobility: Relationships Among IQ Score, Education, and Occupation in Two Generations," *Social Biology* 18 (1971): 252–59.
17. Arthur R. Jensen, *Bias in Mental Testing* (New York: Free Press, 1980) chap. 8.
18. J. D. Matarazzo, *Wechsler's Measurement and Appraisal of Adult Intelligence*, 5th ed. (Baltimore: Williams and Wilkinson, 1972) chaps. 7 and 12.
19. R. S. Ball, "The Predictability of Occupational Level from Intelligence," *Journal of Consulting Psychology* 2 (1938): 184–86.
20. John Lewis, "The Relationship Between Academic Aptitude and Occupational Success for a Sample of University Graduates," *Educational and Psychological Measures* 35 (1975): 465–66.
21. R. L. Thorndike and E. Hogen, *Ten Thousand Careers* (New York: John Wiley & Sons, 1959).
22. Coffman and Mahoney, "A Follow-up Study of Yale Phi Beta Kappa Graduates," in *Educational Testing Service Annual Report, 1966–67* (Princeton: Educational Testing Service, 1967) pp. 98–99.
23. Terman and Oden, *The Gifted Group.*
24. Joe L. Spaeth, "Occupational Attainment Among Male College Graduates," *American Journal of Sociology* 75 (January 1970): 632–44.
25. L. A. Munday and J. A. Davis, "Varieties of Accomplishment after College: Perspectives on the Meaning of Academic Talent," ACT Research Report: no. 62 (Iowa City: ACT, March 1974).
26. M. S. Olsen, "Majority in *Who's Who* Not Top Students," *Phi Delta Kappan* 46, no. 441 (1965).
27. L. Bevier, "College Grades and Success in Life," *Education Review* 54 (1917): 325–333.
28. C. M. Cox, *Genetic Studies of Genius: The Early Mental Traits of Three Hundred Geniuses* vol. 2 (Stanford, Calif.: Stanford University Press, 1926).
29. D. W. MacKinnon and W. B. Hall, "Intelligence and Creativity," in *Colloquium 17: The Measurement of Creativity, Proceedings, XVIIth International Congress of Applied Psychology*, vol. 2, Liege, Belgium: 25–30 July, 1971 (Brussels: Editest, 1972) pp. 1882–90.
30. E. Paul Torrance, "Creatively Gifted and Disadvantaged Gifted Students," in *The Gifted and the Creative: A Fifty-Year Perspective*, J. C. Stanley, W. C. George, and G. H. Solano, eds., (Baltimore: Johns Hopkins University Press, 1977).
31. H. Chauncey and T. L. Hilton, "Are Aptitude Tests Valid for the Highly Able?" *Science* 148 (1965): 1297–1304.
32. M. A. Wallach, "Tests Tell Us Little About Talent," *American Scientist* 64 (1976): 57–63.
33. E. E. Ghiselli, "The Measurement of Occupational Aptitude," *University of California Publications in Psychology* 8, no. 2 (1955): 101–216.
34. E. E. Ghiselli, *The Validity of Occupational Aptitude Tests* (New York: John Wiley & Sons, 1966).
35. Alfred B. Carlson and Charles E. Werts, "Relationships Among Law School Predictors, Law School Performance, and Bar Examination Results," in *Reports of LSAC Sponsored Research: Volume II, 1970–1974* (Princeton: Law School Admission Council: 1976) p. 284. •

36. R. Watkins, *The Comparability of Grades on the California State Bar Exam Obtained at Different Administrations,* SR-68-1-WO (Berkeley, Calif.: Educational Testing Service, March 1968).

37. D. A. Lind and S. A. Yarbrough, "The Relationship of Law School Grades to Passing the Bar Exam: Empirical Evidence," *Toledo Law Review* 5 (Winter 1974): 426–31.

38. Leonard L. Baird, "A Survey of the Relevance of Legal Training to Law School Graduates," *Journal of Legal Education* (Spring 1978).

39. Erwin O. Smigel, *The Wall Street Lawyer* (London: Free Press, 1964).

40. Marcia Guttentag and Joseph Dewhirst, "Report on the Job Placement of Harvard Law School Graduates 1971–1974," unpublished report to Dean Sacks, Harvard University, Cambridge, Mass.

41. David A. Wise, "Academic Achievement and Job Performance," *American Economic Review* 65 no. 3 (June 1975).

42. David A. Wise, "Personal Attributes, Job Performance and Probability of Promotion," *Econometrica* 43 no. 5–6 (September–November 1975).

43. Lois A. Crooks and Joel T. Campbell, "Career Programs of MBA's," monograph, (Princeton: Educational Testing Service, 1974).

44. Lois A. Crooks, Joel T. Campbell, and Donald A. Rock, *Predicting Career Progress of Graduate Students in Management* (Princeton: Educational Testing Service, February 1979).

45. T. W. Harrell, "High Earning MBA's," *Personnel Psychology* 25 (1972): 523–30.

46. M. S. Harrell, T. W. Harrell et al., "Predicting Compensation among MBA Graduates Five and Ten Years after Graduation," *Journal of Applied Psychology* 62 (1977): 636–40.

47. Jeffrey Pfeffer, "Effects of an MBA and Socioeconomic Origins on Business School Graduates' Salaries," *Journal of Applied Psychology* 62 (December 1977): 698–705.

48. Ann Stouffer Bisconti, "Who Will Succeed? College Graduates as Business Executives," *Special Topic Series,* no. 3, CPC Foundation (1978).

49. A. G. Weinstein and V. Srinivasen, "Predicting Managerial Success of Master of Business Administration (MBA) Graduates," *Journal of Applied Psychology* 59 (April 1974): 207–12.

50. D. S. Bridgman, "Success in College and Business," *Personnel Journal* 9 (1930): 1–19.

51. Roy W. Walters, Jr. and Douglas W. Bray, "Today's Search for Tomorrow's Leaders," *Journal of College Placement* 24 (1963): 22–23.

52. R. P. Calhoon and A. C. Reddy, "The Frantic Search for Predictors of Success," *Journal of College Placement* 28 (February–March 1968).

53. Brian S. O'Leary, "College Grade Point Average as an Indicator of Occupational Success: An Update," PRR–80–23 (Washington, D.C.: Office of Personnel Management, GPO, August 1980) p. 16.

54. P. M. Muchinsky and D. P. Hoyt, "Academic Success as a Predictor of Occupational Success among Engineering Graduates," *Measurement and Evaluation in Guidance* 6 (July 1973): 93–103.

55. R. Perrucci and C. C. Perrucci, "Social Origins, Educational Contexts, and Career Mobility" (paper read at American Sociological Association, San Francisco, August 1967).

56. G. A. Pierson, "School Marks and Success in Engineering," *Educational and Psychological Measurement* 7 (1947): 612–17.

57. D. E. Rice, "A Study of Incomes of Technically Trained Men," *Scientific American* 109 (1913): 116–17.

58. Walters, "Scholastic Training of Eminent American Engineers," *School and Society* 13 (1921): 322–29.

59. John E. Rolph, Albert P. Williams, and A. Lee Laniear. *Predicting Minority and Majority Medical Student Performance on the National Board Exams,* R–2039–HEW (Santa Monica, Calif.: Rand Corporation, November 1978).

60. Robert M. Bell, *Medical School and Physician Performance: Predicting Scores on the American Board of Internal Medicine Written Examination,* R–1723–HEW (Santa Monica, Calif.: Rand Corporation, August 1977).

61. J. M. Richards, C. W. Taylor, and P. B. Price. "The Prediction of Medical Intern Performance," *Journal of Applied Psychology* 46 (1962): 142–46.

62. Peterson et al., "An Analytical Study of North Carolina General Practice," *Journal of Medical Education* 31, no. 12 (1956).

63. P. B. Price, J. M. Richards, C. W. Taylor, and T. L. Jacobsen, "Measurement of Physician Performance" (paper presented at American Association of Medical Colleges, Second Annual Conference on Research in Medical Education, 1963.

64. P. B. Price et al., *Measurement and Predictors of Physician Performance: Two Decades of Intermittently Sustained Research* (Salt Lake City, Utah: L. L. R. Press, 1971).

65. John R. Wingard and John W. Williamson, "Grades as Predictors of Physicians' Career Performance: An Evaluative Literature Review," *Journal of Medical Education* 48 (April 1973): 311–12.

66. Jonathan R. Cole, *Fair Science: Women in the Scientific Community* (New York: Free Press, 1979) p. 169.

67. Derek deSolla Price, *Little Science, Big Science* (New York: Columbia University Press, 1963) p. 40.

68. Jonathan R. and Stephen Cole, *Social Stratification in Science* (Chicago: University of Chicago Press, 1973).

69. J. A. Craeger, "The Use of Publication Citations in Educational Research," *Journal of Educational Measurement* 3 (1966): 243–59.

70. William B. Schrader, *Admissions Test Scores as Predictors of Career Achievement in Psychology*, GREB No. 76–1R (Princeton: Educational Testing Service, September 1978).

71. Alan E. Bayer and John Folger, "Some Correlates of a Citation Measure of Productivity in Science," *Sociology of Education* 39 (Fall 1966): 381–90.

72. C. R. Harmon, *Validation of Fellowship Selection Instruments Against a Provisional Criterion of Scientific Accomplishment* (Washington, D.C.: National Academy of Sciences, 1959).

73. D. W. Taylor, "Variables Related to Creativity and Productivity among Men in Two Research Laboratories," in *Scientific Creativity*, C. W. Taylor and F. Bannon, eds (New York: John Wiley & Sons, 1963) pp. 228–30.

74. K. E. Clark, *America's Psychologists* (Washington, D.C.: American Psychological Association, 1957).

75. C. W. Taylor and R. L. Ellison, "Biographical Predictors of Scientific Performance," *Science* 155 (3 March 1967): 1075–80.

Index

Index

Index

ance in, 91, 203–4; admissions policies of, 46; anti-Semitism in, 65; college performance and admission to,
127; of education, 4–5; level of enrollment in, 8; minorities in, 160; professional, see Business schools; Law
schools; Medical schools
Great Britain, admissions policies in, 49,
189–90
Griliches, Zvi, 118, 213, 239n 12
Group representation, see Diversity;
Minorities; Women
Guttentag, Marcia, 219

Hall, W. B., 218
Hand, Learned, 186, 187
Harmon, C. R., 226
Harrell, M. S., 222
Harrell, T. W., 221, 222
Hartog, Joop, 135, 214
Harvard Business School, 5, 9, 134; ad-
missions policy of, 18, 42–45, 47
Harvard College, 3, 6, 7, 234n 15, 239n
23; admissions policy of, 17, 18, 23–
31; evolution of admissions process
at, 52–55; faculty incentives at, 77;
"happy bottom quarter" at, 74; incentive effects of, 79; interviews for,
137; later-life success and, 123, 124,
127–29; minorities at, 155, 188; social
value added and, 61
Harvard *Crimson,* 56
Harvard Graduate School of Arts and
Sciences (GSAS), 17; admissions policy of, 18, 31–35, 46
Harvard Law School, 5, 80, 128, 140,
219; academic requirements of, 78;
admissions policies of, 17, 18, 35–39,
229n 34; tryout system at, 59
Harvard Medical Alumni Bulletin, 41
Harvard Medical School, 5, 13, 183–84;
academic requirements of, 78; admissions policies of, 17, 18, 39–42, 49,
230n 43; Admissions Review Committee of, 193; interviews for, 137,
138, 191; minorities at, 80–81
Harvard University, 3–7, 14, 105, 157,

165, 191, 193, 240n 2; academic standards of, 10; changing educational
objectives of, 8–10; Committee on the
Faculties of, 186; diversity and, 72;
Divinity School, 17, 134; grades com-
pared with other educational inputs
at, 111; perceived value of education
at, 118; quality of applicant pool for,
8; size of, 57–58; see also Harvard Col-
lege *and specific graduate schools*
Hauser, Robert, 239n 26
Hecht, Lawrence W., 253n 16
High school: grades in, 91, 108, 196–
202; influence of admissions policies
on, 76
Hilton, T. L., 218
Hispanics, 159
Hogen, E., 216
Holton, Gerald, 232n 19
Homogeneity, 72–73, 75
Honeywell, 149
Horace Mann School, 74
Howard, Jeffrey, 188
Howard University, 72
Hoyt, Donald P., 129–30, 223
Hunter, John E., 101
Husband, R. W., 125, 239n 23

Incentives, effects of admissions policies on, 60, 61, 75–79
Income: and academic performance,
212–14; nonacademic variables and,
134–35; as success measure, 119–21,
129
India, 81, 187, 232n 35
Indiana State University, 110, 197,
200
Indonesia, 187; alternative selection
systems in, 101; minority representation in, 156; preferential treatment
policies in, 168
Intelligence tests, 91
Interest tests, 144
Interviews, 15, 18, 91, 133, 137–39, 186,
191–92; for business schools, 47; and
Graduate School of Arts and
Sciences, 33; for Harvard Medical

Index

Index

Index